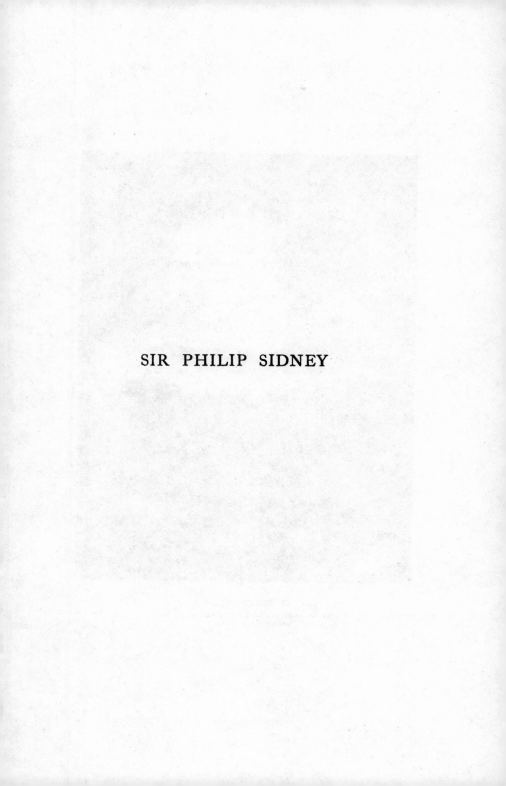

# SIR PHILIP SIDNEY

SIR PHILIP SIDNEY

FROM A PAINTING, BY AN UNKNOWN ARTIST, IN THE HEAD MASTER'S HOUSE AT
SHREWSBURY SCHOOL

# SIR PHILIP SIDNEY

BY

## PERCY ADDLESHAW

WITH TWELVE ILLUSTRATIONS

KENNIKAT PRESS
Port Washington, N. Y./London

SIR PHILIP SIDNEY

First published in 1909
Reissued in 1970 by Kennikat Press
Library of Congress Catalog Card No: 77-113304
ISBN 0-8046-1005-3

Manufactured by Taylor Publishing Company      Dallas, Texas

# PREFACE

I HAVE consulted the acknowledged authorities, also many authorities not universally accredited. The conclusions I have drawn may, reasonably, be disputed. Their parent facts are, I believe, correctly stated.

I cannot pretend that my summary of a remarkable ten years should satisfy everybody. I may fairly plead that such knowledge as I have gained is the result of earnest study.

I would thank, among many others, the Dean of Christ Church, the Rev. Prebendary Moss, late Headmaster of Shrewsbury School, and Lieut.-Gen. Sir Reginald Pole-Carew, K.C.B., for courteous letters. Also my acknowledgments are due to Mrs. Churchill Osborne, to Professor Elton, of Liverpool University, Mr. J. B. Wainewright, of Lincoln's Inn, and Mr. Caulfeild Osborne, of New College.

I regret keenly that his lamented death prevents my thanking Mr. Fox Bourne. His knowledge of the period here treated was profound. To others working on this period, he was the most cheery and sympathetic of advisers. It is a real grief to me that I cannot tell him how greatly I valued his friendship and his kindness.

In conclusion, I wish to mention my beloved master, York Powell. He urged me often to write. In writing,

though I realised he would at times have controverted the
views I have put forward, I have regarded my task as
a sacred duty owed to him.    I like to think he is still, as
he always was, my kindest critic.

PERCY ADDLESHAW

The Hillside, Hassocks, Sussex

# CONTENTS

# LIST OF ILLUSTRATIONS

xi

# SOME OF THE AUTHORITIES REFERRED TO

Hollinshed's Chronicles, vol. iii.

The Processions at the Obsequies of Philip Sidney.  (Lant, 1587.)

Life of the Renowned Philip Sidney.  Fulke Greville.

The Blakeway MSS.

Memoirs of the Lives and Actions of the Sidneys.  Edited by Arthur Collins, 1745.

Langueti epistolæ ad P. Sidneum.

—— Perse's Translation and Introduction to same.  (Pickering, 1845.)

Wright's Elizabeth and her Times.  1838.

Lives and Letters of the Devereux, Earls of Essex.  Devereux.

Calendar of the Carew Papers.  Brewer and Bullen.

Zouch's Life of Philip Sidney.  (1809.)

Gray's Life of Philip Sidney.  (1829.)

Elizabethan Worthies.  Sidney Lee.

Philip Sidney, Type of English Chivalry.  Fox Bourne.

Sidney.  J. A. Symonds.

Etc., etc.

# SIR PHILIP SIDNEY

## CHAPTER I

### THE PHILIP SIDNEY OF LEGEND AND FACT

Elizabethan worthies—The Catholic - Protestant quarrel—Philip's short career—Its difficulties to a biographer—The Philip of legend—The Sidney of fact—Politics and religion—Philip's portraits—Elizabethan painters

"**A** BORN courtier with a becoming confidence," was the high compliment Elizabeth paid to each of her Devon worthies. She might have said the same, with greater truth, of Philip Sidney. For he was nobler than they, despite their glittering merits of patriotism, courage, and devotion to their Queen.

His aloofness detracts from the value of Philip as a subject for the writer to this extent, that his conduct shut him off from the society of many brilliant men of his day. His aims were only theirs in part. It is impossible, too, to avoid feeling that he was never quite "hail fellow" with them. Noble he was, generous he was, quixotically honest he was ; but also the qualities of the prig and the bigot are apparent. His very virtues make these blemishes the more conspicuous. He seems never to have laughed heartily. His conversation was, probably, of the same nature as his letters. These were improving, not entertaining. A pleasantry becomes heavy when instantly

weighed down by a classical quotation, always very
seriously applied. The lighter side of life was a region
he never explored. To most modern ears his excessive
puritanism is offensive, or should be. It is curious, too,
that he did not, as did others less wise and less serious,
quite understand the purely political aspect of the Catholic-
Protestant quarrel. Most of the champions on either side
would have been hard put to it had they been asked to
explain the theological points at issue.

When La Bruyère declared, " C'est la profonde ignorance
qui inspire le ton dogmatique," he spoke no more than the
truth. One so all-embracing is unhappily rarely understood even to-day. When Philip Sidney lived there was
no one who could have, even dimly, perceived what the
philosopher meant. In all the dismal fights, the acrid
squabbles, wherein blood was spilt and noble lives lost,
Philip's among them, each combatant believed that his
opponent merited instant death. It was impossible to
love or trust the man who held a different opinion on
a matter concerning which the contending parties were
equally ignorant. This ignorance bred a fierce hatred
among men who should have known better, and would have
known better had they lived in the twentieth century. To
understand the conduct and attitude of a Sidney we must
remember that were he translated to our own times and
walked in Fleet Street, or Manchester, at this moment, it
would not have seemed odd or wrong to him to see Hang-
ing Ditch or the Griffin adorned with the heads of Mr.
Page Hopps, Dr. Clifford, or the Archbishop of West-
minster. He would have been shocked to see Mr. Frederic
Harrison's there, because this great thinker adopts no form
of Christian belief. Philip's theory was, and more experienced men accepted it, that you might be a Christian or
not ; but being one you must, at the risk of incurring great
and grievous penalties, accept the particular doctrines
himself affected. He hated the Catholics, for no reasons

save political ones, though he imagined others ; he was not friendly to such Protestants as had the pluck to denounce the particular sort of Protestantism he favoured.

The greatest blot on his career is his loathing—it was little less—for those of the old faith. Justification of his attitude, except politically, is difficult. The conduct of neither party was beyond reproach. In judging of the dispute it must be remembered that the reasonable severity of one age is often regarded as an excess of cruelty by the next. He, however, hated all Catholics with a bitterness quite unwarranted by facts. The Smithfield massacres were terrible, but the martyrdom of Catholics began earlier and lasted longer. It must be remembered, however, that he witnessed, as a boy, the horrors of St. Bartholomew ; he could never understand that the demoniac nights were inspired by a wicked and shameless Queen, working on the terrors of a lunatic son. Philip was a great deal more in earnest on the purely religious aspect of the dispute than any one except, it may be, Languet and du Mornay. The great Prince of Orange, a nobly and godly-minded man, renounced his allegiance to Catholicism only when it menaced the political independence of the Dutch. He was stirred by a wholehearted love of freedom more than by a devotion to the niceties of the reformed doctrines. Unluckily for what was good on the Catholic side Philip of Spain, a cruel fanatic, ruined his cause by an undue severity. He desired a personal power that would have made every one in Europe, except himself, a slave. It is easy to realise this now ; distance clears the sight. But Philip Sidney died a young man ; he was fervently religious, he did not understand a difficult problem. His untoward experiences in Holland, when he discovered that Protestant and angel are not necessarily synonymous terms, if they opened his eyes, opened them too late. Bigotry of a sort that has smeared the pages of recent history, casts something of a shadow across his fame. It is foolish to ignore this defect, though he was inspired by his prejudice to brave the anger of a Tudor, and was willing to allow an active spirit to chafe under the tedium of many idle hours rather than support what he conceived to be, rightly or wrongly, a lie. Fortunately with him were the poet's gifts of reverie and reverence for the beautiful. The gods did not desert him in his days of inactivity. These days are numerous, when we think at how early an age he died. With a sigh—from what we know of him he sighed—he contented himself by paying the homage due to Elizabeth and England to the muses of poetry and romance. Here, again, he showed that failure is truer than success : the half better than the whole. Absolute sincerity made at once Philip's failure and Philip's glory. Men of his own time, without complete understanding, saw this ; in our own day, laugh as we will at a man whose greatest defect was a lack of humour, there are tears in our laughter, and his very faults make him dear to us. It is comfortable to remember that a paragon can be human, for us who are not immaculate.

Another reason, as though his aloofness were not a sufficient difficulty to overcome, besets his biographer. His career was so mercilessly short, his years so jealously numbered, that the material to one's hand is scanty and unsatisfactory. Pæans of undiscriminating praise echo through the succeeding centuries ; were they printed in a collection they would manufacture a portly volume. But they all give us a single aspect of the man—the seraphic aspect. His fellows claimed for him almost saintlike qualities, and posterity has accepted their verdict. But at an age when other men, if they are to win fame, are spoken of as giving promise of illustrious performance he had already passed—

"To where, beyond these voices, there is peace."

At his death the greatest poets vied with humbler singers in praise of unequalled virtue; men of lax morals were for the moment struck with shame; good men and scholars mourned one who, by general consent, was the flower of European knighthood. Princes sorrowed, we are told, and there were those in Spain who rendered willingly the tribute of a heartfelt sigh. We cannot find in authentic history a man whose conduct so fixedly impressed his own and succeeding generations, yet whose claim to adoration is supported merely by panegyric and the foreshadowing of good work. And this short life of his is a real difficulty to those who would write of him. So considerable a portion of it was spent in trivial embassies, important for the moment only; of real history in the making his part was necessarily insignificant. The facts we have scarcely warrant the panegyrics of his contemporaries, at least as judged by modern eyes. Yet for Fulke Greville and others he was almost a perfect man, knowing neither spot nor stain. And this unison, in which there is no jarring note, could only have been excited by conspicuous virtues and graces. Succeeding writers have been misled by these acclamations and lamentations; they overdo the praise, they lose their critical acumen. Thus his name has been handed down from generation to generation as the model on whom every schoolboy should arrange his own actions and character. A nobler ideal it is not easy to suggest. Yet the ideal is a Sidney of legend rather than of reality. He had grave faults; even the few facts we have prove them.

That he was bigoted is not to be wondered at. Religious controversy was conducted in a temper and manner that made many sane men, we may be certain, loathe all religion. Their motto would have been, had they dared to show it, "a curse on both your houses." We must remember, too, that the quarrels in which he took so great an interest were political no less than theological.

A King of Spain had helped the Protestants, a free-
thinking King of France had burnt heretics.  An English
King had embraced the doctrines of Luther in order to
achieve his own ends and annoy the Pope.  Henry VIII.
was not a bad man, and in many ways he was a fine King.
Probably only cardinals and bishops and reformers, whose
reformation did not always apply to their private conduct,
really troubled about dogma.  The vital issue was liberty
or slavery.  Roman Catholicism, as hated by Sidney, really
meant Spain.  Philip only half realised this.  When he
discusses religious matters he is violent and not logical.
He was no wiser, no more temperate, no more philosophical than his neighbours.  Of a reserved temperament,
he knew intimately only a few.  He was like a snail,
except on occasion, content within the confines of his own
shell.  With the will-o'-the-wisps of the Court he had
nothing in common.  Men admired and worshipped, but
they admired and worshipped from afar.  This attitude of
theirs is not astonishing ; his grave and sober demeanour
awed them into respect.

The portraits extant of Philip are disappointing.  The
picture Veronese painted of him in Venice, which Languet
grew to like, is lost.  Until it is found we must content
ourselves as best we may with those unsatisfactory pre-
sentments of his features that are to hand.  Much
difficulty is experienced tracing in them his reputed
grace of figure and courtly attitude.  Features confront
us that do not betray unusual intelligence, and they are
not handsome.  Artist, not model, must be at fault.  His
face gave pleasure to beholders, and it was illuminated by
the fire of his genius.  Faces were fortunes at the Court of
Elizabeth, where gallants ruffled it bravely that they might
please the eye of the Queen.  Hers was a Court where, as
at the Cloth of Gold, men "wore their castles and forests on
their backs."  Yet his pre-eminence is not disputed even
by those who were, or thought themselves, his rivals.

QUEEN ELIZABETH
FROM THE PICTURE AT ROUSHAM

Unfortunately painters of the later Tudor era seem incapable of catching a likeness. If their records are true, we hold to-day greatly different notions of grace and beauty. Stately, for example, Elizabeth certainly is in her portraits, but beautiful she is not. Yet the many references to her loveliness cannot be merely fulsome adulation, for these compliments were not all paid directly to her, and were made by many who had no personal ends to gain.

Curious similarities haunt the features of all those whom Elizabethan painters limned. A distinctive legend adorns the frame, but the high foreheads and hooked noses seem to have been fashioned in the same mould. To the historian and reader, this failure to convince us that current estimates and appreciations were justified is an irreparable loss, which we must accept with what equanimity we can.

# CHAPTER II

## EARLY INFLUENCES

Penshurst, its history—Sir Henry Sidney—His early life—His devotion to Edward VI.—His conduct after Edward's death—Philip's mother—Tudor notions of religious freedom—Protestant dissensions—Johann Sturm—The Jesuits—Spain and the Papacy—Impossibility of tolerance

PENSHURST has been so often the theme of panegyrist and poet, that nothing new is left to be said. Its supreme natural beauties are added to by the recollection that it is a cradle of the Sidneys, though it was not their first home in England. For though more honest and patriotic Englishmen have not lived and moved among us, it was in Anjou that they first made a bid for fame. Sir William de Sidnei, the pioneer of his race on English land, was Chamberlain to Henry II., and accompanied that prince when he left France. Quietly and steadily the Chancellor's descendants achieved more and more distinction, till at last Sir William Sidney gained the favour of Henry VIII. In war and peace he was alike distinguished, and was chosen to represent his master on more than one embassage of importance, when he became the recipient of signal honours. He had won his knighthood on the field of Flodden, and not long after he represented his King when that King's sister was crowned as Queen of France. We can still read how he and his nine companions, clad in green, tilted for the honour of St. George against the chivalry who claimed St. Denis as their saint. He was with his King on the Field of the Cloth of Gold, where extravagant courtiers carried their estates upon their backs, and ostentatious pronouncements of friendship failed to produce a permanent peace. For Sidney, however, the sun shone steadily, and he was dubbed a Knight of the Garter, a great though not quite unique honour for a commoner, as well as chamberlain and tutor to Edward, Prince of Wales. From this prince he received as a gift the stately manor of Penshurst, " with the adjoining lands, meadows, and pastures, woods and trees," the stateliest demesne in all England.

There had been many owners of Penshurst, and more than once it had reverted to the Crown because the occupier lacked an heir. The De Porchesters held it for two hundred years, and from the last of the race it passed to Sir John de Pulteney. To him the place owes much, for having obtained permission to embattle the building, he contrived to beautify it in many ways. As an example of a feudal house at its grandest it was probably unrivalled then as now. Pulteney is credited with having devised, or at least caused to be built, the noble hall with its strikingly beautiful timber roof and central hearth, nor did he forget the claims of music, a minstrels' gallery crowning his design. Once, at least, he was the host of royalty at this noble Kentish home, entertaining for the Christmas festivities the Black Prince and his wife Joan, called the Fair Maid of Kent. After Pulteney, who had no heirs, Sir John Devereux, Warden of the Cinque Ports, became its owner. He, like his predecessor, built considerably, and added a long wing to a residence already majestic enough. Love of building, a mania not unknown in our own day, and architectural taste, almost unknown, beyond the common, impelled him. There was no one to whom he could leave his possessions. A bewildering succession of owners confronts us, till at last, in 1552, Sir William Sidney, but a few months before his death, became " fyrste of his name who was Lorde of this Mannor." Sir William died, and Henry became lord of the fair demesne, and at the same time, as we know, or almost at the same time, the companion of Edward VI. " At the young King's accession he was reputed for his virtues, fine composition of body, gallantry, and liveliness of spirit, the most pleasant young gentleman in Court. And for the singular love and entire affection that virtuous prince had ever shown him, he was made one of the four principal gentlemen of his privy chamber. And such delight had he in his modest and ingenuous conversation and company as he rarely gave him leave to be absent from him." That Sir Henry was the king's bedfellow—the custom of the time providing for this, to our ideas, curious arrangement— meant that even as a child he had become a person of importance. Readers of Grammont will be familiar with the lengths to which a habit, in itself inoffensive, could be pushed nearly a hundred years later. The somewhat startling details set forth in the Count's enter- taining volumes need not be repeated here. Wives and husbands held a more generous notion of the claims of friendship than is popular in our sedater times. To be chosen as the Prince's bedfellow was important; and, apparently in the reign of Charles II., by Divine right King and Fidei Defensor, Nell Gwynne was more respect- able than some of her rivals. This custom, however, of appointing a bedfellow to a person of distinction is interesting.

Henry Sidney- became lord of Penshurst. There are half-a-dozen descriptions of the place extant. Not one gives the faintest impression of the beauties that greet us to-day, yet it was more beautiful, in itself and in its sur- roundings, in Philip's day than in ours. The valley of the Medway was then, we cannot doubt, pleasant and agree-

Equs Auratus

HENRICUS SYDNEIUS

Quo me Fata vocant

SIR HENRY SIDNEY
FROM AN ENGRAVING

able.   It is said to be so now by enthusiasts, whose imaginative powers strike our envy.   Penshurst is still beautiful,
and Sir Henry found it convenient.   It stood even nearer
to London then, comparatively speaking, than it does
now.   The couplet, in praise of one corner of the park,
runs—

> "Where Pan and Bacchus their high feasts have made,
> Beneath the broad beech and the chestnut shade."

There is no reason why the revels of these deities should
not be recorded in the present tense.   Ben Jonson is
peculiarly the laureate of Penshurst.   Convention bids us
admire his lines, and we admire them conventionally, just
as conventionally we admire "The Alchemist" or "Every
Man in his Humour."   But few sit down willingly to study
these ponderous effusions.   Were it not for the vile
slanders of Drummond of Hawthornden on their author
even bookworms would not burrow into their recesses.
The stage has done with them.   They were written for
the stage, and they have not held the stage.   That is the
only comment that can be made concerning them.   A
few pious people in every age will continue to praise them
and forget to read them, literary piety being no more
capable of explanation and quite as bigoted as that which
belongs to the Churches.   The following verses, however,
are often quoted concerning Penshurst, and may be re-
quoted here.   They are neither good nor very bad.   They
are also non-committal.   Cumberland says of Jonson that
he "stocked his mind with such a mass of other men's
thoughts that his imagination had not power to struggle
through the crowd."   The powerlessness of his imagination
so to do is evidenced in the following lines :—

> "Thou art not, Penshurst, built to envious show
> Of touch or marble, nor canst boast a row
> Of polished pillars or a roof of gold ;

> Thou hast no lantern, whereof tales are told,
> Or stairs, or courts, but stand'st an ancient pile,
> And—these grudged at—art reverenced the while.
> Thou joyst in better marks of soil, of air,
> Of wood, of water ; therein art thou fair."

Here we have the classic description of the place, which would not describe a yard, and a gift of lamentably halting and uninspired verse into the bargain. Giffard's volume of Jonson, the best, gives us, including the index, over eight hundred pages, and each page is printed in double columns. From this terrifying jungle we may pluck a few stanzas of merit, and some fewer of exceeding beauty. The major part of this prolific poet's output is no better and no worse than his lines on Penshurst. To read most of his effusions is a direct incentive to compose " a fit of rhyme against rhyme." But it is necessary to allude to this poet's works in passing, for he affected to draw inspiration from Penshurst, and Philip Sidney spent his childhood there.

> "And though thy walls be of the country stone,
> They're reared with no man's ruin, no man's groan ;
> There's none that dwell about them wish them down,
> But all come in, the farmer and the clown,
> And no one empty handed to salute
> Thy lord and lady, though they have no suit."

To this Mr. Fox Bourne puts a note as follows : " The lord whom, with his lady, Ben Jonson honoured was not Sir Henry Sidney, but his younger son Robert, afterwards Earl of Leicester. Yet the praise was perhaps more appropriate to Sir Henry and his good wife than to their son and daughter-in-law." This note, coming from so great an authority, must be treated with respect. Yet one agrees that it has two unintended merits—it does not praïse verses that endeavour, haltingly, to do honour to Penshurst, and it invites us to consider, and by doing so discover, how the second Lord Leicester was far the greatest master that Penshurst knew. The life of Sir Robert Sidney is well worth writing : how well worth the perfunctory sketch in this volume can only hint.

Philip Sidney was born at Penshurst on October 30, 1554 ; he died on October 17, 1586, not quite thirty-two years old. Within that narrow compass his life's history is comprised ; of his first ten years we have the scantiest records. In great measure he must have been left to the care of servants, seeing little of his mother and even less of his father. This was not a desirable, though it was an unavoidable, bringing up. The involuntary absence of his parents from Penshurst would have hurt a less serious nature ; but their duties were peremptorily demanded elsewhere. The forced separation of his early years did not cool either his love or his obedience. He had, too, every reason to be proud of father and mother, not alone on account of their personal merits, but on account of the illustrious name he bore. A famous critic contends that Philip put no undue value on noble birth. Here we have a somewhat intemperate eulogy. Most emphatically Philip held his descent in high value, declaring once in defence of Leicester : " I am a Dudley in blood ; that duke's daughter's son ; and do acknowledge, though in all truth I may justly affirm, that I am by my father's side of ancient gentry ; yet I do acknowledge, I say, that my chiefest honour is to be a Dudley." So vigorous a pronouncement nonplusses the critic and refutes his assertion. No stronger proof is needed that he did not look upon himself as a mere commoner. Throughout his short life he never once allowed his rank and importance to be called in question.

It has been said that, " If the truth must be told Sidney, as we now know him, is not an eminently engaging or profoundly interesting character." Boasts such as the one just quoted are not meritorious, they are foolish ; in this

boast Philip was speaking as a youngster dazzled by the
surface splendour of Leicester. Such youthful vainglory
is not, however, to be condemned roughly. In his heart
of hearts he was a Sidney. I think his conduct proves it.
Yet without at all accepting the critic's dictum, it must none
the less be acknowledged that much of the young man's
charm is to be taken on trust. Our usual estimate of him
is too clearly the phantom of a long tradition to be really
accurate. Tradition never absolutely lies, but tradition
exaggerates.

Sir Henry Sidney, himself the son of a distinguished
father, had little credit or kindness during his life ; less
than " bare justice " has been accorded to him since his
death. Yet Philip was his son. One would hardly claim
for him that he was " eminently engaging," though his
career and himself should arouse interest and must command respect. Never a favourite among his contemporaries, he knew how to make his will felt among those
whom he was sent to govern. Compliments he could not
coin, but he knew how best to intimidate rebels and evolve
some sort of order out of chaos. His honesty was
conspicuous and his courage beyond the shafts of
calumny. As an administrator he many times showed
unusual ability ; his services were always in request.
For all tangible reward he was, at gracious intervals, permitted to sit " on the carpet of hope smoking the pipe
of expectation." He was no poet, and had little time to
exercise the talent of verse-making had he possessed it.
But, man of affairs though he was, he rejoiced in his boy's
accomplishment.

Born in the July of 1529, a comfortable and brilliant
career seemed Sir Henry's destiny. Little of comfort
was to be his lot. Not only had he all the advantages
of considerable rank : he inherited a good fortune, and
was early taken into Court favour. As we have seen,
he was chosen to be the playmate and often the bedfellow

according to the custom of the time, of Prince Edward.
His father and mother were, respectively, his highness's
chamberlain and governess. His aunt, on his mother's
side, was "in such place as, among meaner personages, is
called a dry nurse."

On few children could fortune have smiled more favourably. In addition to conspicuous advantages, his own
merit stood him in good stead. He writes: "As the
prince grew in years and discretion, so grew I in favour
and liking of him." Favour and liking were continued to
the end of Edward's life of sixteen years. Sir Henry
was an only son, but he had four sisters, one of whom,
Frances, married Fitzwalter, later Earl of Sussex. To her
posterity owes a real debt of gratitude. She promoted the
advancement of sound learning, founding the College of
Sidney-Sussex in the University of Cambridge.

When Edward succeeded to the throne he lost no time
in conferring favours on his old playmate. Four coveted
distinctions were conferred on him, who was quaintly
described as "the odd man and paragon" of the Court.
As royal cipherer he received the desirable sum of
£33 6s. 8d. a year. On the same day and occasion as
the future Lord Burleigh he received the honour of a
knighthood. Following rapidly on this already quick
promotion he was nominated one of the four grooms of
the bedchamber. Then he was entrusted with a mission
to France, where he did his business so well that he was
despatched on a second errand, this time to Spain.
Apparent good fortune did not end here. The Duke of
Northumberland, full of false religion and subtle scheming,
fixed upon Sir Henry for a son-in-law.

So Sir Henry and the Lady Mary Dudley were married.
For them the alliance was a most happy one. In weal
or woe—and they had more of sorrow than happiness to
meet—the two were ever lovers and friends. That this
consummation should be arrived at was a matter of no

interest to the Duke.  His crafty head was full of a plot
for the almost regal betterment of his family and, most of
all, for himself.   Dangers from the Papists, from rapacious
enemies, were adroitly rumoured.  The King's health was
known to be feeble, and he had no heirs of his body.  The
unfortunate, much maligned, but bigoted and kind-hearted
Mary was the next heir.  Fear and a vague unrest brooded
over the land.

In this nervous condition of men's minds Northumberland
saw his own chance.  His unmarried daughter he gave to
Lord Hastings, and then made his unscrupulous and daring
bid for permanent power.  His son was the husband of
the Lady Jane Grey.  With inconceivable audacity he
determined to make this beautiful, clever, innocent girl
Queen of England.  As her consort he thought his son
would directly influence her, and that he would be able
easily to influence his son.  The propriety of this daring
scheme he trusted to make apparent to Lady Jane by
means of those subtle arguments he well knew how to
use.  An example of how vaulting ambition may o'erleap
itself was the result, a result not confined to Northumberland's own ruin, that was a deserved retribution, but
embracing the destruction of innocent and gentle people.
Meanwhile events, till the fatal June 21st, seemed to
march in the plotter's favour—to play into his hand.  At
the earnest request of the Duke the King appointed his
kinswoman as successor to the throne.  Edward was too
weak to perceive the fragility of the arguments used on
the occasion.  Fervent Protestant as he had been schooled
to be, any thought of the possibility of Mary succeeding
him was an additional pang to the bodily pains he endured.
Mere boy, and a dying boy, he cannot be blamed for not
realising that it was Northumberland's ambition and not
the reformed faith for which the artful councillor was
pleading.  Had real zeal for religion been his inspiration,
or animated his least word, he might have advocated the

claims of Elizabeth, whom no Protestant deemed illegitimate, nay, regarded as a true daughter of Henry VIII.,
and a royal princess. Of course, such a solution of a
supposed difficulty would not have suited itself to Northumberland's plans. His arguments could convince no
sane man ; it was to a sick king, yet in his teens, that
they sounded plausible and even convincing. Protestantism
—his Protestantism—appeared triumphant to the Duke,
and he deluded himself into the belief that his machinations were beyond discovery, and must be successful.
A fortnight later Edward died in Sir Henry's arms. His
last words show the temper of the time and the ease with
which a scholarly boy was duped. "Oh, my Lord God,
defend this realm from papistry and defend Thy true
religion." Save for a brief moment the answer to this
"complaint unto the Lord" was decidedly unexpected
and inconvenient. Within a fortnight Mary was on the
throne that was hers by right, and a few days later the
usurpers were in prison.

Sir Henry saw, and quickly, that he had been befooled
in assenting so readily to the Duke's scheme. He was
among the first, after Mary's accession, to ask for forgiveness. Mary did not forgive easily, and no wonder, but
his pardon was granted quickly enough. This craving for
forgiveness has brought some contumely on his memory.
No less an authority than Mr. Fox Bourne writes that "if
allowable it was hardly praiseworthy." Surely this is less
than justice ; for there are powerful reasons why he should
have made his submission. His wife, whom he loved, was
a daughter of the guilty Duke and a sister of the sham
Queen's husband. The truculent attitude of his father-in-
law must have influenced so young a man. Persuasion
and argument, from such powerful lips, influenced him to
sign what he ought not to have signed, to place himself in
a position a more experienced man would have avoided.
Then, too, this Reformed Faith, so in danger, was the

creation of his first patron, who had chosen him for his son's friend ; that son whose succession was to solidify, and establish firmly, all that the great King—for great he was though his crimes were leviathan too—had brought about. His subsequent career, which will be noted in some pages that follow, makes clear proof that cowardice, a desire to spare himself, did not animate his submission. He loved his country greatly. Is it not reasonable to believe that this very love inspired him to be at her call in the hour of her danger ? And one argument weighed with him more than all others. It is a sentimental reason, and a powerful, for Sir Henry was too noble a man to care whether the epithet sentimental were hurled at him or not. He had been devoted to his boy friend, knew and loved him better than any one else could have loved him and known him. He had received rewards, but not sought them. Edward must have talked with him over Northumberland's scheme, and stated his approval. Such a bias towards the exclusion of Mary and the elevation of Lady Jane, coming from the monarch himself, must have clouded his judgment. With Edward's dying words ringing in his ear, with knowledge strengthening each one of the fifteen days in which the plot failed, it is not extravagant to suppose that he thought he would best obey his master's wishes by making friends with the unrighteous, for a time, and so preserve, as far as he could, quietly, not without success, the interests of that cause his master so truly loved. He knew the dangers that threatened the kingdom. Here, it may plausibly be suggested, lay the whole motive of his conduct at this crisis. Humane and affectionate men may, and do, honestly reason thus. Hearts at times speak more wisely than brains. Mistakes are sometimes made in the interpreting of a man's actions because the exact circumstances that prompt them are forgotten. Sir Henry was a brave man, a firm supporter, as his son after him, of the Reformed Church. No one

knew better than he that his conduct was open to miscon-
struction. Facts are stubborn in his support. To do his
duty was his one ambition. He never sought honours or
titles, his work spelt incessant toil and scurvy recognition ;
his courage, honesty, and consistency were used gladly,
but his exercise of such virtues made him daily poorer.
The document he had signed, for signing which he is
sneered at, had attracted the signatures of judges, privy
councillors, and bishops. An ailing king, who was his
playfellow, whom he loved, had persuaded him to give
the Letters Patent the credit of his name. Logic is
excellent when all goes smoothly ; it is a pretty rapier
enough. But if only logical reasons animated men we
might as well be machines. Queen Mary, at least, was
not vindictive. Restored, not to favour, at least to useful
work, he was appointed, and there is a touch of poignant
humour here, to travel in the Duke of Bedford's suit to
Spain to "fetch" the royal bridegroom, Philip. He procured the release from the Tower of his near relatives.
For himself he did not ask reward, but he obtained one
honour paradoxical and extraordinary, in the light of later
history. A son was born to him, and that son Philip
Sidney. The most ardent enemy of Spain and the
Catholic religion began life as the godson of " The Most
Catholic King."

Of the boy's mother not much is known, and what little
we do know makes us wish for further details. Though
born to high rank she was not favoured by fortune. Her
father, the Duke of Northumberland, perished, as he
deserved to perish, on the scaffold, but the same fate,
undeserved, befell her brother, Lord Guildford Dudley,
and his wife, Lady Jane Grey. From her brother Leicester
she could hardly expect genuine sympathy or affection.
Yet she was patient and uncomplaining, a serene, good,
Christian woman. The few letters of hers that are preserved are mostly requests for money, of which she always

had a plentiful lack, though she lived quietly, when she could, in her little house by St. Paul's Wharf. Passionately fond of her husband, whom she sometimes accompanied to Ireland, she was devoted to her children. It was for their sakes that she at times pleaded her poverty and asked for assistance. Of herself she seems to have thought but little ; content to do her duty, she neither sought for nor desired promotion and honour. This modesty, inherent in her character, was accentuated by the terrible malady that permanently disfigured her. Yet the ignoble Queen whom she had loyally nursed back to life, thus herself contracting the small-pox, never deigned to relieve her from the pettiest and meanest worries. No word of complaint on this score seems to have escaped her, though she might well have claimed some sign of interest and affection from the woman whom she had snatched from death at so great a cost. As were so many of the faithful and virtuous, she also was ignored and put aside when the service required had been fully rendered and reward, however slight, reasonably expected. Only a Court poet could be blind enough, or foolish enough, or mendacious enough, to hymn a—

> "Great Eliza, the retreat of those
> Who, weak and injured, her protection chose,
> Her subjects' joy, the strength of her allies,
> The fear and wonder of her enemies,"

for such a person did not exist, and only the fourth line contains a truth.

Indeed, the loyalty of such exceptionally level-headed people as Sir Henry and his wife is one of the most puzzling facts that face a historian dealing with this period. It is far easier to understand the devotion inspired later by the Stuarts. A belief in the divine right of kings, even of kings who " govern wrong," had become an article of a creed which men, often of great intelligence and courage, were able to understand. But previously to the

LADY MARY DUDLEY
FROM AN ENGRAVING BY E. HARDING

Stuarts the formula of divine right had not been actually proclaimed. Moreover, in addition to the still shadowy conception of such a doctrine, no one of importance had volunteered a theory that kings were less than an advantage to a nation and might be expeditiously removed. The popularity of Charles II. is, of course, partly due to his own inherent qualities of careless good nature and real kindness of heart. No sane men could regard the austere and ambitious Cromwell with other feelings than those of aversion; not that the Protector was a bad man, he was not: but because under his intolerable despotism the trifling amenities of life were choked, and to vigorously minded people existence became a melancholy burden. An oft-repeated dictum of Macaulay's that the Puritans forbad bear-baiting, not out of a feeling of sympathy and pity for the bears, but because they hated to see others enjoying themselves, is a perfectly just estimate of the real spirit that actuated these people. However greatly England was feared and respected abroad during Cromwell's reign, it is not conceivable that life was even tolerable at home. But when the King, whom Dr. Johnson admired so outspokenly, despite his mistresses and rather lax code of morality, came back, existence was smoother for everybody, and the manners and customs of Whitehall were, at least, amusing. The grim respectability of the Protector's Court was, it may be suggested, less healthy than the easy manners encouraged, or at least allowed, by the second Charles. Hence it came about that in men's minds, and those of Churchmen especially, was strengthened a belief in the doctrine of divine right. Before, and during the Tudor period, kings fought kings; afterwards the people, not for the first time but more systematically, fought the king and claimed and exercised a right to depose him if necessary. The first effort of a democracy to rule in this country led to a tyranny by a section worse than has ever been known before or since. Seeing that the substitute was more dangerous to civil and religious liberty than anything that preceded it, the cause of a more real freedom was effectually encouraged by a compromise when William III. came to the throne. Intelligible reasons can be given why men supported the Crown or the Parliament. It is harder to understand, before the two became antagonistic forces—especially before the sovereign, in the eyes of many, was acclaimed as almost divine—how men and women could be found to sacrifice their lives and their happiness to the whim of cruel and arbitrary despots, of whom Henry VIII. was not the most cruel or Elizabeth the most considerate, though she was certainly the most selfish.

A French poet declared of Kean, the actor, that the dazzling tragedian was

"Si mauvais acteur dans sa propre histoire."

The same comment may be applied in the conduct of their lives to Sir Henry and his wife. Their loyalty and their devotion brought insult and contumely ; and no reason is discoverable, save personal attachment to a disagreeable woman, why they should have sacrificed their happiness, as they both did, to her pride and her caprice. Yet they were ever far more loyal than were those who reaped substantial benefits. And, very curious to observe, those who bit the hand that fed them were always the most readily forgiven. To tell the truth was an error of judgment on the part of the speaker that the Queen never forgave. Work had to be done, especially on the borders and in Ireland, requiring consummate tact, invincible energy, and remarkable courage. These tasks were accomplished, and in the main well, with the most conspicuous loyalty and courage by men who received abuse instead of praise, who so far from being enriched were constantly impoverished. It will always be a mystery how this zeal, the formulated theory of divine right being absent, was aroused ; still more will it be a mystery how this eagerness continued despite constant affronts and studied injustice.

Some writers suggest that a zeal for the Protestant religion animated men. This may be so, and in the case of many of the best men it was so. Busy people, like Sir Henry, however, had scant time for theology, and such as he had he took from a boy he loved. Lady Mary, excellent woman and worthy of all honour, was not a theologian. Philip's very decided attitude of mind makes it curious that a Tudor, and an Elizabeth Tudor, should inspire respect. Henry protested because he wanted a divorce. He could not get one, so he still more loudly protested and became a Protestant. I am, of course, not discussing a great controversy irreverently or with bias. And I favour neither side in the dispute. Very unfortunately matters of difference had to be decided, and rival armies were marshalled. But the commanders on both sides cannot command much of our respect. In the rank and file many men were found of the highest virtue who could, and would willingly, have loved each other had an opportunity of doing so been allowed to them.

But there is an argument, quite unanswerable it seems to me, that needs consideration. Henry was only a Protestant in so far as he derived pecuniary benefits from his opposition to the Pope. He was never one in the sense that Wycliffe and his Lollards were antagonistic to the Papacy. He had more wit and less conviction. Every sort of device, afterwards declared idolatrous, was supported by Henry, and ignored at the risk of pains and penalties rather rigorously enforced. Elizabeth encouraged a form of worship more ritualistic than any the most ritualistic parson of our own day has ventured to suggest, and certainly has never dared to put into practice. Moreover, Elizabeth horrified her best supporters by pretending to be in love with a man who, if he had an inkling of religion, which is doubtful, leant to the side many earnest men opposed. The Tudor instinct for the furtherance and control of religious observances comes as a curious phenomenon at the very time when men of all creeds and parties were actively interested in religious controversy. Controversy to a Tudor mind meant that a despot exacted, and had a right to exact, implicit obedience, both in thought and deed, from all who were their subjects. In many ways this imperious attitude was not intolerable, only intolerant. It cannot be suggested, with any show of argument, that they cared in the least which direction the trend of thought flowed so long as their own authority was blindly acknowledged. The cruellest Pope was not so cruel as Henry, the most imperious less malevolent than Elizabeth. These people, Henry and Elizabeth, cared nothing so long as they got their own way; and they adopted, on occasion, unpleasant methods of attaining the objects they had in view. That they were tolerated is, I think, due to this : they hated Rome, because Rome opposed them ; it was to their worldly advantage to support every enemy of the Roman Pontiff. Their own largeness of mind is exhibited by the instances, of which there are many, where they attacked everybody who dared to oppose their will in any way whatsoever. Their idea of religious freedom was to substitute a Tudor for a Pope. And it is, to the observant and unbiassed student, somewhat curious that the problem they considered was, not whether there should exist a Church with bishops and a head, but whether any one should be allowed to live who had the temerity to declare that a Tudor was not the chief of all Christian people, and the one entitled to decide who should be the authoritative ministers unto them.

Consequently it is remarkable to find men of real religious instinct standing by the very sovereigns who were without religion. The reason is, putting aside the rather biassed attitude of those who became wealthy, that, within certain limits, some free discussion was tolerated. This tolerance was an advance, and a novelty ; but it was a toleration that had its root in an intolerance as un-mitigated and as dreadful as any it usurped. The men who fought for Protestantism cared for all that Pro-testantism meant. The sovereigns, who for their own ends shielded their efforts, cared nothing about it at all. Some of the punishments inflicted by Elizabeth on those who disobeyed her mandates were very cruel and drastic, as we shall see. Unfortunately a belief in intolerance was universal, and no ruler or statesman thought for a moment that he could, by any possibility, be in the wrong. It therefore happened that a real zeal for the right led men to do the most abominable deeds. And this zeal, as we shall see and refer to, was not confined to a Catholic Mary and a Protestant Elizabeth. Each tiny sect that separated itself from the two chief opposing factions can show its list of executioners and martyrs. The same spirit that stirred men to adventures by sea and on land, the same courage that led them to rely on their own initiative at a moment of danger, is traced in their various attitudes towards religious and ethical questions. In England a temper of sturdy independence was gaining strength under the, apparently, growing absolutism of the Tudors. Nor is this phenomenon at all wonderful, for the Tudors were in reality attempting the experiment of subordinating action and thought to individual authority. Naturally, at first, kings could assert their authority with comparative ease. But even Elizabeth's power grew weaker towards the end of her reign, and James, had he been as wise as he was learned, would have realised that very little personal authority remained to a king.

Signs of change, though not wanting, were hardly apparent when Philip Sidney first appeared on the stage, and his advisers do not seem to have understood exactly what the mental unrest and clamour signified. Neither to them nor to Philip would it have been possible to foresee the end. They could not know that before the world was much older amazing events were to happen, events of a kind not seen in England before, when the people, united for a brief moment, set up their own sovereign, only to find he was King Stork and not King Log.

Other affairs than those directly inspired by religion, or the want of it, agitated the minds of contending factions. But even in the settlement of these it was always, when reduced to a common denominator, found to be a question between the acceptance of a Pope or one of the many Popes the anti-Roman parties set up for themselves. The good that the Reformers accomplished was most seriously hindered at the outset by the absurd quarrels they started among the seceders. They were like a body of Italian banditti who, in the face of a powerful antagonist, ignored the common danger, each one being eager to avenge a personal affront, to settle a vendetta the conclusion of which weakened their own forces and left a united enemy more powerful than ever. It is difficult to read of these feuds with patience, yet it is impossible to avoid mention of them again and again. The lack of any sort of Christian charity or any approach to honesty on the part of the combatants is astonishing to contemplate. In the mad conflict as to which party should control the bucket, Truth herself was left shivering at the bottom of the well.

An example of the folly of the Protestants may be taken from the history of a man to whose care Robert Sidney was confided. Johann Sturm was the friend of Roger Ascham and of Languet. His learning was great, his piety universally admitted. As Rector of the Gymnasium at Strasburg, he won such honour for the institution and such fame for himself that the Emperor Maximilian raised the place to the status of a University. Yet this man, after forty-four years of devoted service, was dismissed by the Lutherans, who showed their good sense, gratitude, and Christianity by hating him on account of his Calvinistic principles, treating him with ignominy. The disgrace attaching to such an act remains theirs, not his.

Controversies of a religious kind are invariably bitter, and in them the real points of value and edification are always forgotten or ignored. It is often asserted that in the Elizabethan age the universal activity in every sort of human endeavour is to be expected in theological matters as in others ostensibly of more worldly concern. There is this reason partially to justify such a theory. An awakening of the public mind had come about in poetry, drama, music : men began to strike out new lines for themselves, to think for themselves more freely than they had ever done before. It seemed no more difficult to reform a religion than to reform the sonnet, to discover a new verity than to exploit a new continent. What was most materially worth having in the world belonged to those of the older faith. Business zeal and religious zeal became partners. Often rank injustice and bare-faced robbery were viewed with undisguised approval by men of considerable piety. The bigotry and power of Spain were not commendable ; but the bigotry of her opponents, of which England and Holland were chief, was not less aggressive and unpardonable. It cannot be doubted that the riches from the Spanish Main formed a powerful incentive to adventurous spirits to adopt any new form of religion that gave a halo of sanctity to performances not of themselves peculiarly remarkable for honesty.

It is, of course, easy for us, living in an age when our disputes are, comparatively speaking, of little more than parochial size, to misjudge the actors and their motives in a drama greater than any in which we have been called upon to play a part. Yet we have an example before us,

even to-day, of how bitterly faction fights are still fought,
over very minor issues, when the words " faith," " religion,"
and the like, are hurled by opponents at each other.   The
ignorance and brutality sometimes shown in these
squabbles concerning the government of a parish school,
exhibitions of temper quite unwarranted by the importance
of the points at issue, the perversity of rivals, sensible
enough in most controversies, lest a reasonable compromise should be arranged, show us that this strange
antagonism between supporters of truths none dispute,
though dying, we may hope, is not yet dead.   Therefore
it is not altogether impossible for us to realise how
tremendous the conflict was more than three hundred
years ago.

All walks of life were rendered dangerous to the
traveller, for at every step he was either tripped up or
applauded, according to the particular form of Christianity
affected by the spectators.   Very fortunately for ourselves
we save life and limb, however much our reputations
suffer.   When Sidney lived, no opponent, on any side,
escaped unscathed if his adversary were skilful enough
to waylay him.   The big bonfire of religious intolerance
was lit in the sixteenth century ; it only smoulders now.
Here in England a few faggots emit sparks dangerous
enough to be uncomfortable, but unlikely to cause any
fresh conflagration.   Mrs. Varden always consoled herself
with Foxe's " Martyrs," not at all a book to be relied on.
Mrs. Varden was a descendant.   Lord George Gordon
stirred up the embers of a fanaticism no civil power could
control.   At first even actors took sides, and in their plays,
a profound scholar tells us : " It is odd enough to see
quoted in a dramatic performance, chapter and verse as
formally as if a sermon were to be performed.   There we
find such rude learning as this :—

" ' Read the v. to the Galatians, and there you shall see
That the flesh rebelleth against the Spirit,'

or in homely rhymes like these :—

> " ' I will show you what St. Paul doth declare
> In his Epistle to the Hebrews and the x. chapter.' "

Mr. Disraeli comments as follows, justly : " They curiously exemplify that regular progress in the history of man, which has shown itself in more recent revolutions in Europe : the old people still clinging, from habit and affection, to what is obsolete, and the young ardent in establishing what is new ; while the balance of human happiness trembles between both."

Of the Jesuits strange stories were told and believed. " Political calumny," says the author just quoted, " is said to have been reduced to wit, like that of logic, by the Jesuits. This itself may be a political calumny. A powerful body, who themselves had practised the art of calumniators, may, in their turn, often have been calumniated." They were, of course, calumniated frequently, and as they were, not without reason, recognised as the brains of the Catholic party, their condemnation was never the sober verdict of a fair trial. Such doctrines as those crystallised in the *Medulla Theologiae Moralis* are startling : " Whoever would ruin a person or a government, must begin this operation by spreading calumnies, to defame the person or the government ; for unquestionably the calumniator will always find a great number of persons inclined to believe him, or to side with him ; it therefore follows, that whenever the object of such calumnies is once lowered in credit by such means, he will soon lose the reputation and power founded on that credit, and sink under the permanent and vindictive attacks of the calumniator." Busembaum's decidedly frank advice really represents accurately what Philip Sydney and others were taught to believe was Jesuit policy, though the expression of it may not have been presented to them so concisely. And what makes a belief in such a perversion the more curious is, that they had knowledge enough to know that such doctrine would not have appealed to Ignatius Loyola.

The Catholics, however, were scarcely less happy than their enemies. As Hume says pertinently of Philip of Spain : "Where his reasoning was weak was in the assumption that the cause of the Almighty and the interests of Philip of Austria were necessarily identical." There was little chance of immediate peace between opposing parties who hugged an identical fallacy. And it must be remembered that the Protestants who confused the issue, and thought of the Pope and Spain as almost interchangeable terms, were not without excuse. This attitude was encouraged by the then weakness of the Papacy as such, and the exploitation of the Papacy in the interests of Spanish arrogance. "The gradual slackening of the bonds which bound the Spanish Church to the Papacy, and the laxity of the ecclesiastical control which was a consequence, had brought about scandalous corruption amongst the higher cloistered clergy. The general tone of religion, indeed, at the time, seems to have been one of extreme looseness and cynicism, accompanied by a slavish adherence to ritual and form. The terms in which the King and his ambassadors in their correspondence refer to the pontiffs and to the government of the Church in Rome are often contemptuous to the last degree. . They are always regarded as a simple instrument for forwarding the interests of 'God and your Majesty,' the invariable formula which well embodies Philip's own conception of his place in the universe. Nothing is more curious than the free way in which religious matters were spoken of and discussed with impunity, so long as the speakers professed profound and abject submission to the Church, which in this case really meant the semi-political institution Spain."

To onlookers who saw evidence of this submission on the part of the haughty, and not infrequently cruel, Spaniards. To Rome, it was not revealed how bitterly

the Church resented the hidden insult it was powerless
to prevent. They thought that from Rome all Spanish
policy was dictated; the two were hand in hand. To
fight Spain was to fight Rome; to attack a Papist was
to attack a Spaniard.

We may look back with horror and disgust at much
these lamentable divisions and misunderstandings brought
about. Our own record to-day, though not spotless, as
any report in any current journal will show, is cleaner.
But we know more, and are, therefore, the majority of us,
at least, decidedly inclined to tolerance. Such an attitude
was almost impossible during Elizabeth's reign, and nobody,
save those who in modern phrase are called "wire-pullers,"
quite understood the points at issue. Names were bandied
without any very precise idea as to whether they were
appropriate or the reverse. Men even gloried in an
abusive epithet, and converted it into a sign, which they
wore on their breasts or attached to a chain round their
necks, as badges of distinction and honour. When the
party so branded accepts the insult and wears it boldly
in the face of the insulter, that very affront is a virulent
weapon of offence in the hands of the injured. The
boomerang of the Australasian savage returns to the
hand of the thrower. But the opprobrious terms hurled
at the enemy were not expected to possess this home-
coming quality, and they caused consternation in the
ranks of those who had flung them.

It is necessary to dwell for a few pages on this turmoil
agitating Europe at the date of Philip's birth. Without
doing so there is no possibility of understanding the
passions and thoughts and ambitions that led him and
others to act as they did. Though it seems unaccountable
that so many good and great men faced each other as
enemies, believing themselves to be fighting for the truth,
we find no solutions to hand in our perplexity. A
cautious legal maxim, " *Cujus est regio, illius est religio,*"

gives us the only explanation we shall get. It is not
completely accurate, though it has more truth in it than
most maxims, even legal ones. Up to a point it describes
a conflict which, with important exceptions, set the
northern half of Europe against the nations of the
south.

# CHAPTER III

## SCHOOL AND COLLEGE DAYS

Philip's first preferment — Sent to Shrewsbury School—Public
school life in the sixteenth century—Roger Ashton chief master
—The daily task—Greville's estimation of Philip as schoolboy—
Sir Henry's letter to Philip—Wrangles between the school
authorities and Corporation — Philip goes to Oxford — A
marriage project that fails—Philip is ill—He goes to Paris—
Is placed there under the care of Walsingham

BEFORE Philip was ten years old he received, by
proxy, his first preferment, being appointed
Rector of Whitford, in Flintshire. The complacent Rector of Skyneog appeared before the no less
complacent Bishop of St. Asaph. The Pope was duly
denounced, then an oath of allegiance to the Reformed
Church and its saintly head, Queen Elizabeth, as cordially
sworn. While yet in his nursery Sidney declared war
on Rome. The babyish oath was faithfully kept. But
it is strange to read of this induction. In a country
wracked to the very heart by religious controversy the
simplest decencies were violated without comment. Even
in a frankly material age such a scandal would provoke
criticism. A deputy, of course, was appointed, and probably
not overpaid ; but no one protested against a little boy
receiving sixty pounds a year for the nominal cure
of souls. Church and State in all ages can show a
plentiful record of scandals : there is not one more curious

33

than this.   We may be quite certain that it was not the
only  transaction  of  its  kind.    These  proceedings  were
regarded  with  absolute  equanimity  by  men  who  would
willingly  kill  each  other,  and  torture  each  other,  over
a  difference  of  opinion  on  abstruse  theological  questions,
imperfectly  understood  on  either  side.

Of  Hugh  Whitford,  the  outgoing  incumbent,  little  is
known.   Perhaps  he  was  an  old  man  and  desired  rest ; and
it  is  likely  enough  he  was  paid  to  retire.   There  is  no
evidence  that  he  was.   It  has  been  suggested  that  he  was
a  Papist,  but  here  again  there  is  nothing  stronger  than
mere  conjecture  to  support  the  theory.   At  any  rate  he
lived  undisturbed  in  his  parochial  duties  for  five years  after
the  accession  of  Elizabeth.   They  who  paid  homage  to
" the  Whore  of  Babylon "  usually  got  shorter  shrift.   These
contumacious  persons  were,  however,  occasionally  overlooked.   Some  villages  on  the  Lancashire  coast  are  to  this
day  practically  untouched  by  the  Reformation.   In  these
the  dominant  feeling  is  still  for  the  old  faith.

Many  men  are  glad  to  become  rectors  years  after  they
leave  college.   Circumstances  and  opportunity  made  Philip
one  the  year  before  he  was  sent  to  school.

The  choice  of  a  school  was  easily  made.   With  that
practical  common-sense  which  always  distinguished  him,
Sir  Henry  decided  to  send  his  son  to  Shrewsbury,
although  then  quite  a  young  school.   Her  traditions, very
glorious  ones,  really  begin  from  the  day  his  name  first
figured  on  the  books.   Under  the  wise  guidance  of  Ashton
the  place  flourished  exceedingly.   No  other  school  in
England  had  so  large  a  muster-roll  of  scholars.   From
every  part  of  the  country  the  nobility  and  gentry  despatched  thither  their  sons,  so  that  a  contemporary  wrote
" there  is  no  better  filled  school  in  all  England."   Apart
from  its  deservedly  great  reputation  there  was  another
strong  reason  for  Henry's  choice  of  an  academy  for  his
son.   Lady  Sidney  was  in  constant  attendance  on  the

Queen, and could look to see but little of him in whatever place he prosecuted his studies ; whereas Sir Henry himself, as Lord President of Wales, had his official residence at Ludlow.  His duties often called him to Shrewsbury, and for the next few years, doubtless, he had hoped, his pleasure also.  Unfortunately the scheme failed, for he was shortly sent to Ireland, where his wife accompanied him.  That he took a deep interest in his boy's progress and pursuits is certain.  It must have been a delight to him to be an eye-witness of his youthful triumphs.  Philip never had reason to regret the choice, for here it was he cemented that deep affection for Fulke Greville, Lord Brooke, whose love was so great that " friend to Philip Sidney " was his own epitaph.  If in those days men expressed their hatreds with freedom, and pursued revenge with remorseless diligence, they were not ashamed of boasting openly of their affections.

The Blakeway MS. gives us many attractive glimpses of public school life in the sixteenth century.  To Thomas Ashton clearly belongs the chief credit, seeing that it was during his governance that Shrewsbury at once took rank with older and illustrious foundations.  The original charter dates February 10, 1552 ; but owing to difficulties with bailiffs and burgesses, who, having asked for a school wished to control it, no great headway was made at first.  These disputes between masters, governors, and the town authorities were continued for many years.  Ashton's firm hand, however, was soon felt, and he had Elizabeth's support.  Almost at the beginning of its history the school suffered by the visitation to the town of the " sweating sickness."  It was not till 1561 that Ashton entered into possession of his kingdom at the not very munificent salary of £40 a year, less than Philip received from his rectory.  But Ashton had, probably, other sources of income.  A favourite of the Queen's, he was often employed by her on delicate missions.  Indeed, at

her request he brought about a reconciliation between
the Earl of Leicester and the Earl of Essex, a task requiring very nice diplomacy to be successful.   More than once
he expressed a wish to be relieved from his duties as
master.   The Queen always promptly dissuaded him.   He
received in 1571 a notable reward ; for he was permitted
the right to make ordinances for the .good and general
government of the school, a privilege he had desired for
ten years.

We have a complete account of a school day, which,
though dated a half-dozen years later than Philip's time,
shows us how Ashton controlled his scholars.   The school
year was divided into halves.   From Lady Day to All
Saints' Day the hours of attendance were from six o'clock
in the morning till eleven, the dinner hour.   In the after-
noon the boys studied from a quarter to one till five
o'clock.   Prayers were recited at the beginning and close
of the day.   If a holy day occurred in the week it was
a play day ; but usually the weekly day for games was
Thursday.   One custom then begun is still observed in
our own time.   At "the earnest request and great entreaty
of some man of honour, of great worship, credit, or
authority," an extra holiday was granted to the boys.
The judges of assize, when visiting Shrewsbury, are still
accustomed to ask for, and obtain, this boon.   This they
are persuaded to by a greeting in elegant Latin verse
addressed to them by the head boy.   Games were, apparently, strictly regulated.   The senior boys were compelled, before beginning their sports, to perform an act
of a comedy.   After the dramatic performance came a
" chesse play," a curiously severe form of pastime for boys
whose working hours were long, shooting the long-bow,
wrestling, running, and leaping.   It used to be said in my
time, though I will do no more than accept the probability
of the theory, that the " new " boys' races on the first
Monday of term are a mutilated relic of these earlier

activities of the leisure hours. Modern schoolboys would
not approve of the scanty vacations accorded to their
forerunner. Christmas gave them eighteen days, Easter
twelve days, and Whitsuntide only eight. Candles, for
some mysterious reason, were supposed to promote the
plague, and, in any case, there were sufficient reasons for
appointing the longer holidays in the shorter days. How
serious the plague and other dangerous sickness was at
this time, we have ample evidence. They who enjoyed
every care and could afford to enlist the best advice, were
frequently stricken by small-pox and other dreadful
maladies. Lady Sidney was herself a severe sufferer. Yet
it sounds oddly to modern ears to read that provision was
made in the case of a master "infected with any loathsome, horrible, or contagious disease."

Considerable learning was required from those who
would enter the school. There are not many boys of ten
years old in these days who could satisfy the examiners.
Few will be found to lament the fact. Some of us get
through life, not brilliantly, it may be, but with credit,
knowing far less of "accidence without books" than
Philip was expected to have acquired. How many of us
could "make a latten by any of the concordes, the latten
words being first given him"? Sir Henry, once Philip
had satisfied his examiners, paid six shillings and eight-
pence as his son's entrance fee. Had Philip been the son
of a lord, the sum required would have been ten shillings.
His father being only a knight, saved three shillings and
fourpence.

The boys could not all be accommodated in the main
buildings, therefore many were put out to board with reput-
able householders, who were strictly enjoined to use watch-
ful care over the pupils. One obligation laid upon them was
to "cause and see" that they attended with decent regularity "their pairshe churche everie Sondaie and holy daie
to heare divine service at morning and evening prayer."

The modern system, common to most great schools, of monitors chosen by the headmaster was inaugurated. To them was given the task of reporting at the various churches on the misbehaved and the absent.

It is interesting to read a list of the books Philip and Fulke Greville studied. They are : Tully, Cæsar's " Commentaries," Sallust, Livy, Virgil, Ovid, Horace, and Xenophon. These most schoolboys know something, not very much, about. But Ashton himself had contrived a torture, under which we moderns have not been compelled to suffer, "two little books of dialogues drawn out of Tully's ' Offices ' and ' Fodovicus Vives.' " Then, as though all this were not enough, the Greek Grammar of Cleonarde, the Greek Testament, Isocrates and Xenophon's " Cyropædia " are considered necessary. Philip and Greville delighted in their tasks : their future position as men of learning and fine scholarship proves that their early labours were a pleasure. They were not, however, quite normal men, and, as boys, must have been somewhat unusually seriously and studiously minded.

I have already noticed that a comedy, or an act from a comedy, was played every Thursday. Shrewsbury would seem to have been a nursery of interlude and drama. Ashton was a master of pageants, and these exhibitions gave employment to himself and his boys. The verses that have come down to us are not of conspicuous merit, though they are not without fancy. Sir Henry Sidney seems to have been the chief sufferer from them. He had to listen while youthful orators declaimed. Our modern speech day is not an unmixed blessing to audience or performers. But on one occasion, at least, the function lasted fourteen days, and the governor of the Welsh marches lodged opposite the school, at the Council House, during this period, entertaining everybody who desired his hospitality, and listening to peculiarly indifferent verse. Neither the headmaster nor the youthful poets

believed that brevity was then, as now, the soul of wit.
Once, when he was leaving the town by water, some
picked scholars surrounded his barge, and, the salutes of
musketry and cannon over, made " lamentable oracons to
Sir Henry, sorrowing his departure." " Apparelyed all in
green," with "green willows on their heads," they may have
looked picturesque. We are told that their grief was so
effectively uttered, many were seen to weep. His Ex-
cellency himself was reported to have " changed countenance." It is not to be wondered at that he did ! Here
is an example of the poetry to which he was compelled
to pay a civil compliment :—

> " An will yr. honour needs depart,
>     And must it needs be soe ;
> Would God we could lycke fishes swyme
>     That we might with thee goe.
>
> Or else would God this lytill ile
>     Were stretched out so lardge,
> That we one foot might follow ye
>     And wait upon thy bardge.
>
> But seinge we cannot swim,
>     And Ilelands at an ennde,
> Saffe passage withe a short returne
>     The myghtie God thee sende."

These are very creditable verses for a schoolboy, but it
is conceivable Sir Henry often suffered from a surfeit.
Indeed, the chronicler of this particular occasion does not
hesitate to give it as his opinion that the lamentations of
the nymphs were " somewhat tedious." Such pleasures as
these, however, Philip indulged in with his schoolfellows.
Nor can it be held that a glimpse of the life he lived
at a great public school is without interest or value.
Bishop Butler, centuries later, in encouraging theatrical
enterprise among his pupils, was but preserving the
Ashton tradition. Some of the performances not only

drew all the rank and fashion of the county, but won the applause of no less a person than Dr. Parr, who was accorded both pipe and spitoon that he might view them with the greater comfort from the depths of his easy chair.

Philip himself seems to have taken very kindly to his surroundings. He worked hard, and became a brilliant scholar. That he played his part in the pageants and dramatic exercises cannot be doubted. Whether he wrote any of the verses sung on these occasions is not certain; but it is not rash to hazard a guess that he helped to make some of the rhymes, for his "very play tended to enrich his mind." How far he would have engratiated himself to-day among a crowd of modern schoolboys is a problem that needs consideration. Certainly those virtues and qualities so eulogised by his companion make rather portentous reading. It must be remembered, in ex-tenuation of so much excellence, that boys in his day thought that study, rather than play, was their main business. Nor do they seem to have shirked the un-doubtedly heavy tasks imposed on them. Here is Greville's character sketch of him at this period, and it is pleasant to speculate what the Salopian or Etonian of the twentieth century would think, were it applicable to himself or his companions :—

" I never knew him other than a man : with such staidness of mind, lovely, and familiar gravity, as carried grace, and reverence above greater years. His talk ever of knowledge and his very play tending to enrich his mind : so as even his teachers found in him something to observe, and learn, above that which they had usually read or taught. Which eminence, by nature, and industry, made his worthy father stile Sir Philip in my hearing (though I unseen) *Lumen familiæ suæ.*"

Whatever may be our secret opinion of so precocious not to say austere, a disposition in one so young, it is evident that the child was father to the man. His worth, so early visible to boys and masters, certainly did enable him, in Greville's fine phrase, " to sail through the straits of true virtue, into a calm and spacious ocean of humane honour."

Additional interest attaches to his utterance when compared with an often-quoted letter Philip received from his father in 1568. Herein the President sets out a scheme of conduct for his heir, and very closely did Philip adhere to it. Few letters are more noteworthy for simplicity, dignity, and honest pride in a hope that he felt sure would become a reality. He loved his son, and was not ashamed to show it ; he trusted his son, and his son proved then, and afterwards, more than merely fit to be trusted. It is, however, very difficult quite to understand these people. The Lord President is an easier problem than Philip. Every one, if he has had luck, knows a seemingly rough man with a very gentle heart. There are no finer humans than these, and Sir Henry was of them. The precocious Philip, who knew Greek before he was twelve, sometimes makes us wish he was like Porsons's Germans, and the wish should make the ghost of Hermann tranquil. It is odd, none the less, to find that the stream of learning could be defiled by the mud of so much bigotry. Here we must acknowledge Sir Henry not wholly without blame. I have not been able to discover another of his letters, though there must be more : and the most serious student would welcome gladly another postscript.

" SON PHILIP,—I have received two letters from you, one written in Latin, the other in French ; which I take in good part, and will you to exercise that practice of learning often ; for that will stand you in most stead in the profession of life that you are born to live in. And now, since this is my first letter that ever I did write to you, I will not that it be all empty of some advices which my

natural care of you provoketh me to wish you to follow, as
documents to you in this your tender age.

"Let your first action be the lifting up of your mind to
Almighty God, by hearty prayer; and feelingly digest the
words you speak in prayer with continual meditation and
thinking of Him to whom you pray, and of the matter for
which you pray. And use this as an ordinary act, and at
an ordinary hour; whereby the time itself shall put you in
remembrance to do that you are accustomed to do in that
time.

"Apply your mind to such hours as your discreet master
doth assign you earnestly; and the time I know he will so
limit as shall be both sufficient for your learning and safe
for your health. And mark the sense and the matter of
that you do read, as well as the words: so shall you both
enrich your tongue with words and your wit with matter,
and judgment will grow as years grow in you.

"Be humble and obedient to your masters, for, unless
you frame yourself to obey others—yea, and feel in yourself what obedience is—you shall never be able to teach
others how to obey you.

"Be courteous of gesture and affable to all men, with
diversity of reverence, according to the dignity of the
person. There is nothing that winneth so much with so
little cost.

"Use moderate diet, so as, after your meal, you may
find your wit fresher and not duller, and your body lively
and not more heavy. Seldom drink wine; and yet sometimes do, lest, being enforced to drink upon the sudden,
you should find yourself enflamed. Use exercise of body,
yet such as is without peril to your bones or joints: it will
increase your force and enlarge your breath. Delight to
be cleanly, as well in all parts of your body as in your
garments; it shall make you grateful in each company,
and otherwise loathsome.

"Give yourself to be merry; for you degenerate from
your father if you find not yourself most able in wit and
body to do anything when you are most merry. But let
your mirth be ever void of all scurrility and biting words
to any man; for a wound given by a word is oftentimes
harder to be cured than that which is given by the sword.

"Be you rather the bearer away of other men's talk
than a beginner and procurer of speech: otherwise you

shall be accounted to delight to hear yourself speak. If you hear a wise sentence or an apt phrase, commit it to your memory with the respect of the circumstances when you shall speak it. Let never oath be heard to come out of your mouth, nor word of ribaldry; so shall custom make to yourself a law against it in yourself. Be modest in each assembly, and rather be rebuked of light fellows for maiden-like shamefastness than of your sad friends for pert boldness. Think upon every word that you will speak before you utter it, and remember how nature hath ramparted up, as it were, the tongue with teeth, lips—yea, and hair without the lips, and all betokening reins and bridles for the loose use of that member.

"Above all things, tell no untruth; no, not in trifles. The custom of it is naughty. And let it not satisfy you that for a time the hearers take it for a truth; for after it will be known as it is to your shame. For there cannot be a greater reproach to a gentleman than to be accounted a liar.

"Study and endeavour yourself to be virtuously occupied. So shall you make such a habit of well doing in you as you shall not know how to do evil, though you would. Remember, my son, the noble blood you are descended of by your mother's side; and think that only by virtuous life and good action you may be an ornament to that virtuous family. Otherwise, through vice and sloth, you may be counted *labes generis*—one of the greatest curses that can happen to man.

"Well, my little Philip, this is enough for me, and too much, I fear, for you. But if I shall find that this light meal of digestion nourish in anything the weak stomach of your capacity, I will, as I find the same grow stronger, feed it with other food.

"Commend me most heartily unto Master Justice Corbet, old Master Onslow, and my cousin, his son. Farewell! Your mother and I send you our blessings, and Almighty God grant you His, nourish you with His fear, govern you with His grace, and make you a good servant to your prince and country!

"Your loving father, so long as you live in the fear of God.

"H. SIDNEY"

Here is a very noble letter, and the postscript from Lady Sidney is not less admirable, despite its crudity of phrase and spelling :—

"Your noble, careful father hath taken pains with his own hand to give you, in this his letter, so wise, so learned and most requisite precepts for you to follow with a diligent and humble, thankful mind, as I will not withdraw your eyes from beholding and reverent honouring the same— no, not so long as to read any letter from me. And therefore at this time, I will write you no other letter than this ; whereby I first bless you, with my desire to God to place in you His grace, and, secondarily, warn you to have always before the eyes of your mind these excellent counsels of my lord, your dear father, and that you fail not continually, once in four or five days, to read them over.

"And for a final leave-taking for this time, see that you show yourself as a loving and obedient scholar to your good master, to govern you yet many years, and that my lord and I may hear that you profit so in your learning as thereby you may increase our loving care of you, and deserve at his hands the continuance of his great joy, to have him often witness with his own hands the hope he hath in your well doing.

"Farewell, my little Philip, and once again the Lord bless you!

"Your loving mother,
"MARY SIDNEY"

So ends the letter : and at fourteen the recipient was considered old enough, and wise enough, to proceed to Oxford, where he entered at Christ Church in 1568. On the same date Fulke Greville became a student at Broadgates Hall, now Pembroke College, and only the street of St. Aldate's separated the two friends.

At first sight the choice of a University for these illustrious scholars is not a little perplexing. From its beginning Shrewsbury School has been most closely bound to Cambridge, and especially to St. John's College there.

The master and fellows appointed the ushers, they intervened in the interminable quarrels perpetually happening between schoolmen and townsmen. These disputes were often of a very bitter character. Sometimes they do not reflect any credit on the school authorities: but far less often had the town any reason to boast. Luckily the Mayor and Corporation were no match for their opponents, or Shrewsbury would not to-day be in the proud position that distinguishes her. It is unnecessary to revive the memory of old quarrels, except in passing. But Cambridge saved the school on many occasions: and though the wrangling had not taken on an acute form in Sidney's day, it was a Cambridge headmaster and his staff that Philip and Greville had been bidden to revere and obey.

Of neither University, at this period, is there much of good to say. At the great centres of learning abroad there was far more mental activity, and pupils thought more of the master than the college. Cambridge was better than Oxford, just as Burleigh was wiser than Leicester; but neither at Cambridge nor Oxford could a scholar learn much that was worth knowing. If mere pedantry comprises knowledge then, it may be, Oxford was wiser than Cambridge. Whatever Philip acquired of scholarship, and he seems to have acquired a great deal, he owed to Shrewsbury. At school he was treated, quite frankly, as a boy. At Oxford, though a boy still, he was supposed to be a man. Gibbon's criticism of Oxford is, of course, famous and ill-natured. What he wrote, none the less, would apply with some accuracy to the place when Philip entered Christ Church. Undergraduates were tiny boys, and though high-born ladies read their Greek and Latin with facility, the scholar near Carfax knew little of either. He did not receive any enthusiastic encouragement to pursue his studies, and when he left the University he was nearly as ignorant as when he entered it. As a modern historian tells us, " the spacious days of great

Elizabeth" were not inclined to foster learning in the two
places where we might have expected to find it flourishing,
or at least tended. There is nowhere to be found a
suggestion that the "hard-drinking fellows" of a later
generation were conspicuous in Philip's day. There is
much evidence to show that they were not. References
to the "Three Tuns" and the "Mitre" are difficult to
discover. A very much worse sort of inebriety was, however, a common failing among the fellows of colleges,
whether situated on the banks of the Isis or the Cam.
If not much learning was instilled into their youthful
charges by easy and learned pedagogues, a great deal of
prejudice was, and very determinedly. A curious mental
epidemic invaded both places. That people of intelligence
really expected to see the Pope of Rome invade England
and destroy such poor liberties as her people possessed
may be doubted ; but they were assiduous in propagating
their absurd theories. Such success, indeed, crowned their
missionary labours that Philip all his life was quite unable
to think logically or reasonably on this matter of importance. The only definite bit of knowledge he carried from
Oxford may not have been knowledge at all. Whether
it was knowledge or ignorance, he was taught the good or
the evil by his Oxford teachers : on some subjects he never
had an unbiassed and sane opinion.

Religious controversy was a less popular pastime at
Cambridge than at Oxford. But the instructors of youth
at both places were neither broad-minded nor over-
scrupulous. Their example and precepts encouraged
violence and cruelty in the rising generation. Even so
late as the reign of Charles II. an English justice of the
High Court could pass with satisfaction such barbarous
sentences as this on religious opponents :—

"That you be conveyed from hence to the place from
whence you came, and from there be drawn to the place
of execution upon hurdles. That you be hanged by the

neck. That you be cut down alive. That your bowels
be taken out and burnt in your view. That your head be
severed from your body ; that your body be divided into
four quarters, and your quarters be at the disposition of
the King. And the God of infinite mercy be merciful
to your soul. Amen."

This atrocious sentence was common form, as a reference to the State Trials shows. It is easy to believe that
it gave a Scroggs or a Jeffreys intense gratification to
pronounce it. But men, otherwise humane and admirable,
pronounced it too with the conviction that they were
repeating words grateful to the ears of a God of " infinite
mercy." Gentle and simple approved, and the rabble
applauded, each successive incident of the revolting
tragedy, even when, as in one case, the victim was a man
more than eighty years of age, paralysed, blind, and deaf.
King Charles hated these persecutions, though circumstances compelled him to sign the death warrants. Whatever may have been his faults, he believed in religious
liberty, perhaps the more so because he could not attain
it for himself.

The reason for deciding upon Oxford is none the less
one of substance. A Chancellor of Oxford University is
always an important personage, even when his honours and
dignity are for the most part decorative and dignified.
Doubtless in Elizabeth's day this exalted official exercised
more individual power. The Earl of Leicester was Philip's
uncle, and the Earl of Leicester was Chancellor. Mr. Fox
Bourne does not state this directly as a reason for the
choice, but he lays some stress on the point indirectly.
He points out how, among other advantages, he procured
for Sidney permission to eat flesh in Lent. At this time
the boy seems to have been delicate. The same admirable
historian also points out that, even at Oxford, it was the
Cambridge Chancellor, Sir William Cecil, who kept the
more careful watch over the lad. Herein, one may suggest,

lurks the reason.   Leicester was the Queen's favourite.
She trusted Cecil in affairs of State ; it may be doubted
if his personality attracted, though in such matters it
dominated her.   Sidney had to carve a career ; here was
not an affair of State, but a purely personal and domestic
matter.   Sir Henry was not at all popular ; his brains
were picked and, incidentally, his pocket.   Material profit
enriched neither him nor his.   Small wonder, then, that in
his extremity he put his well-loved son under the man of
the moment, who, in his casual way, was not bad-natured,
only conceited and extravagant.   From the intimate
friendship afforded the Earl by the Queen much might
reasonably be hoped.   Leicester was vain, but Philip was
not old enough to be a rival, and the unscrupulous nobleman would be quite ready to keep one who could not
challenge his own pride of place.

Fulke Greville says little about Philip's career at the
University.   A few important points, however, come to
light.   We read of him that, while at Oxford, "an excellent stock met with the choicest grafts ; nor could tutors
pour in so fast as he was ready to receive."   He certainly
differed as much from the average undergraduate as he
had from the average schoolboy.   Even a Dean of Christ
Church, if he ever devises his own epitaph, is not so far
impressed by a pupil as to commemorate that pupil's
name upon his own tombstone.   This is exactly what Dr.
Thornton did, and on the slab at Ledbury was recorded
"preceptor of Philip Sidney, that most noble Knight."
Oxford may have been "heavy with the indolence of fat
fellowships," as has been asserted, but at least the fuller
fatness of a deanery did not dull Thornton's brain or
acumen.   In fact, much of Bruno's often-quoted talk of
the Oxford at this period, or a very few years later, is not
quite according to knowledge.   A small list of the men
who graduated on the banks of the Isis at this decade
might be drawn up not less notable than the honour rolls
of rival universities, whether English or foreign, can show.

Sidney did not take a degree, but he hardly needed one. His perfection of scholarship was not disputed, and the mere hall-mark of academical honours was of no use to him. He had learnt enough to move easily among scholars, as he could stand on terms of virtual equality with princes. Such at least appears to be Greville's view, who writes thus of Don John of Austria's attitude towards the young man : " Giving more honour and respect to this hopeful young gentleman than to the Embassadors of mighty Princes." No wonder Europe was amazed, for from Scotland's King came eulogies and marks of friendship, while of Henry of Navarre it is written that " he found out this Master-spirit among us, and used him like an equall in nature, and so fit for friendship with a King." Whatever the faults of Oxford, it was she had taught him to merit these royal honours ; and one still greater, when Mendoza, " a secretary of many Treasons against us," acknowledged openly : " That howsoever he was glad King Philip his master had lost in a private Gentleman, a dangerous enemy to his Estate ; yet he could not but lament to see Christendome depriv'd of so rare a Light in these cloudy times ; and bewail poor widdow England " (so he termed her) " that, having been many years in breeding one eminent spirit, was in a moment bereaved of him by the hand of a villain." The chronicler goes on to add : " Indeed, he was a true modell of worth."

Other projects than those for the acquisition of learning were agitating the minds of his protectors by the time he was sixteen. It is usual for modern chroniclers to speak of the present day as an age of hurry and bustle. Compared to the middle and close of the sixteenth century we live, though active, prosaic and somewhat drab lives Philip at sixteen had become an accomplished scholar, knowing all that a great school and a great university could teach him. When this mature age was reached he was accounted by his friends fit to face the world under the patronage of his uncle Leicester. At the time when Philip was writing to that nobleman in Latin, the Earl was negotiating a marriage for his kinsman. The project fell through, as might have been expected. Very good reasons made the proposition a barren one. Leicester and Cecil hated each other, and it was Cecil's daughter whom the great courtier had chosen as Philip's bride. Sir Henry was only useful, and no courtier as a woman understood it; he was very poor, and the peerage eventually offered him he could not afford to accept. Cecil, though a real patriot, was not blind to his own advancement. The position of the brilliant Earl could not have seemed over-stable to the shrewd and silent Burleigh. So, with all courtesy, he declined the honour of the alliance—probably with his tongue in his cheek, for he was never caught napping, but nodding, according to the veracious Sheridan. The lady was betrothed to the Earl of Oxford, a most undesirable match from her point of view, but a politically expedient one from her father's. He prided himself on showing a becoming blend of worldly wisdom and paternal solicitude. Sidney fell ill about this time. One biographer asserts firmly the sickness was due to chagrin; another declares that concerning a boy of sixteen such a supposition is ridiculous. May it not be that both writers have missed the exact significance of Philip's ailment? He was never strong, and while at Oxford was allowed to eat flesh during Lent. He would certainly know of the plans being made for him, if not in detail, at least their general tenour. He was inordinately proud, not conceited; and this wounded pride, it is reasonable to suppose, he felt more keenly than would one of maturer years. Moreover there is no reason why, as a boy, he should not have imagined himself in love, as boys do even in the twentieth century. Again, the splendour of the match dazzled him. To one who, early, took life so seriously would come the temptation to brood over, unduly, this first check. He would say little.

And a stinging insult had to be faced when he learned that a blackguard was his chosen rival and successful suitor. Enough, and more than enough, was there here to make the sensitive victim ill; and Dr. Parker wisely put no limit to a meat diet. Wherein he was wiser than the scoffing chronicler.

Another point is forgotten by him, a point it is odd that so learned a man should have overlooked. Early marriages in the families of people of position were very usual in the sixteenth century. Nor is it astonishing that they were. It was an age of unrest; stupendous events were happening that were altering the aspect of the world no less than agitating men's minds. An age of vast discoveries by land and sea, it was also an age when in the region of thought men had become adventurous. A new religion, or perhaps one should say a novel form of an old religion, had won adherents. Antagonisms were bitter in consequence, and where princes trembled for their thrones, nobles and gentlemen trembled for the safety of their emoluments and estates. The friendship and alliance with a powerful family was naturally desired and sought by those oppressed with uncertainty and anxiety. Just as the rulers of kingdoms thought to prop their thrones through the alliances created at the altar, men of wealth and station trusted by the same means to given stability to their fortunes. The ages or wishes of the bride and bridegroom were not consulted. They were not the real contracting parties. Knowing as we do how proudly Philip bore himself, not rendered unduly complacent by a contemplation of his own merits, for he was genuinely and unaffectedly modest in all that touched his own personality, because of his ancestry the blow must have been a severe one. Coming, as it did, at a time when he was ill and sickly, the affront was one to aggravate his ill-health.

The plans for this proposed alliance between the houses

of Cecil and Sidney were discussed carefully and in full
detail. They were elaborate enough to have attracted
Philip's attention, and he must have known of the negotiations and approved. For he was admitted to family
councils at an early age, as "the light of the family"
naturally would be. How far Burleigh seriously considered the question is open to debate. He could not
offend Sir Henry, nor would he wish to, for the knight
was useful though poor. But it would scarcely appeal to
the Chancellor to hear that, as Sir Henry writes, "I mean
truly, loving your daughter as one of my own, regarding
her virtue above any *dot*, and your friendship more than
any money you will give. And for my boy, I confess if I
might have every week a boy, I should never love like
him, and accordingly have dealt with him, for I do not
know above a £100 a year I have not assured to him."
This protestation of the value of affection above money
probably made Cecil nod that wise head of his. But
Cecil, not a bad or ungenerous man, was opposed to
romance. Sir Henry, on the contrary, is often a belated
and sorrowful figure of romance. He was more than Sir
William's equal in the best sort of ability, but he became
poorer and poorer in a strenuous and heart-breaking
service. The other grew more and more rich, and
cherished personal ambitions, creditable but not sentimental. He even behaved kindly and stood as godfather
to Philip's youngest brother, and named the child Thomas;
perhaps a hint, if rightly understood, that too ostensible a
relationship with Cecil was not desirable. Leicester
seems to have behaved well in the matter. Arrangements
were made by him through which the suggested bridegroom and his heirs were to be quite decently endowed
for their joint start in life. The fact that Leicester supported the match may have temporarily pointed to a
successful solution of the problem. "Marriage money"
before and since Philip's day has proved a stumbling-

block. Cecil never meant the wedding to take place, but would not hurt Sir Henry's feelings by dismissing the suggestion of such a contract hastily. It is easy to realise, even as events came about, that Sir Henry was hurt, for he writes : " If I might have the greatest Prince's daughter in Christendom for him, the match spoken of between us, on my part, should not be broken." The Lord Deputy was only allowed to think. He was poor, struggling to avoid debt, his Queen was contemptuous but exacting. He complains of his health, and had reason. Not long after the question of the alliance was put gently on one side, and an impoverished gentleman saw another assume the dignity of a peerage and a position of even greater importance than hitherto.

But if Philip had cause to complain, Sir Henry also was not without a grievance. Cecil, we see, did not at once scout the suggestion of an alliance between the two families. The Lord Deputy was simple-minded and far too honest, most able man though he was, to understand the methods of the schemer. Cecil invited Lady Henry to spend her Christmas at Hampton Court, and even asked Philip. It seems that they accepted the invitation. Not content with this show of favour, and in spite of the press of work that claimed his attention, Cecil wrote more than one letter full of Philip's praise. He goes so far as to say, " Your Philip, in whom I take more comfort than I do openly utter for avoiding a wrong interpretation." This is a subtle and characteristic remark, but one quite calculated to hoodwink Sir ·Henry, and this the more especially as it is followed by the sentence, " He is worthy to be loved, and so I do love him, as he were mine own." The only interpretation of such a passage that could occur to Sir Henry's mind is the one he longed for, which, for the moment, Cecil wished him to accept. In another letter, a few weeks later, the wily statesman writes, during an access of apparently unrestrained enthusiasm, " I thank you for your free offer made to me by your letters concerning your son, whom truly I do so like for his own conditions and singular towardness in all good things as I think you a happy father for so joyful a son.  And as for the interest that it pleaseth you to offer me in him, I must confess, if the child alone were valued without the natural good that dependeth of you his father, I could not but think him worthy the love I bear him, which certainly is more than I do express outwardly, for avoiding of sinister interpretation.  For, as for the account to have him my son, I see so many incidenties in it as it sufficeth me to love the child for himself, without regard therein of my daughter, whom surely I love so well as, so it be within my degree or not much above it, I shall think none too good for her.  Thus you see a father's fondness, which to a father I dare discover, and so for this time it sufficeth."

Explanation of this enigmatic epistle is impossible.  It was certainly ably calculated to deceive Sir Henry.  The meaning, I suggest, is this.  "Your son pleases me more than any lad I know.  My daughter deserves the most worthy of husbands; the most worthy of husbands shall be hers."  There is no mention here made of money, and after the eloquent eulogy passed on Philip, Henry Sidney might easily have forgotten its importance for the moment.  The clever wording of the letter gave Cecil the chance if, as it did, it should come to him of choosing a rich suitor; also he could point to his praises of Philip if the girl were unmarried and the turn of events made an alliance with the house of Sidney at all useful and desirable.  The father was deceived by the artful wording of the letter, and the son shared in the deception.  If his parent's hopes and plans were outwitted, the mortification of Philip must have been great.

Meanwhile Philip consoled himself as best he could by eating flesh in Lent.  There is a certain grim satisfaction in realising that Lord Burleigh, as he now was, had little reason for self-congratulation. His daughter married the Earl of Oxford. This nobleman was a favourite at Court. The Queen so far forgot her prejudices as to agree to the marriage, and Oxford was his father-in-law's ward. It was unkindly suggested that the young woman married the Earl. Gossip has a habit of twisting the truth into knots difficult to unravel. We need take no more notice of the tattle of yesterday than we should of the idle chatter of to-day. Burleigh made a bad bargain, and, though he does not say so, knew it. Writing to the Earl of Rutland he says : " And surely, my lord, by dealing with him I find that which I often heard of your lordship, that there is much more in him of understanding than any stranger to him would think." Here is an adroit way of unfavourably commenting on the mental capacity of the successful nobleman in order to soothe Rutland, an unsuccessful suitor. And the great statesman had to derive what consolation he could from an ingenious bit of insincerity. Rutland had been earnest in his pursuit of the lady's favours. Doubtless he had to be pacified. He was a person of substance and rank. For the rest, it may be supposed that Burleigh said little of his failure as a matrimonial agent. Sir Henry was not the man to say anything save to his familiars. The two families re mained on terms of intimacy and friendship. But one grew richer and the other poorer. Maybe Sir Henry was a little sorry, even in the middle of his own disappointment, for the astute statesman. It can hardly be pleasant to reflect that while directing your country's destinies with superb success, you have contrived to marry your daughter to a dissolute ruffian, who kills his cook, dissipates a princely heritage, prefers other women, and cheats poor men. The noble Earl was a proficient in all these accomplishments.

Yet from one point of view Burleigh regarded the match with equanimity. Oxford was a first favourite at Court, for what reason save his good looks is not apparent. The Queen may have tired of him as a lover, but wished to retain him as a friend. However this may be, she rather promoted than retarded his marriage, and kept him in high esteem. So, varying her usual custom, in great good humour she smiled pleasantly on the Earl and his lady. Oxford and Philip met in a tennis court some years later, and the nobleman did not shine in the encounter. It is not extravagant to suppose that they, from the first breaking off of Philip's contemplated marriage to Anne Cecil, disliked each other. Burleigh seems quite incorrigible, for the crafty man writes of this reprobate: "I do honour him as much as I can any subject, and I love him so dearly from my heart as I do mine own son, and in any case that may touch him for his honour and weal I shall think mine own interest therein." This sentence throws a peculiarly instructive light on the character of Burleigh. In such terms as these he had eulogised Philip. "Mine own interest," though, was always a most potent advocate with him; indeed, his own advancement and his country's glory were all he cared for. He contrived to make both himself and his country successful. Oxford was a scoundrel, but he carried a great name—a name he eventually disgraced. Doing this he was for the first and last time in his life successful. His literary efforts are of no importance; his performances when a husband disgust decent-minded people; his cowardice was asserted and caused derision. Anne forgave his infidelities, and on such matters Elizabeth, once she had permitted a marriage, was indifferent. They may have amused her; they were powerless to anger her. So for longer than he deserved Oxford cajoled his wife and kept his footing at Court. Anne was pleased to be a countess, the earl delighted being allowed to do as he chose, and Burleigh was satisfied to find that if his son-in-law did not assist his plans he retained sobriety enough not to interfere with them. Yet at a very early date the Chancellor felt bound to utter a protest, and he wrote to Oxford a letter, more clearly worded than most of his compositions, in which he recalls the errant husband to his duties. He asks that " all hard and vain speeches of his unkindness to her may cease, and that with his favour and permission she may both come to his presence and be allowed to come to do her duty to her Majesty, if her Majesty shall be therewith content ; and she shall bear with as she may the lack of the rest." " The rest " is the love that "a loving and honest wife ought to have."

Yet the man to whom he writes thus is the same man of whom he wrote such fine compliments and found himself able to honour as a son. Philip and Oxford were in Holland together. It was the third and last time their names are linked. Oxford's ending was a sad one : he died in poverty and disgrace. A princely fortune was unequal to the drains upon it caused by his extravagance and debauchery. He had posed as the friend and patron of poets, he ended as a cheat. The man he defrauded was poor and stood in need of help. Churchyard was not a great poet, though he was often a meritorious one. Frequently he was starving. To him the Earl, when old and needy, applied for help. He sought a lodging, which Churchyard found for him ; but the poet, after helping him as generously as his slender resources could, was left to pay the bill. An earl had disappeared, and with him disappeared Philip's rival ; but Philip and Burleigh had long gone before.

We hear often that blood is thicker than water ; money would seem to be thicker than a solution of the two combined. This at least is certain that, on a blood basis, a Cecil was far from being the equal of a Sidney. From every point of view, save that of lucre and personal aggrandisement, the match originally proposed would have been a subject of legitimate boast to every member of the

Cecil family. Doubtless Philip understood this, and, hot-tempered and proud, was more hurt by the realisation of an insult than he cared to brood over or than his genuine Christianity would allow him to express in adequate terms. He probably was hard put to it to keep his temper ; and, it may be suggested, was glad enough to seize the offered opportunity of a visit to France. There were other reasons why the chance must have been eagerly grasped. Elizabeth, great Queen though she proved, was exacting and selfish beyond belief. To assist a Tudor was reward in itself, no matter how disastrous a result befell the servitor. Lady Sidney, with a quiet, uncomplaining devotion beyond the impertinence of praise or criticism, once nursed the Queen through an attack of small-pox. Thanks to this devotion the royal mistress recovered ; the attendant—and not less nobly born lady—was disfigured for life. She would not go into society lest she should disgrace her lord, who, splendid man that he was, loved her more than ever. Sir Henry had his own troubles. He was ill, overworked, affronted and needy. His great services received no tangible reward, and no doctor had skill enough to restore him to health. At forty-three he was an old man. He was misunderstood, and too blunt of speech to explain his position. He had none of the graces of a courtier, and probably despised them. He had carried worthily an illustrious name ; his son, he felt, would enhance its reputation. At Ludlow, doubtless, he and Philip discussed matters.

Sir Henry was no longer Lord Deputy, for inefficient reasons he had been removed from the ill-paid but stately dignity. The barren offer of a peerage was merely a stately insult. He could not accept it ; as has been well said, " She," meaning Elizabeth, " paid the late deputy for his long service and heavy losses by a compliment, his non-acceptation of which left her with a seat in the House of Lords at her disposal."

President of Wales Sir Henry still was.  To him and
his son came the rumour that was disturbing the political
world.  The Queen once more contemplated, what she
seldom allowed others to contemplate, a marriage.  This
time she affected to desire an alliance with France in the
person of the Duke d'Alençon.  There were some good
reasons for, and a great many better ones against, the
match.  The Duke was a poor creature.  He was younger
than the Queen, and could hardly have been expected to
be faithful to her.  Protestantism in France was struggling
heroically, but with vague prospect of success.  For a
French, and on paper very Catholic, prince to marry a
Protestant queen no doubt seemed sagacious politics from
a Protestant threshold.  Walsingham was busy in Paris,
Lord Lincoln was ordered to join him, and required an
escort suitable to his rank.  Gentlemen of repute and
position would naturally be looked for in the train of an
Ambassador Extraordinary.  Henry of Navarre was
affianced to the King's sister, or supposed to be ; the
wicked Catherine de Medici was pretending a friendship
for the Huguenots ; and France and Spain were at deadly
enmity.  So Philip's advancement and the advantage of
the Protestant cause seemed to pull in the same direction.
Small wonder, then, that Philip hastily accepted an invitation to join the Paris mission.  His religion and his
interest gave him a joint call.  Though his pious aspirations were doomed to a bloody disappointment, and his
own advancement was not appreciably furthered, he won
a wise friend who was later to become a gentle father-in-
law in the disgracefully treated Walsingham.  This man
died so rich in honour that his name stands nobly for all
time on the roll of English worthies.  He died so poor
that he was buried at midnight, lest the poverty of his
funeral should inspire derision.  Elizabeth had brains but
no heart, and Walsingham shared with Sir Henry the
uncomfortable honour of being one of her victims.  It is

impossible not to wish sometimes that she had been less
magnificent as a princess and nobler as a woman. Her
treatment of these two faithful and able servants is, unfortunately, not the only instance of her vanity, cupidity,
and meanness.

WILLIAM CECIL, LORD BURGHLEY
FROM THE PORTRAIT BY MARK GERARD IN GRAY'S INN HALL

# CHAPTER IV

## PHILIP'S ENTRANCE INTO PUBLIC LIFE.
## ST. BARTHOLOMEW

Elizabeth contemplates marriage—Walsingham's ignorance—Philip
goes in the Earl of Lincoln's suite—Is made a baron—Catherine
de Medici and her schemes—The Peace of St. Germain—
Margaret's marriage to Henry of Navarre— Pageants and the
wedding ceremony—The Duke de Guise arrives unexpectedly—
St. Bartholomew—Philip leaves France

TO the care of Mr. Francis Walsingham it was
decided to confide Philip. That great man was
ambassador at Paris, and wise though he was,
utterly ignorant of the trend of events in the excitable
capital. In France he seems to have believed that all things
made for peace and prosperity. Coligni, chief of Huguenot
leaders, was honoured greatly, and a French princess was
to marry the Protestant King of Navarre, the merry
fellow who afterwards thought Paris worth a mass, if
legend is accurate, as it probably is not. But a greater
reason than these actuated the boy's friends in hailing the
suggestion that he should accompany the Earl of Lincoln
to the Court of Charles IX., in reality the Court of
Catherine de Medici ; though even the astute Francis
Walsingham seems to have been ignorant of the fact.
Elizabeth had once more decided to marry. Such was
her determination, she declared, and every one seems to
have believed her declaration. Her advisers, fearing

Scotland, counselled her to take a consort. She fooled every sapient Polonius to the top of his bent; but like Hamlet, at the obsequious absurdities of Rosencranz and Guildenstern, was not fooled at all. There is no evidence to show that she wanted a husband : she had lovers in plenty; and there is nothing to prove her people desired her to share her throne with another. The vast majority would never have heard of an alliance till months after it was concluded. Then they would have shrugged their shoulders, tended their flocks, busied themselves with a hundred occupations, and gone to sleep at sunset with supreme serenity.

To her immediate attendants the plans of the Queen were as clear as daylight. She took great thought, always and at all times, to make them so. During a long reign she hoodwinked everybody ; there is not a scrap of evidence that she ever hoodwinked herself. She was always professing herself in love, or quite willing to simulate affection for all sorts of impossible people. She never was even attracted by any of them. Her councillors were so anxious to see her married that she delighted in humouring them : on this matter she was far too cunning to take their advice. A great dynastic alliance meant that he who shared her bed would, practically, share her throne. But the throne, at least, was sacred. She was like unto " The Fair Serpent " of the poet's fancy—

> " A serpent, woman-headed,
>   With loose and floating hair.
>   Beware, O fool! how you touch it,
>   Beware for your soul, beware."

Playing the game at which she was an adept, for her own amusement and her country's good, the Queen let it be known that she was prepared to consider the advances of the Duke d'Alençon. He was a quite indifferent creature in himself, and brother to a king who, by charity, it must be conjectured was mad. Eleven years later a similar proposal was made, but came to nothing. Meanwhile it was felt that a decent cavalcade should proceed to Paris. It would evince the greatness of the Queen, while showing a proper respect to the chosen husband. So the Earl of Lincoln, in the May of 1572, left London and took Philip with him. Leicester wrote to Walsingham calling Philip "raw" and "young," commending him to the Ambassador's care. The epithets are not very well chosen. The lad was not "raw," he only had much to learn; his manners and scholarship had extorted admiration. Young, also, he was not: for he had never been young, and the unexpected experience before him was not likely to make him more youthful. "You have too little mirthfulness in your nature," wrote Languet to him a few months later. St. Bartholomew was not an event to enliven; in his case it only served to emphasise a sombre, though gentle, habit of mind.

Philip was empowered to take three servants and four horses. Who was directly responsible for this outlay is not to be discovered. Perhaps Leicester did more than write an amiable letter. The money was forthcoming, and he set off on his journey. A delightful reason for his departure is that he would find opportunities for perfecting himself in foreign languages.

Within a fortnight from their setting out the illustrious voyagers reached Paris. His companions, their mission done, were to return to England, but Philip was to remain for two years under Walsingham's protection, in France or elsewhere. Doubtless Paris was a strange city to him; strange both to his eyes and his notions of comfort. He saw the "frog-faced duke," and was received in audience of the King. So impressed was the royal imbecile that he conferred the honour of a barony on the young man. It may be conjectured that the recipient accepted the distinction gravely and without demur; as also the post of groom of the bedchamber. As the horizon seemed clear, these marks of eminent favour were doubtless a subject of congratulation.

The rapid downpour of events during his four months' visit to France have produced a flood of literature. Explanations, refutations, and recriminations are scarcely less familiar than the alphabet. What no one at the time seems to have realised is that Catherine, for her own ends, was instigating a farce the last act of which should be a tragedy. She wanted money, she always did, a novel position for one of her family to face. She was not scrupulous as to the means by which it might be obtained, being "the Jezebel of our age," according to Sidney himself; she thirsted for power, and she hated the Protestants.

Her elaborate schemes cannot ever be understood fully. To marry Margaret to a Protestant king and allow a puppet king to be gracious towards the emissaries of a Protestant sovereign were clever moves enough. Yet these very ambassadors had come about a project of great moment, which her conduct, directly their backs were turned, made dust and void. This is mysterious, for she hated Spain, and Spain hated her. The only explanation of the terrible event following Lincoln's return is that religious bigotry so distorted men's minds they could not think or see clearly. And a wicked woman, cloaking herself in the studied pretence of religious fervour for a secret and private ambition of her own, opened the gates of hell and smiled at the consequences.

The internal affairs of France at this period were of too intricate a nature to be dwelt upon here. Various treaties had been patched up between the contending factions. By the Peace of St. Germain a settlement of some stability had, it was thought, been arrived at. Certainly, on paper at least, the Protestants might well congratulate themselves. Such easy terms had never before been accorded to them.  They were allowed to garrison their four cities of La Charité, Cognac, La Rochelle, and Montauban. Even Calvinists were not to be debarred from office. Worship according to reformed rites was permitted in two towns of each province.  Favours so great and generous dispelled the fears of the recipients.  At last it seemed, to the better disposed of both parties, an era of peace had dawned when differences might be amicably adjusted and an impoverished country grope her way back to comparative prosperity.  Catherine bearing gifts was, as events proved, more to be feared than when she brandished a sword.  With Italian shrewdness she saw that it was useless to continue a fight in which all her victories were barren, to prolong a war in which her enemy seemed to become stronger with each defeat.  This Peace of St. Germain—"a traitorous, violated peace, the perdition of those who trusted it "—was a master-stroke of policy.  She had schemed for two years, it is said, and now felt certain of her triumph.  The King was her tool, whether because he loved her or because he feared her is not known.  He was swayed, probably, by the combined feelings of fear and love.  Devoid of principles, destitute of compassion, without honour, he did what his mother told him to do.  He agreed readily to the marriage of Margaret and, as we see, was graciously inclined towards the members of the English embassy, and to Philip in particular.

But even the first act of the play was not all comedy. Margaret was in love with the Duke de Guise.  He may have been an ardent lover, certainly he was cruel and cowardly.  Ordering the stabbing of a man already nearly dead is not a sign of heroism.  He could achieve more monstrous deeds than this.  The husband chosen for Margaret was a gallant gentleman.  Complete respect-ability in another was not expected at this time, for no one was anxious to find too high a standard of morals demanded from himself.

Henry of Navarre arrived for the ceremony. He was then the hero of the Protestants in France, even as Elizabeth in the Low Countries was their protectress. French Protestants had to mourn later that the king was won by a bribe ; and it would not be pleasant reading to learn what Holland and La Rochelle thought intimately of the powerful English Queen.

Seemingly one heart alone was sad in all France : that of the unwilling bride. Her entreaties and prayers were of no avail ; yet the pomps and ceremonies pretending her gladness must have increased her misery. Whatever the rumours at the Court may have been Philip, even if he heard them, had not time to test their accuracy by his own observation. If he considered the matter at all he would find in this alliance fresh hope for the Protestant cause, giving it, therefore, his mature approval. For him the day of the great peace, that 18th of August when bride and bridegroom met before the altar of Notre Dame, was henceforth to be regarded as sacred. At last the Reformed Faith would be above and beyond persecutions, its adherents as safe as though they were honest merchants in Cheapside.

Meanwhile much happened to delight Philip. The love of pageant and pageantry, fostered at Shrewsbury, was gratified to the full. With the memory still young in him of masque and revel upon the Severn, he could watch everything with the eye of an expert. Knightly tournaments appealed to his own knightly instincts. As he watched the chivalry of France contend, one thinks of his fine sonnet :—

"Having this day my horse, my hand, my lance."

He probably thought, as nearly every boy has thought, that nature had in truth made him "a man of arms."

These costly amusements served the end at which they
were aimed.   That end was not to encourage a love of
swordsmanship or horsemanship, nor was it to increase
further the affection for taste and display, already evident
enough.   They served their end because men felt safer
and happier than they had before.   They seemed to ratify
the feeling, then prevalent, that friendships would not be
broken between those who thought differently, that the
wicked years of persecution were over, that kinsmen would
be once more united in the common bond of blood, no
matter how they differed in matters of religion.   This
feeling permeated the atmosphere of that gay August of
1572.   Not for the last time in her history France sang
the hymn of toleration on the very threshold of terror.
Apparent triumph of Protestantism must have made the
jousts seem even brighter than they were, to one of
Sidney's temperament.

They came to a close at last, and the sun rose on the
promise-giving 18th day of August.   An ingenious compromise was affected between the adherents of the
contending faiths.   The ceremony was to be celebrated
in the great cathedral of Notre Dame, but two services
were to be performed so that each party might be satisfied.
It is curious that shrewd Walsingham could not prophesy
danger from the splendid meeting of the two processions
within the walls of the noble church.   But he, like the
rest, was blind to the immediate future.   Sidney was,
it may easily be asserted, present.   His new dignity of
baron, apart from the fact that he was under Walsingham's
protection, would procure for him a place.   What he saw
must have astonished and perturbed him.   Margaret to
the last resented the part she had to play, and refused
to notice the formal questions put to her.   She loved De
Guise, who hated Navarre.   She would not speak or make
any sign that she understood even the purport of what the
priest said.   Charles was furious, and, seizing her roughly,

pushed her head forward as a visible form of consent. This involuntary movement was her sole contribution to the marriage vows.

Paris had plenty to talk over in this untoward incident. On the top of it came another more dangerous. De Guise, furious at the marriage, rode into Paris at the head of his soldiers. Every one feared trouble, though few were prepared for the terrible happenings that fell, quick as lightning, on the unhappy city. The King professed alarm at the Duke's arrival. All the recent gaiety was to be changed to lamentation, the marriage to funerals, peace to the semblance of war. Adroitly instructed by his mother, the man of weak intellect played his part with a cunning almost devilish. Sending for Coligni, he poured out his fears into the old man's ears. The Admiral listened, and did not perceive the trap laid for him. It was asserted that there must and would be trouble now that this stormy petrel De Guise had flown into their midst. Means must be taken, it was urged, to minimise all danger as much as possible. If more troops were summoned, it was pointed out, the likelihood of a serious disturbance would be minimised, Protestants would be protected and the citizens safe from violence. Some such arguments clearly were used, for the wise Coligni agreed to the importation of the troops ; and foredoomed Huguenots approved a step taken ostensibly for their well-being.

The story now moves rapidly. The citizens, lulled in security, were suddenly startled by the awful news that the old Admiral had been killed. Incredible though the tidings seemed, it was fatefully true that he had been badly wounded. An unknown assassin had shot the hero venerated of all good men. Beyond promises, so easy to make, nothing was done to trace the murderer. It is quite certain that he was acting under orders. Despite the shock of horror dealt by the vile deed, jousting and revelry began once more. Sidney must have shared the general horror, but has left no comment dated at the time.

Within the first two hours of August 24th the evils, to which this murder was a presage, had begun. Paris was fast asleep, many dreaming of the dying Coligni, more of the glitter of the day's tournament. All was peaceful when, suddenly, through the silence, hoarse voices yelled "For God and the King!" Adding to the tumult the Palace clock was sounding. Paris was in a moment illuminated by ten thousand lights held by shaking hands. A frightening spectacle met the eyes of peaceful onlookers. The streets were full of armed men, wearing on their sleeve the cross they were about to defile. A hideous slaughter began ; men, women, and children fell. Huguenots found no quarter, Coligni least of all. Lying ill from his wound he must have heard the disturbance, perhaps even congratulated himself that he had consented to the reinforcement of the soldiers. If this were so his satisfaction was short lived indeed. One of these brutes, mad with blood, rushed into the chamber where he lay and stabbed him to the death. The Duke de Guise was pleased. "It is well," he told the fellow. Then, by his orders, the old hero's body was hurled into the street, and the savage kicked it furiously until his rage somewhat abated. His thirst for blood was strong, however. He rushed off to satiate it, shouting that what his followers did was the King's will. Strange though it seems, he spoke the truth. The massacre lasted for seven days ; its tally of victims is still untold. A hideous episode closes with a scene grotesque in its horror, that of a maniac king standing at his bedroom window, gun in hand, screaming, "Kill! kill!"

During these orgies of slaughter, rape, torture, and nameless horrors Philip was kept safely within the doors of the English Ambassador's house. But he heard and saw enough to fill him with undisguised horror and disgust. He never forgot these hideous nights and days, and his

mind, naturally biased against all that was Catholic,
absorbed from their contemplation a still bitterer hatred, a
more profound animosity. It must have been that he
chafed at the restraint friendly hands placed upon him.
It is asserted, with authority, that he longed to get
away from a country "where such evils were possible."
I think he would have preferred to stay where he was,
conceiving and executing plans for the alleviation of the
sufferers. This, whichever theory is right, is mere conjecture. One thing is certain, he cannot have plumed
himself on his new title of Baron, conferred by a king who
was a puppet, a madman, and a murderer. Nor can I find
that he referred to it during his later life.

A mistake, perhaps a natural one, that he made was
this, he confused the murderers and the creed they found
it useful to assert. To associate the Duke de Guise and
Catherine with any form of religion is to pay them an ill-
deserved compliment and do real faith an injustice. Good
men, whatever their beliefs, were appalled ; but he was too
young to understand this. A man may rise superior to
circumstances ; it is doubtful if a boy can when they come
to him in the guise of massacre and cruelty and deceit.
Sidney, to his credit, was only a little more convinced,
more aggressive, and more stubborn in his notions. He
was one of those men of whom it might be said that they
formulate their opinions in their cradles. Such an event
as this made it harder for him to modify them. A narrow
mind is often, however, the body-servant of virtue. A
St. Bartholomew is likely enough to make a narrow mind
narrower. In all else but religion he was broad and
sympathetic. There was not much of the Puritan about
him, as the word Puritan is understood. After the "crowning glory of Worcester," Cromwell found a militant psalm
more in accord with his victorious mood than—

"Stella, think not that I by verse seek fame,
Who seek, who hope, who love, who live but thee."

At the same time there are the kindlings of the Puritan fire in Sidney's soul; St. Bartholomew's awful doings did much to make the flame leap more certainly. The churlish suspicion he is by some accused of was engendered by these events.

When the news of the massacre reached England consternation was universal. No further talk, even in whispers, of Elizabeth's marriage was possible with the man of whom a sister said, that if fraud and cruelty were banished from the world, himself could easily repeople it with devils. Sidney was not forgotten, despite weightier affairs, and he was recalled, or rather ordered to leave the country. So he left France, never to return, and journeyed to Lorraine with Dr. Watson, a learned divine and future bishop, as his guide, philosopher, and friend.

# CHAPTER V

## PHILIP VISITS ITALY AND GERMANY

Philip visits Strasburg—He lodges with Andrew Wechel—Meets
Languet—Visits Hungary—Decides to visit Italy—Languet's
opposition ignored—He goes to Venice—Reasons for opposi-
tion—Fears for Philip absurd—His correspondence with
Languet—Is prevented visiting Rome—Quarrels with Coningsby
—Death of his sister—Starts for home—Well received at Court
—Meets Penelope Devereux at Kenilworth while attending the
Queen—Received at Essex House—A marriage project—
Accompanies Essex to Ireland—Death of Essex

CONTRAST could scarcely be more emphatic
than the lurid extravagancies of St. Bartholomew
and the near future surroundings of Philip's life
presented. From an atmosphere of passion and crime he
passed to one of calm and devout learning. From Strasburg he visited the Rhine, the river of history and legend,
saw Heidelberg, and rested at Frankfurt. By this time he
had probably recovered his nerve, dominated his nausea.
A more personal matter certainly worried him. He had
very little money, and frankly said so : for he had to seek
temporary help from a gentleman, and writes to the Earl
of Leicester asking him to treat the lender with consideration. Meanwhile, in the eye of the world, he maintained
his modest dignity, accepting, as his right, the hospitality
and courtesy of princes and men of note and position.

His lodgings were at the house of the illustrious printer
Andrew Wechel, of whom much might be written. Here

it is enough to note that learned men sought his society, and that Philip found himself happy under the printer's roof for more than four months.    Two reasons explain this sojourn.    He met at the worthy and learned crafts-man's many it was good to meet; since every traveller who cared for books and art and learning deemed Wechel's roof covered the best hotel in the town; a reputation the hospitable printer would not have changed for the possession of a principality.    Moreover, the solemn, greatly wise, and admirable Languet lodged there too. He was a man after Sidney's heart, and, indeed, was of the aristocracy of learning; to his words Sidney listened with reverence.    He loved him with an affection it is a little difficult for many nowadays to understand fully. Languet could offer little except knowledge, but know-ledge was an asset in the Elizabethan age.    Its acquire-ment brought in no riches, but it commanded an honour the most noble could not by mere rank obtain.    The printer, and the scholar who lived in the printer's shop, were princes to Sidney's vision: the palaces, where the Duke de Guise flaunted were, by comparison, merely shambles.

Languet was as learned a man as Europe could discover He not only absorbed but he distilled knowledge.    Custom of the time, a meritorious one, made him the equal in con-sideration and esteem of all men howsoever great their rank.    He was austere and at the same time gentle, very wise yet not unduly severe, cultivating a piety according to the rule of his master Melancthon.    To him as looker-on, illustrating the adage, the game of European politics was clearer than the players thought.

They lived together for three months, a quiet time for both.    For Languet, too, had witnessed the atrocities of St. Bartholomew, and remembered them.    Rest was needful for master and pupil.    After three months Languet was called to Vienna, and the young man accom-danied him.    By this Sidney seems to have grown tem-

porarily wearied of high philosophy and sound theology.
He determined to be "like a bird that has broken out of
its cage." Announcing that he intended to spend a few
days at Presberg, he left his preceptor and mapped out a
fairly extensive tour for himself in Hungary. He travelled
for several weeks, but no precise record of his movements
exists. This is unfortunate, for Hungary, then as now,
presented many problems to thinker and statesman.
Languet condoned the runaway's offence, though he seems
to have felt the unexpected separation somewhat keenly.
He reproached Sidney with having concealed his designs,
for a fitting and sufficiently erudite travelling companion
might have been found. " I could have procured you such
a companion, had you told me what you were going to
do." The rest of the letter is amiable and pleasant : but
one is almost glad to remember that Sidney escaped the
attentions of one who could "discourse to you in the
course of your journey, or instruct you about the manners
and institutions of the people you visit, conduct you to
learned men, and, if need be, serve as your interpreter."
Free from restraint, it is to be hoped Sidney committed
some follies during his tour. St. Bartholomew and
Languet were tending to make him superhuman.

But except that he heard Campion, the famous Jesuit
priest and poet, preach in Vienna, there are too few
records of his wanderings extant to be of value. It is
mentioned in Campion's Life that his hearer was decently
impressed by what he heard, a result which Languet would
have disliked, and of which he was not informed. Not
much scholarship is needed to translate " *Dulce est decipere
in loco*," nor much common-sense wanted to act upon the
advice of the cheery maxim. For once Sidney was "out
of school," the only time in his life, a life almost too
strenuous to be quite attractive. Stevenson's " Apology
for Idlers" would never have convinced him, though it
appears conclusive enough to most of us.

On his return from his wanderings Sidney spent a
month with his elderly friend. A spirit of unrest possessed
him, and he once again decided to travel, this time in
Italy. Languet was shocked at the suggestion, and did
what he could, by argument and persuasion, to nip the
project in the bud. To him, as to Ascham, Italy was a
garden of Circe, an isle of Sirens. Atheist or papist, he
would have been puzzled to decide which was the worse
Sidney was bound to become. The sturdy old reformer
was unable to realise the possibility of a man preserving
his mental balance once his eyes had rested on the fair
plains of Lombardy. His fears were shared by many an
instructor of youth : nor was such nervousness always ill-
founded. Young travellers in Italy did become atheists or
embrace Catholicism. Greybeards wagged and thought,
even mumbled, of the wrath of Heaven and judgment to
come. Wise as they were, the old birds of evil omen could
not perceive the immense gulf that separates the most
rigid of all faiths from the miserable condition of no faith
at all. Stupid and wicked people had done stupid and
wicked things in the name of Rome, and men's minds
were not willing, or not able, to understand. Sidney, however, really suffered little danger. His piety, narrow and
insular to an unpleasant degree, was vigorously sincere.
He had already made up his mind about God, as he had
about everything else. The problem for him was ridiculously easy of solution. Qualms such as Languet felt
were unnecessary and idle. That so stern a Protestant
should be, for a second, lured by the glamour of Papal
magnificence and tradition, or even historical reasons for
its assumption of Divine power and wisdom, was, on the
face of it, an absurd supposition. Atheist was a word the
mere sound of which would cause him to recoil with
horror. And though Languet, worthy man, was anxious,
he had no reason to be so.

Yet absurd though his tremors may appear, Languet did

not suffer them alone.  To the modern mind they are in-
comprehensible ; to the men of Sidney's age this world
and the two next worlds also, could only be gained,
understood, and faced, with all their problems, by first
rightly adjusting one's mind as to the correct attitude
to adopt between papist and Reformer.  Each believed
the other damned, each was convinced of his own salvation.  Sidney is mostly famous as hero and poet.  He
was both of these ; but the chief aim of his life was to be a
Protestant, and often an unpleasant one.  His temperament was to some degree responsible, and he was not very
fortunate in his tutors and choice of friends.  To them,
indeed, the blame mostly attaches.  Theological argument
has its merits ; but theological argument petrified into
cruel assertion is a species of discussion to be avoided.
Europe was a battle-ground whereon nimble wits dis-
ported themselves ; and while the wholesome, if pot-house
reared, drama was distributing an infinity of good, the
dogmas of rival creeds were scattering the seeds of pesti-
lence.  It is usual to regard the life of Sidney from one
vantage-ground : that molehill gives a survey of his
character at once misleading and mischievous.  He was a
poet, and sometimes wrote fine verses : he was a polished
advocate, and contrived " A Defense of Poesy " ; his was a
slipshod, but not wholly unattractive, skill in the weaving
of romance.  " Arcadia " had imitators and has had
successors.  It is hard to read, and not very pleasant,
coming from the hand of so pious a man.  In fact, a great
deal of it is muddy enough, for which we may make Sidney
or his age responsible as we choose.  Even Walpole disliked
it.  This fact, at least, is certain, though it is glossed over
by his commentators, that however much poetry and
romance attracted him, true religion as he understood it,
and frightful bigotry was what concerned him most.

These considerations make Languet's opposition to the
Italian tour, pathetic in its iteration, the more astonishing.

Impressionable youth, it is obvious, might easily have fallen under the spell of the land that every artist in dream or deed has loved. But Sidney was quite safe. He knew, or thought he did, "the ultimate will of God"; so Philip Sidney might walk unscathed through any number of dangers. He was quite aware that Venice, his destination, had, in morals, a bad name. He was equally aware that he could pass between her palaces unsmirched. Contriving to accomplish this feat, he came back as ignorant as he was accomplished. There was a great problem to be solved, and English statesmen to-day in their various ways are busy with its counterpart. They cannot explain away the difficulty; Sidney never saw there was a difficulty to be tackled. Yet his qualities as statesman have been lauded often enough. He saw in Venice what the average man of education would see. It is no fault of his that he saw no further. The fault lies with his panegyrists. What Sidney found was the most comfortable city in Italy. Art paid homage to riches, and wealth gave tribute to art. Internal dissensions did not exist or, if they did, the walls of the Doge's palace were discreetly silent. Discontent was as hushed as the lapping of the waters in the green canals. Venice was serene and magnificent. All that money could buy was hers, all good that taste could command belonged to her also. Victorious, mighty, arrogant, a republic of tradesmen patronised the world. But this same splendour and surety meant ultimate ruin. Sidney did not foresee this : he was as blind as on the eve of St. Bartholomew. Venice was at the apex of her fame ; revelry and debauchery, often shameless, were already sounding her death-knell. It is quite easy to discount Roger Ascham's perfervid sigh of horror. London was not Paradise, but London was not Venice. As yet the Jew and the financier had not begun to plot her ruin. But the Queen of the Adriatic was already forced to

measure the weight of her debts.   Sidney only saw a city
buzzing with life, blazing with colour ; there was more of
amusement to be obtained there than in any other capital
of Europe.   He does not seem to have availed himself of
his chances.   The letters we have, written to Languet, are
earnest, sometimes humorously eloquent.   But the wretched
theological bias, which ought not to have influenced a boy
of his years, he was now nineteen, is irritatingly easy of
detection.   A modern schoolboy has this advantage, that
he only hears he has a soul on Sundays and forgets the
fact the other six days of the week.   Eccentric indeed are
the tasks to which this Admirable Crichton set himself.
Cosmography, thus earning Languet's approval, and
astronomy were but a small part of the studies which he
pursued.   He forgot to write to Languet sometimes in
the multiplicity of his labours.   A sharp reprimand
follows each omission.   It is not very easy to follow the
reasoning in these letters of the sage.   In one he tells his
pupil that he has in him "too little fun," while in another
he exclaims, "By omitting one dance a month you could
have abundantly satisfied us."   Apparently Sidney did
not give up his monthly dance.   Anyhow the querulous
protests at a supposed slackening of affection grow monotonous.   Perhaps it was not good for Sidney to receive
these letters, he would not have been human if he had
felt no annoyance at the receipt of more than one of
them.   They had a most emphatic effect on his character,
they narrowed his outlook.   But after all he was glad to
get them, and writes, in a spirit of enthusiasm, "I had
rather have one pleasant chat with you, my dear Languet,
than enjoy all the magnificent magnificences of these
magnificoes."   It must be confessed that the letters are
not exhilarating, I doubt if the pleasant chats referred to
were either.   The letters have received their meed of
praise, and to the student they have their interest.   In
them none the less we find that grim and grey spirit that

cloaks enthusiasm, as a fog clouds the sun. The extraordinary melancholy that such austere Protestantism as
Languet's engendered was not a wholesome beverage. It
was not good for a boy recovering from fever to read that
his illness seemed to the philosopher " worse than death ";
and the petulant assertion that Sidney preferred to see the
" galley slaves of Genoa " rather than stay at home and
talk to an eminently worthy teacher is a ridiculous and
jealous gibe.

Still Languet's letters did exercise this great influence
over their recipient. They comprised a study, to quote
the words of one of them, " which will make you still more
grave." Discussions on death and its advantages are
morbid and monotonous reading, even for a serious boy,
though relieved by a few touches of unconscious humour,
as in one where Sir Thomas More, who died for a faith
not theirs, is quoted with approval. It is difficult to
understand the attitude of men who quote what suits their
argument and assertions while they endeavour to refute
every other belief that same authority advances. However,
Languet easily performed the feat, and his pupil was apt.
Count Philip of Hainau was perhaps not too desirable a
companion ; for he was a bigot, though a good man and
brave ; so there was no need for letters perpetually harping
on these grave religious topics, making the poet's outlook
narrower than it need have been. Apparently men could not
escape from these piteous discussions. There is nothing
quite like them in English history, except during the
Tractarian Movement, when the healthy businesses of life
were put aside and unhealthy uncertainties lived and eat
and slept with all men.

When Sidney suggested extending his tour to Rome
and Constantinople he disturbed a hornet's nest. Not
much to his credit he was persuaded by arguments quite
foolish and thoroughly unchristian. Let it be remembered, however, that the Pope and Mahomet were anti-

Christ, and he had been taught to believe, and willingly
accepted the absurdity, that of the two the former was
much the worse.   Moreover, Mahomet was suffering under
defeat, Catholicism had at most experienced a snub.
True Alva was, or had lately been, on the warpath.
His name inspired horror for no very adequate reason.
John Knox was quite as cruel and a great deal more
impertinent.   Philip's going to Rome would not, in any
case, have helped the famous Spanish general, and might
have worked considerable benefit to the young traveller.
But Sidney allowed himself to be persuaded, and stuck
to Padua or Venice, Protestantism and cosmography.
With the fairest intentions it is difficult not to be angry
with the foolish old man whose knowledge was not always
according to wisdom or charity.   This is not the verdict
usually passed on the worthy Burgundian ; even so able
a scholar as Mr. Fox Bourne, if one less learned may
speak, praises him too highly.   He meant well, but his
knowledge did not always conduce to salvation.   Much
that he said Sidney remembered ; what was said was
honestly enough meant, but, judged by the light of later
times, was often particularly unwise.

Sidney, deprived of his visits to Rome and Constantinople, did manage to enjoy himself according to his own
austere manner.   He got himself painted by Paolo
Veronese.   As he was not well provided with money it
would be interesting to know what the fees of the great
artist were at this time.   The portrait has been mislaid,
and the late John Addington Symonds suggests that it is
"buried in some German collection."   Another performance of Sidney's was less creditable.   Perhaps the
pugilistic school of Protestantism in which he had been
reared had discovered too promising a pupil.   He lost his
temper, before reaching Venice, over a matter of but little
importance.   Setting out on his journey a gentleman and
kinsman, Thomas Coningsby, accompanied him.   Not

much is known of him, save that eventually he married
his companion's cousin. On the other hand, nothing is
known against him. Unluckily we do know that Sidney
was hot-tempered and peevish. Because an innkeeper
was a cheat Sidney accused Coningsby of being a rogue.
He roundly charged his friend with theft, and wrote to
Languet saying that his companion was nearly as bad as
the Pope. Naturally he had to withdraw this babyish
complaint. There was not a word of truth in it. But the
episode is worth noticing, since later incidents in his career
are not more satisfactory and display some undue quickness to anger and want of judgment.

Languet, out of sheer weariness, was calling for the
death he dare not seek : his letters are lugubriously
pompous. Sidney was not seeing Venice as he ought to
have seen it. It is, all things considered, well that in
the summer of 1575 he was called home. A sister was
dead, the other was about the Queen's person. One
fact told for sorrow, the other for encouragement. The
future, when he first faced it, looked brighter than it
proved.

The death of Ambrosia, save in so far as it grieved his
parents, cannot have caused Philip more than a passing
sigh. He was still young, and she only a girl. Companionship between them had perforce been infrequent.
Different, however, was the care with regard to his elder
sister Mary. The Queen, whose conduct towards the
Sidney family was full of contradictions, at one moment
friendly at another harsh, even ungenerous, had signalled
the girl out for royal honour and advancement. Sir
Henry hard worked as he ever was, none the less struggled
under the shadow of a haughty disapproval. Such benefits
as his wise conduct produced were accepted, without
thanks ; their necessary price was always grudged, and, at
times, absolutely ignored. So it was something for Philip
to know that his sister could speak privately to the sover-

eign on occasion.  For the young man determined to be his
father's champion, resenting bitterly the indignities thrust
upon him.  His hopes for a betterment of this state of
affairs was founded also on a further reason.  His own
popularity was great, and he was immediately taken into
favour at Court.  Not only in London was his attendance
demanded, he was bidden to take part in the stately
progress of the summer of 1775.  He was present at the
famous tournament at Kenilworth, where Leicester entertained the Queen with princely magnificence.  There is
no doubt that of all those who did homage to Elizabeth on
this occasion Philip himself was not less interesting to the
spectators and visitors than was his uncle the Earl.
Leicester having no children, it seems to have been current
gossip that the brilliant nephew would succeed as heir.
The favourite did nothing to dissipate the rumours of
which he must have had knowledge.  Consequently
Philip's comings and goings were certain to be duly
noted and commented upon.  After leaving Kenilworth
the Court proceeded to Chartley Castle, where it was
entertained graciously by Lady Essex, whose lord was in
Ireland.  Here an important meeting took place, the
result of which eventually caused Philip an appreciable
amount of sorrow and unhappiness, and, as a compensa-
tion, created him a poet of distinction.

Lady Phoebe Devereux was only a girl of thirteen,
and Philip still a boy.  But it must be remembered
that, among people of their rank, maturity was gained
earlier than with us.  Whatever Philip may have thought
at the hour of meeting, his stay at Chartley furnished
him food for thought and reflection.  When Essex returned, not many weeks later, the young man was
already a constant visitor at Durham House.  Reason
for his visits seemed too obvious to need explanation.
Essex viewed them with entire approval.  He showed
his feelings in a practical way.  Philip was to stay

WALTER DEVEREUX, EARL OF ESSEX
FROM AN ENGRAVING AFTER THE PICTURE AT BLYTHFIELD

for a period with his father, for the third time Lord
Deputy, in Ireland.  Essex, in the July of 1576, returned
there as Earl Marshal.  He took Philip with him.  Philip
once more, to the casual onlooker, appears as a favourite
of Fortune.  Within six weeks after their arrival in
Dublin the fair prospect suffered eclipse.  In the far wilds
of Galway news came to the Sidneys that Essex was
dead.  Rumours that he had been poisoned were frequent,
but it has not been suggested that either father or son lent
ear to them.  Neither were of a temper to have believed
the suggestions and taken no steps to avenge the crime.
On his deathbed Essex sent Philip a message : " Tell him
I sent him nothing, but I wish him well ; so well, that if
God may move their hearts, I wish that he might match
with my daughter.  I call him son, he is so wise, virtuous,
and godly."  Then the dying man added : " If he go on in
the course he hath begun, he will be as famous a gentleman as ever England bred."  Clearly, the marriage details
apart, had been definitely decided upon.  Nor was it a
project as yet only discussed in private between the two
families.  It was frequently discussed by others ; one writes
declaring that "if it is prevented it will turn to more
dishonour than can be repaired by any other marriage in
England."  For a time at any rate no decided steps in
the affair were advanced.  The death of Essex was a blow
under which the Sidneys staggered.  They were very
poor, and Sir Henry grew daily poorer.  Lady Mary, at
her wits' end, turned to Burleigh for such comfort as she
could get and that astute statesman felt inclined to
bestow.  The arrogant and ungenerous Ormonde was
doing his best to undermine whatever little influence Sir
Henry possessed with the Queen.  At first it seems
strange that they should not have turned to their powerful
and splendid kinsman Leicester.  Perhaps they knew
more of that nobleman's designs than is apparent to us ;
or, what is equally credible, did not care to worry the man

from whom such great benefits were confidently expected. Leicester liked himself a great deal better than he liked Philip. As soon as he decently could he married Lady Essex, and all dreams of future fortune and prosperity ended as such dreams usually do. When Philip returned to England his prospects, once all sunshine, contained clouds much larger than a man's hand.

# CHAPTER VI

## PHILIP'S FIRST MISSION

Mission to Rudolph of Hapsburg—Protestantism not Penelope his mistress—Languet joins mission — Money difficulties—Conflicting parties among Reformers—Well received by the Emperor and Court—Rudolph's character—Philip received by Emperor's mother and daughter—Social successes in Prague—Notices increasing power of the Jesuits—Starts homewards—Leaves Languet at Cologne—Meets William of Orange at Dorddrecht

A T Court he found little to encourage him. Intrigues and abuse were further damaging his father's reputation ; his mother lived in retirement, as she had ever since the small-pox disfigured her ; his sister was a favourite, but had little influence, if any.

Philip's lot was not enviable, but fortunately his courage and his pride were not easily damped. His return was noticed, he was also received graciously, and soon set off on his travels again, the bearer of an important mission. Full of political ambition, an ambition Languet assiduously nursed, he accepted the position gladly and, with Fulke Greville as companion and a numerous retinue, left London for the Court of Rudolph of Hapsburg. They carried with them the congratulations of their mistress on the accession of that prince to the Imperial throne.

The task was honourable, if only formal : Sidney may well have thought that to confide it to so young a

man was a proof of further and more exacting labours
to be hereafter allotted to him. He took very good care
to act his part with dignity and splendour. At each stage
on his journey he caused a tablet to be set up over
the lintel, bearing the impressive words, a delightful
comment on his supposed humility : " Of the most
illustrious and well-born English gentleman, Philip Sidney,
son of the Viceroy of Ireland, nephew of the Earls of
Warwick and Leicester, Ambassador from the Serene
Queen of England to the Emperor." It has been suggested that this high-sounding announcement did not
display a lack of modesty, but merely set forth the dignity
of his office and the greatness of his Queen. Affording
pleasant reading, as it does, it hardly needs an apology,
but no one can gravely assert that it shows an undue
diffidence in the heralding of his own claims to consideration.

His journey interested him, but caused him also grave
anxiety. How deeply he was in love we have no means
of knowing. Yet any reference to the lady of his choice
is now, when it might have been made with all propriety,
not to be discovered. Protestantism rather than Penelope
was once more his mistress. Germanised Europe certainly
gave him ample material for thought, and a grave young
man was set a considerable number of grave problems
with which to wrestle. Still his very earnestness of
purpose at this period may conceivably have annoyed the
young girl.

> " And this inconstancy is such
>     As you, too, shall adore :
> I could not love thee, dear, so much
>     Loved I not honour more "

was a potent and eloquent excuse in Lovelace's beautiful
verses, and they were addressed directly to the lady.
Philip made no such apology ; his excuse, had he offered
one, for his abstraction would scarcely have proved as con-

vincing as that of a gallant warrior risking personal
danger, nor so romantic and picturesque. Hard though
the conclusion may seem, Philip was at this time a
laggard in love and lived to regret his dilatoriness. In
the words of Fulke Greville : " Above all he made the
religion he professed the firm basis of his life." And
in a generous tribute to his friend declares : " This was it
which, I profess, I loved dearly in him, and still shall be
glad to honour in the great men of this time : I mean, that
his heart and tongue went both one way, and so with
every one that went with the Truth ; as knowing no other
kindred party or end." Lady Penelope may be excused
if she estimated each virtue of less account than a few
more compliments from the man people regarded as her
suitor.

Philip, however, was the politician, not the lover. To
one of his particular mould of mind his expedition was
exactly of the nature himself would have chosen. That
he laboured hard is proved by evidence beyond controversy. Luckily Fulke Greville was with him, the friend
he best loved, to share his anxieties and encourage the
full accomplishment of his schemes. Philip had no intention of merely congratulating the Emperor and condoling
with the brother princes in the Palatine. A much more
serious duty was imposed upon him, at his own request,
though this object of his journey was not made known
publicly, nor would it have been politic to let Europe
into the secret. To make his journey a real service to
his sovereign he was able to " procure an Article to be
added to his instructions, which gave him scope (as he
passed) to salute such German Princes, as were interested
in the cause of Religion, or their own native liberty."
Fulke Greville tells us this, and his testimony all through
the tour is valuable and clear. Before the party reached
Heidelberg it was joined by Languet. The meeting must
have been agreeable for both, perhaps especially agreeable

to the elder man.  His presence, too, added still further lustre to the little party.  For Languet's reputation as a scholar filled Europe, and they who hated him most hated him because they feared him.  Taking no ostensible part in public affairs, his advice, it was no secret, was frequently asked and often accepted.  The old gentleman in his quiet lodgings wielded a subtle influence more powerful than that exercised by many a ruling prince. To him the mission upon which Sidney was employed would seem one of importance because of that special clause inserted in Philip's instructions.  He, like many others, saw in his pupil and friend the saviour of Protestant Europe.  Philip had affected to grumble at the task conferred on him : he said it was only fit for a boy, and made other foolish statements to Greville.  His method of conducting his mission, and the sometimes rather absurd pomp he affected both in speech and manner, show that he did not need Languet's stirring to make him satisfied with his trust and with himself.

The venerable scholar was deeply distressed at the trend of events in the great world, and feared the danger that threatened a greatly loved cause.  His voice was rich with counsel for the ear of the youthful diplomat.  It is easy to trace his influence throughout Philip's public utterances, for behind their florid periods and wordy, if elegant, declamation there is the knowledge that can only come of years and ripe experience.  Many historians praise freely these persuasive efforts of Philip's ; and he learned his lesson well and spoke it effectively, if not always to the great pleasure of his listeners.  Oratory and splendour belonged to Philip, but " the voice is the voice of Jacob."

Sir Henry Sidney seems to have been satisfied with his son's advancement, for out of his impoverished fortune he sent his heir three hundred pounds, a large sum then. Elizabeth considered the honour sufficient of itself and

contributed meanly enough towards the equipment of her
representative.    This   profuse   spirit   of   economy   was
probably a characteristic quality of "anointed greatness,"
concerning which not the least able of her eulogists waxes
amazingly eloquent.   Elizabeth's parsimony was due to
two causes : early  years  at  Hatfield  and  vanity.   And
much as we dislike this rigid counting of the pennies
in one who had no need to count them, it is only fair to
consider the reasons that actuated her.   She had been poor
and despised and was mighty ; but even to the powerful comes a fall sometimes, and she knew this.   Further,
she  delighted  to  be  considered  beautiful  and  was,  no
doubt, gratified to discover that men were willing to serve
her even for a frown as payment.   Men were so willing,
the best men of the century in England.   A glow of
romance animated them, and it was married to a flame of
piety.   The  combination  told  for  the  Queen's  comfort.
Protestants abroad looked to her for advice and help ; she
gave  them  the  first  and  withheld  the  latter.   Yet  no
one complained, or if any one did he complained in
secret.

Sidney—for he was Sidney now, his able father is henceforth only Sir Henry, though he had to pay Philip's boot
bill, a big one—was soon successfully launched on his
affair.   His   first   resting-place  of  importance  was
Heidelberg.   Here he hoped to meet Lewis, the new
Elector of the Palatine.   The Prince was absent, but his
brother, Count Casimir, was more than willing to play
the host.   Primed by Languet, as he certainly was, Sidney
could not have been astonished at the news the Prince
poured into his sympathetic ear.   The late Elector had
thrown all his energy and devotion on to the side of the
Calvinists.   They  flourished,  and  were  decent  citizens.
This may be said of their hard creed, that it kept them
honest.   Casimir's brother, the new Elector, was a violent
Lutheran.   He hated the Calvinists as much as he hated

Rome. The Englishman was grieved: he had dreamed of forming a league of Protestants to fight Rome and Spain. The scheme was well considered as practical mundane politics. It was hopeless in view of the way these Christians loved one another. The problem he found himself face to face with was not Rome against the world, but how to tackle Rome if worthy protestors against her power would fly at each other's throats. This exactly was what was happening in Germany and the Low Countries. Nor is the phenomenon to be wondered at. From a multitude of counsellors it is idle to hope to extract much wisdom. Sidney seized the bull by the horns. With the amazing fatuity of the politicians of the day, he busied himself about what he did not understand. Gravely he advises Casimir to "make peace between warring sects." Writing home he leniently assigns "extreme conscientiousness" as the motive which animated the conflicting parties. The excuse is distinctly humorous, as it would have been withheld from a Catholic or atheist. According to this enlightened theologian the two words meant much the same thing. Meanwhile it is curious to note that while advising a peaceful settlement he gives the unfortunate Count not a single hint as to how the arrangement could be most easily brought about. His endeavours were hampered too by a money-lending transaction between Elizabeth and the late Elector. The debt was not large, but the Queen wanted it paid. Casimir explained that he was not personally liable, which was obvious, for he was not the reigning Prince. Also he explained the lamentable condition of the principality financially, concluding, as most debtors or their advocates do, by asking for time. He asserted that in two years the amount would be refunded. The gist of his remarks, which seem to have duly and properly, in this case, influenced Sidney, the ambassador forwarded to London.

By the time he paid his parting visit to the Count

Sidney had learned a great deal. No doubt his brief call at Louvain had in some measure prepared him for the solid opposition his Protestant League was likely to encounter. Don John treated him with every possible courtesy, and paid him a high compliment, but courtesy and compliment did not further the plan Sidney had set his heart upon. His Imperial Highness was not the sort of man to advance any such scheme. So we may believe readily that Sidney and Languet had much talk together on their way to Prague, and scant encouragement attended on their arrival at the Bohemian capital.

Rudolph was proud, taciturn, and determined. He had become a Catholic in his father's lifetime, but the old Emperor had not worried overmuch. As he told the Bohemian Diet, he had so educated his son as to insure that his son should be liberal and fair-minded. The Empress, after whom the Prince took, was careful that he should be neither. Most certainly he obeyed his mother in all things. She was not a lovable woman, but a vindictive bigot. Yet, like our own Queen Mary, she was a good woman, scrupulously honest and fearless in the pursuit of that which her conscience commended as right and true. Philip Sidney knew all about her before his embassy to Prague was even thought of. What he did not know Languet may have been trusted to tell him on the road thither from Heidelberg.

It is not necessary to be a partisan to see that the affairs of Europe were in a parlous state. On one side " Rome's undermining superstitions " aided by "the commanding forces of Spain," on the other a nebulous League stood ready for action. This vision of combined forces Sidney wished to make a concrete reality. The Reform loving princes were poor allies. Left in peace to hunt, ride, and shoot, they cannot be said to have cared acutely what happened outside their own territories. Protestantism was then, as it always has been and must be, a set of warring sects with no authoritative leader. When they discovered that Rome was actively against them they could not combine. One thinks of Erasmus, the Bishop Blougram of his age, sitting in his study watching a combat that, had he lived, he would probably have been able to prevent.

To all appearance the Protestants were bound to lose. Like many other Reformers, each clique insisted on its own leader, and was not nice in its language about the leaders of rival cliques. Most astounding dogmas were preached in various local centres, and one dogma contradicted another, helping to form a maze of bewildering confusion. Some historians assert that these bickerings agitating the Protestant sects are not interesting. They were the heart and sinews of debate and contention at the period now described. Prince and peasant thought and talked of little else. Opposed to the jarring Protestant sects was a power that has never been humiliated, though it has sometimes been silenced. It was absurd for Philip to speak of Rudolph as " Jesuit bound." The great order has had harsh things said of it, borne unjust aspersions so often that its members can afford to laugh. Travellers know what the Jesuits have done, historians are not ignorant, nor lovers of education ungrateful. But "hit a Jesuit if you cannot find a donkey" was a good proverb to act upon, and Sidney agreed that all who did not agree with him were "Espaniolated," by which it may be conjectured an insult was intended, or "Jesuit bound." Rudolph, being no fool, probably knew what the legate would say before he had opened his mouth. He, even as the Prince of the Palatine, acknowledged as father a man of broad views and easy generosity to opponents. These enlightened and humane princes probably believed in peace and quiet, and were not vigorously concerned about any other gifts from the gods. The new Emperor guessed accurately every argument Sidney could advance, and had his answer ready. That he condescended to make a show of answering is to his credit. Sidney had apparently got firmly fixed in his mind that he, Sidney, was a dictator. Great chiefs on their thrones were inclined to think otherwise. Their decision may have astonished him; it astonished no one else. The Emperor received him seriously and with distinction. He was gracious to the envoy personally, nor, so far as patient research can discover, said anything derogatory of the Queen whom he represented. Probably he hated her, as most Catholic princes did. They had a good reason for their aversion.

The controversy between the rival sects is beyond a sane man's comprehension. Their detestation of each other is somewhat ludicrously obvious. And the Protestants by their internal feuds not merely confirmed the absurdity of their position, but emphasised its absurdity. Common ground for alliance the sects did not possess. It has been said that there were as many sects as there were stars in the heavens. Rulers of small states were honest enough in their dislike of both Emperor and Pope; they were not anxious to be "Jesuit bound"; but they did not wish either to attract the attention of princes more powerful than themselves. So for the most part they gave to one or other of the Reformed Churches a flaccid approval, and busied themselves seriously in less serious affairs. We cannot blame them if they preferred hunting to being hunted. If not dignified, their attitude was human. England's position was one of absolute security compared to that of the German principalities.

Before condemning utterly the disorganised condition of the Protestant states, it must be remembered that the peoples and their rulers did not look through equal glasses. The religious indifference of the latter roused grave distress in the minds of men like Languet, distress mingled with angry amazement in the breasts of men so inexperienced and yet so earnest as Sidney. Amazement Languet could not have felt, he was too old a politician. Sidney, though a genius, had everything to learn. The real reason of his disgust lies in the misunderstanding or ignorance of the fact that the crisis in Europe was political no less than religious. This the sluggish princes understood, but their subjects did not. Violent preachers took hold of them, and, politically, these orators were no wiser than their hearers. Dowered with earnestness and fire, each from his own pulpit thundered forth the truth that inflamed him. Toleration had become impossible when each preacher believed the whole truth had been revealed to himself alone. Observers of modern religious movements may trace something of the same spirit animating their organisers, though the fervour is usually chastened by a slight infusion of worldly wisdom and some acuteness in playing the game of politics. The Reformers scorned worldly matters ; their business was to save souls. The business of the princes was to save their crowns, not to interfere in the perilous niceties of theological controversy, and to keep on good terms with their subjects. In so far as a sovereign had duties, this attitude, they conceived, comprised the sum of his obligations. To be at peace with their subjects seemed to them, not unnaturally, the first step towards security. In Germany it was diplomatic to be Protestant, but what particular phase of Protestantism the people adopted was, it would seem, of very little importance. Henry IV. became a Catholic, we may be sure, for much the same reasons as Electors and Land-graves smiled on Lutheran or Calvinist. Sidney cannot be expected to have understood this, nor did he understand their difficulty.

Rudolph showed no tolerance, and his power was too mighty to be carelessly ignored. Left to his priests and his ceremonies, he settled himself calmly to watch with a sneer the frantic quarrels of the rival religious creeds. No wonder Philip quickly grasped the hopeless nature of his self-imposed task, and he viewed with genuine sorrow the

grim future of hapless Protestants in the Emperor's own
dominions. Ten years sooner, in the tolerant days of
Maximilian, perhaps such an attempt as he intended to
make would have been more hopeful. From Rudolph,
schooled by his mother, nothing save the ordinary
courtesies to an ambassador could be expected.

Philip did not flinch from danger or difficulty, but his
heart was heavy as he attended the solemn services in the
Prague Cathedral on Easter Sunday. Yet he does not
seem to have grasped one obvious fact, namely, that how
ever vindictive and prejudiced the Emperor might be they
who would defeat his errors scarcely set that powerful
prince a respectable example either in the matter of
charity or good sense. On Easter Monday the envoy
was received in audience, and more than one account of
the interview has been written. The Englishman bore
himself proudly, and was not to be deterred from speaking
his mind. To an astonished potentate and his obsequious
courtiers he made a very bold speech. Taking as his
text the combined forces of Pope and Spain, and the
danger such a combination threatened he averred that
Germany, for all her industry, her wealth, her resources,
the bravery and numbers of her people, was no match
against this terrible alliance. Theirs was a "brotherhood
of evil," and he pleaded that they who loved liberty and
religious freedom should form a defensive league against
the common enemy. He demanded "a bond of conscience," and with considerable eloquence showed that in
such a compact alone lay the certainty of peace, prosperity, and advancement. Arguments such as these,
though well reasoned and statesmanlike, were not of a
nature to convince their hearer or soften his heart towards
heretics. That he was patient, and curbed his temper,
during the harangue of the fervid boy ambassador is
something to his credit. His answer was perfectly
courteous and adroit.

After thanking the Queen for her congratulations on his accession he told Philip that God was the guardian of the Empire, and he breathed a pious wish that, under the hand of the Almighty, he would find strength and wisdom to act his onerous part, profitably, for his people and with credit to himself. The finger of God, Philip knew, would hardly point, in Rudolph's opinion, to a course of leniency towards those wicked enough to espouse the doctrines put forth by a heterogeneous crowd of Protestant divines. On the analogy of " he who is not for me is against me," not to be a Catholic was to stand condemned as atheist in the Emperor's eyes. And he was sincere and immovably fixed in this opinion. Philip professed to think but little of the Emperor's ability and dubbed him narrow-minded, as he was, as was Philip himself, and nearly all those who busied themselves in ecclesiastical disputes. He also calls him treacherous, but Rudolph had been quite honest during their conversation. It may be that, though Philip knew he could only expect defeat, he anticipated a longer answer, a detailed consideration of his reasons, and therefore cherished a private dislike for this man of few words.

No one, when Rudolph came to his throne, would have seen in him the bigot or the persecutor. He was an amiable man, and, so it seemed, inclined to use all his influence on the side of peace. Anxious about art theories that interested a handful, he was also a dabbler in science. But he fell, at once, under the sway of his mother's evil genius. With quite incredible rapidity the young man of good feeling evolved into the tyrant and oppressor. A wise Emperor had been his father, but Spain was his foster-mother. The traditions of his house were opposed to the policy he adopted. Ferdinand, one of the wisest and most humane of rulers, did not swerve in his loyalty and affection for the Catholic Church. His good sense made him tolerant of those who joined the

Reformers. Even in Austria he would allow no persecutions, and he endeavoured to so bring it about that men of conflicting faiths should live peacefully together. These admirable efforts were continued by his son Maximilian. Always declaring himself a Catholic, he was, none the less, attached to the Lutherans and their doctrines, receiving the communion in both kinds. Persecution was an abomination to him, nor would he tolerate it in his dominions. He contrived some appearance of peace between Lutheran and Catholic, and adjusted their disputes. Unfortunately the protestors weakened position by quarrelling bitterly among themselves. At the close of his life much of Maximilian's generosity and lenity turned to anger, but the measures he decided to take cannot fitly be called persecutions ; prosecutions, not undeserved, is the fitter description. So when Maximilian died Rudolph and the Catholics regained much of the power they had lost. In many districts the Catholics were appointed to benefices held by Reformers, who had to leave the city or province, and Jesuit schools were founded. And these proceedings were accelerated and made easy by the inopportune death of Frederick III., Elector of the Palatine. He had been an enthusiastic follower of Calvin, and, with stupid impetuosity, caused Calvinism to become the nominal religion of his subjects. The new Elector, Lewis, with equal folly, deserted his father's policy and insisted on his bewildered people becoming Lutherans. Confusion caused by the move was worse confounded when the Elector's brother, John Casimir, grimly supported the now ostracised creed. In such internecine warfare, such bitter civil strife, Rudolph and the Catholics saw something more than the mere promise of victory. Had Philip Sidney been older and more experienced he would not have built such high hopes on his self-imposed mission or expected a different welcome from that which he received. His reception was courteous, a cordial and sympathetic welcome was impossible.

Moreover, in the Low Countries the Protestant cause was in difficulties. Don John of Austria, Philip of Spain's near relative, signalised his appointment as Viceroy by persuading the Southern Netherlanders to break the "Pacification of Ghent" in spite of the entreaties of William of Orange. On Sidney's arrival in Vienna events were decidedly hostile to his chances of success in the plans he had brooded over.

A courteous reception also awaited him at the house of Maximilian's mother, where he also met her daughter, ex-Queen of France, herself a widow, Charles IX. being now dead. To them he conveyed the condolences of Elizabeth, and made a further speech. He said that his own Queen hoped the dowager Empress would direct and counsel her son. The lady could not easily hide her dislike of the topic, and hastened to excuse herself from any meddling in State affairs. Retirement from the world was all she desired, she said ; for her its affairs offered neither interest nor temptation. She thanked Elizabeth for her letter of sympathy and goodwill, and sent return messages of a cordial character. On religious and political matters, however, she observed a discreet silence. In the ex-Queen Elizabeth of France he found a more sympathetic listener. This unhappy lady, married to a madman, had done what she could to temper with mercy and sympathy the sufferers who writhed under the power of her unscrupulous mother-in-law Catherine, and the unspeakable follies and cruelties of her husband. When Charles died, haunted by recollections of massacre and torture, she had no wish to play again an active part in life. Scarcely can we wonder that, after the horrors among which she had passed those few terrible years that succeeded her marriage, she sought and found peace within the quiet walls of a convent.

His mission being now done, Philip turned his face sorrowfully homewards, looking for opportunities of sow-

ing the good seed on his progress. Above all, his mind
was bent on meeting and conferring with the great Prince
of Orange in the Netherlands. Before actually starting on
his journey he went frequently into society, and earned a
great reputation in Prague as a conversationalist.

To shine in Prague society demanded merits of unusual
quality. For the first years of his reign the Emperor
made this city his favourite residence. Allowing others to
busy themselves for him in political and religious concerns,
he gave himself up to the pursuit of polite learning, the
arts, and the sciences. For these, as I have said, the
majority of his subjects, noble or simple, cared very little.
But the Court at Prague was brilliant beyond any in
Europe. Tycho Brahe, when exiled from Denmark at the
instigation of jealous and ignorant nobles, found there
honourable refuge. This is a fact not to be forgotten
when we are told how bitterly the Roman Church opposed
the advance of science. Tycho Brahe received his persecution on his own island of Sven at the hands of men
inspired by no feeling of religious enthusiasm. He was
one, too, who had claimed the rank of prophet, and fore-
told the birth of Gustavus Adolphus. So at first sight he
does not seem to us exactly the kind of man to be received
eagerly at Rudolph's Court. Many other foreigners of
great distinction visited Prague, and Philip must have
found agreeable company. But he also found the power
of the Jesuits daily increasing. These brilliant people
utilised every step taken in the furtherance of art and
literature to their own advantage. They were not, and
never have been, foes to learning. Their fault would seem
to be an undue desire to possess the sole direction of
men's studies. Learning they accounted desirable, but
they did not believe in indiscriminate, unorganised, and
undirected speculation. A genius may be trusted to find
his own way, but the mass of mankind stands in need of
leaders. The Jesuits were born schoolmasters, and, with

great wisdom from their point of view, they acquired almost complete control of the children's schools throughout Bohemia. Their success filled Philip with dismay, and in his letters and Languet's, also in Fulke Greville's pages, we find with what horror and terror the Fathers were regarded. Artistic and scientific society in Prague, however, is not likely to have worried much about the Jesuits or the Jesuits about the learned men gathered in the capital. Either party pursued its own course, and the Emperor divided his favours between them impartially. Some of the poets, as Barthold Pontanus, an illustrious and crowned example, became one of the most fervent and eloquent of their preachers. Another, William of Rosenburg, founded a college for poor scholars, which was entirely under the management of priests of the powerful order. Rudolph was only beginning his sovereignty at the time of Philip's visit, but during the two preceding reigns learning had been greatly encouraged, the more easily as the country had enjoyed comparative quiet. But even they saw scholarship and art and science encouraged by the Jesuits. This portent boded no good to the cause he, Languet, and Greville cherished; and Philip, for all his social success, was not sorry to set his face towards home. There he had a right to expect not a few compliments and favours.

Indeed, though unsuccessful in his principal desire, he had covered himself with distinction. Reports that reached England from several sources were flattering in the extreme. His reputation was decidedly enhanced, and he might reasonably look forward to weightier responsibilities in the near future. The Emperor, on his departure, bestowed upon him a valuable ornament. He was busy with his thoughts upon his journey. Pondering over the inertia of princes, whom he describes in very unflattering terms; reflecting on the unedifying wrangles of those who would sooner fight each other than brave in company a common danger, he exclaims, "I grow daily less and less hopeful." Languet went with him as far as Cologne, and the separation was a sad one. He felt he needed all the help and sympathy the old man's gentle wisdom was so ready to supply. The Huguenot himself records that the parting gave him the greatest sorrow of a long life : " I received incredible delight from our intercourse," he writes. Meanwhile the Englishman discussed with Languet a project for visiting, privately, the Dutch prince. Such a project was natural enough, for William's name stood out heroically above the rulers of Europe, and his steady zeal and noble courage in the cause both held dear magnetised the young man. Only with difficulty could he be persuaded to renounce his scheme, for he knew that the famous Dutchman would be friendly, and that he would find his advice doubly precious in this time of dejection. Suddenly out of his darkness came a ray of light. · He was one day met by a letter from England informing him that a son had been born to the Stadtholder. He was bidden to alter the plans of his homeward voyage and carry Elizabeth's felicitations to the Prince.

How gladly Philip received his orders may be easily understood. The choice of such an ambassador seems to have been equally pleasing to the Prince, who met him at Geertruidenberg, and rode with his visitor to Dordrecht. Here good entertainment and every courtesy awaited the traveller. William broke his reputation for silence by writing of his guest most flattering enconiums. Among much else he says : " Her Majesty had one of the ripest and greatest counsellors of state in Sir Philip Sidney that this day lived in Europe." The great silent prince proclaimed thus to all Europe what he thought of his new friend. When the day came for the christening of the heir to the noble House of Orange, it was the young Englishman whom the greatest of the Protestant rulers and heroes chose as godfather for his son. Records of the conversa-

tion of the two men are not to be found. But the clever
and animated conversationalist of Prague must have discussed weighty affairs with more than common gravity to
have been signalled out for so high a compliment. The
jewel, even, that Orange gave to him as a parting gift
would be of less value in the eyes of the Most Catholic
King's godson ; a position he must have detested. A fair
passage brought Philip safely and swiftly home, and,
leaving Greville badly seasick at Rochester, he arrived in
London.

# CHAPTER VII

## THE NEW WORLD

The exploitation of the New World—Philip's early relation with the navigators—Frobisher's adventure in 1576—His return and second voyage—Languet disapproves—The Queen helps—Failure of the enterprise—Indignation against Frobisher undeserved—Philip's magnanimity under disappointment—Languet's letter—He alone sees the real danger of these voyages for gold—War against John of Austria—Sir Henry dissuades his son from visiting the Low Countries—A wise letter from Languet—Is honoured at Court

WHILE Philip was away on his mission great commotions had been stirring men's minds at home, the news of which he soon learnt. Eldorado was on the verge of being exploited, and men were eager for gain and easily acquired riches. Adventure, naturally, was attractive to a man of Philip's bravery. The hidden beauties stirred him as a poet and stimulated his imagination. Discovered riches, so far as he was concerned, should further the cause of true religion and dwarf to insignificance the costly freight hidden in the hulks of Spanish galleons. A new disease had caught hold of every man and woman in the country, a few million peasants excepted. Even Elizabeth was proving herself less mean than usual. Wealth was to pour into the lap of subscribers, beyond the dreams of avarice. Reasons for a belief in this sudden acquirement of money were exactly what they were long before Philip's day, and

are now.  It was a case of practical men believing that
their dreams would materialise; and a healthy disregard
of scrupulous methods to bring about the result was
accounted as common sense.  That if Spain gathered
treasure from the granaries of the New World, England
could much more readily, being specially the favourite
of the Almighty, reap still greater wealth seems to have
been the argument.  How much of the proceeds of
Frobisher's expedition were to be spent on the furtherance of religious work we are not told.  We do know,
however, that whatever Sidney's profits were to be his
religion and his family would share the spoils.

Before touching on this expedition, already under sail
when Philip returned from Holland, it is necessary to
sketch briefly the history of the movement which has
done so much to make the British Empire—for weal or
woe, which the future has still to decide—what it is to-day.
Sebastian Cabot, though not an Englishman, sailed from
the British port of Bristol, on an English ship with West
Country sailors.  His voyage and his discoveries were
made so far back as the reign of Henry VII.  Experiences such as he recounted, added to the stories current of
the greater Columbus, and the flaunted wealth dragged
from a new world by Old Spain, set men's tongues wagging.
Dangers could not intimidate at a time when nerves
were sound.  Also, it should be realised that, just as we
see in our own day, necessarily on a larger scale, men
attracted to what are still called the " new " countries, the
bird in the bush is usually considered a better investment
than two birds in the hand.  Greed of gain instigated the
men of Elizabeth's time, just as it did in the South Sea
Bubble when George III. was king, or, in our own day,
when South Africa and her gold mines enriched the few
and impoverished the many.  " Love of money is the root
of all evil " might have inspired a learned discourse from
countless pulpits.  Congregations were more eager to test

the truth of the assertion by practical experiment than to accept it unreservedly. "Money-mad" was the condition of quite sensible people when Philip returned home. He needed money badly himself, his family even more, and the cause he espoused was poor and necessitous. Little wonder that he, not for selfish and personal ends, joined in the speculation. He did so heartily, and drew upon himself the reproof of Languet for his unworthy folly, as will be seen later.

If we would judge rightly Philip's share in these matters, and he would gladly have given his active services no less than his moral support, it is necessary to look backwards a few years. Honour of his parents was a salient point in his creed, and not the least beautiful and manly. But this high conception of a son's duty itself spurred his enthusiasm. A year and a half before he was born Chancellor and Willoughby were directly patronised by Sir Henry Sidney. The story of their unlucky voyage is too long to quote, and too well known to need repetition. Nor were they the only gentlemen on whom Sir Henry looked with favour. Noble Sir Humphrey Gilbert, who endeavoured to materialise his visions of Cathay, had been the Deputy's lieutenant within Philip's memory. Another officer under the young man's father was Frobisher himself, who was, too, a friend of Philip's uncle, the Earl of Warwick. So he would often have met these rovers, half pirates and wholly heroes. An imaginative boy, he drank in their stories; a sensitive, romantic man, for all his austerity, he fretted at the fate that forbade him to share in their exploits.

Early in 1576 an expedition under Frobisher was projected and arranged. Money had been subscribed in considerable sums, and Mr. Michael Lock acted as treasurer. A list of subscribers is to hand, but it is not necessary to give it in detail. Noblemen, three of them Philip's uncles, merchants of the City, and the staid and sober Burleigh subscribed to the fund. Philip, too, gave a large sum, for him; and doubtless thought he was, if rash, sinning in creditable company. If enthusiasm and generosity were to go for anything Frobisher might have discovered that North-West passage to the Indies, on the finding of which his heart was set. Needless to say, the passage was not found, and, with so shadowy a goal as object, it is difficult to understand in what way the subscribers hoped to cover their risks. The admiral of the two little vessels would be too far north, again, to win bullion and honour at the expense of the Spanish vessels homeward bound from the South Americas.

Be this as it may, enthusiasm was greater than ever when the *Gabriel*, Frobisher's vessel, arrived safely in the Thames. He had a strange story to tell. It seems that when the *Gabriel* and *Michael* were north of Labrador they encountered a terrific storm. Both ships—smacks we should now call them—rode the tempest out in safety, but were separated. Unable to find her companion, the captain of the *Michael* deemed it prudent to steer straight for home. Neither he nor his companions thought it possible that Frobisher had escaped death by drowning. Sorrow was felt, and openly expressed in London, at the news. But a month later sorrow turned to joy and amazement, for Frobisher arrived, big with stories of hardship and adventure, safe and hopeful. His story, incredible but true, was this. After the storm he determined, though only in command of fifteen men, to go forward. Anxious that the coast should be explored, he despatched the ship's pinnace with five men on a tour of exploration. It was the last he saw of either boat or crew. Frobisher then proceeded to navigate the straits that are called after him, but could make few further investigations. He had, however, done a great deal by general observation, and added vastly to men's knowledge of the Arctic regions. Moreover, he brought home with him an Esqui-

maux, who became the, probably, uncomfortable lion of
the season. An amusing account comes to us of the
astonished and astonishing visitor. According to the
treasurer, writing of the welcome given to the survivors
of the expedition, a most cordial one : ' " Their strange
man and his boat was such a wonder to the whole city
and to the rest of the realm that heard of it, as seemed
never to have happened the like great matter to any
man's knowledge." Probably it never had, though the
Esquimaux's views would provide instructive reading.
Certain is it that he proved the only tangible result
of the endeavour ; and he was probably the more persuasive in that he lacked English. The voyagers were
received with honour and acclamation. Lusty speculators
are not discouraged by one failure ; and a second expedition, with Frobisher again in command, was quickly
decided upon, and in the result was considerably more
important than the first. He claimed to have made a
discovery that excited everybody, exciting men more
keenly than ever to risk their savings cheerfully and
eagerly. Philip, in a letter to Languet, gives as good
an account of the whole matter as can be found. It is
quoted here, especially, because it provoked a most
trenchant answer. Philip wrote thus : " After having
made slow progress in the past year, Frobisher touched
at a certain island in order to rest both himself and his
crew. And there by chance a young man, one of the
ship's company, picked up a piece of earth which he saw
glittering on the ground. He showed it to Frobisher,
who, being busy with other matters and not believing that
precious metals were produced in a region so far north,
considered it of no value." The letter goes on to explain
that the young man did not part with his find, but carried
it with him to London. Arrived there, he exhibited his
treasure, with the gratifying result that it was declared to
be " purest gold, unalloyed with any other metal."

Experts in gold mines and horses are not always to be relied upon, though they are frequently believed in. This analyst, whoever he was, whether he had an axe to grind or not, was at once accepted as an unimpeachable authority. News of the treasure buzzed throughout the city; wherever men congregated for business or pleasure the wonderful story was told. Frobisher was the hero of the hour. A Cathay Company was immediately founded, with ostensibly scientific and geographical aims. History, indeed, has repeated itself in many a flotation of our own day. Sober citizens lost their heads, and extravagant courtiers looked for a near future when they would be able to pay their debts. Get gold, plenty of it, and procure it as soon as possible, was the cry. Elizabeth, never backward where money was concerned, became a large shareholder in the speculation. By way of advertising her goodwill she lent a vessel of her own, the *Aid*, to assist the adventurers She was much larger than either the *Michael* or the *Gabriel*, carrying twenty-five soldiers and sixty-five sailors. As men considered of things then she was an imposing and powerful craft. So cautious a lady as the Queen, doubly cautious since she risked her own money, did not intend that her big ship should attempt to find a new route to Cathay. Directly the gold was discovered her captain was ordered to steer straight for the Port of London, with as much bullion as he could conveniently stow on board. Other schemes did not interest her personally. Shrewd people sometimes make a miscalculation, and Elizabeth is an illustrious example of the occasional failure of such.

Horrid and unexpected though the truth was, it got itself believed. The masses of " stuff" brought home, for more than they were worth, might easily with less outlay and greater profit have been raked from the refuse in St. Paul's Churchyard.

Then happened what always happens when gamblers

fail. After a cordial welcome to the heroes, who were not to blame, though they too had to suffer, the spoil was tested. Directly the result became past controversy furious quarrels arose, insults hurled, and charges of corruption and dishonesty clattered, like hailstones, on all sides. Frobisher could not get his salary, and slandered Lock. The blunt seaman, justly angry, called him " a false accountant," a "cozener to my lord of Oxford," "a bankrupt knave," and probably much else besides. Court and city echoed these calumnies, and the treasurer, who had at most only been deceived like everybody else, lamented bitterly and uselessly over the indignity dumped upon him.

From Frobisher it is impossible to withhold sympathy. His part of the business had been honestly and boldly done. All he asked for was his stipulated pay. Anger dulled men's memories of their obligations, and the brave captain would have actually suffered privation, and his family also, had not the Sidneys, who could so ill afford it helped him in his trouble. A fourth voyage, at one time talked of, was speedily abandoned. The scapegoat was the one man whose record was fair. The Queen, whose money he had unwittingly lost, was the last person in the world to acknowledge the courage and devotion of one whose gallant labours had, without fault of his own, produced no substantial monetary success. Her neglect of Frobisher at this time is very disgraceful ; for his endeavours had added a fresh and indestructible splendour to the glory of herself and of her people. "Put not your trust in princes" must have often furnished a text for reflection with those who sought to serve her ambitions and increase her dignity. Yet she never asked for the advice and active help of such men vainly; and was apparently too selfish and self-centred to understand how thoroughly contemptible was her conduct towards them.

Languet's answer to Philip's letter came too late to be of immediate service, but its contents must have often given pause to the enthusiastic young man. The great scholar had long outlived his enthusiasms, if he ever had any. Earnestness of purpose and horror of all but the noblest ideals he still retained. Disappointments many, sorrows acute and frequent, could not shake his belief in a Divine justice and the ultimate triumph of what was right and true. Meditating quietly over the political, religious, and social movements that had passed before him he learned to apprise men and things at their proper value. His letter to Sidney is an extraordinary treatise, very wise, sober, and stately. Its value has not diminished with age. It is pregnant with caution and admonition for the fortune-hunters of to-day :—

" If what you say about Frobisher be true, you have stumbled on that gift of nature which is of all the most fatal and baneful to mankind, yet which most men so madly covet, as it, more than anything else in the world, stirs them to incur every kind of risk. I fear that England, crazed by the love of gold, will now just empty herself into these islands that Frobisher has been finding. And how much English blood do you suppose must be shed for you to keep hold of them ? "

The question has the ring of a prophecy that is to-day even receiving unhappy proof of its truth. The question was rhetorical, not inquisitive. Stirred by his theme, the writer proceeds to tell how: " In old times, when some Carthaginians, on a voyage in the Atlantic, had been carried by a storm to land of some sort, and had come back with wonderful reports of its wealth, the Senate, fearing the people would be tempted to go thither, put to death the men who had brought the report, so that if any wished to emigrate they should have none who could guide them. Do I, therefore, think that you should reject these treasures that God has thrown in your way?

Anything but that. Nay, I thoroughly admire the high spirit, the perseverance, and even the good fortune of Frobisher. He deserves great rewards. But I am thinking of you, for you seem to rejoice in the circumstance as if it were the best thing possible for your country, especially as I noticed in you last spring a certain longing to undertake this sort of enterprise ; and, if Frobisher's foolish hope of finding a North-West passage had power then to fascinate you, what will not these golden islands do, or rather mountains all of gold, as I daresay they shape themselves day and night in your mind? Beware, I beseech you, and never let ' the cursed hunger after gold,' whereof the poet speaks, creep over that spirit of yours, into which nothing has hitherto been admitted save the love of goodness and the desire of earning the goodwill of all men. If these golden islands are fixing themselves too firmly in your thoughts, turn them out before they possess you, and keep yourself safe till you can serve your friends and your country in a better way."

This most noble letter was at once a compliment and a reproof. Nor in all its writer's contributions to the history of the day, save perhaps one other, is a great ideal so ably and conclusively set forth. We have not the means of knowing certainly, but it is safe to assume, that its arrival cooled its recipient's ardour for a time. No evidence can be found that he evinced other than an onlooker's curiosity when Drake set out on the *Golden Hind* upon his famous three-year-long voyage. But, tired of Court life and its vain pleasures, his spirit soon grew restive again ; his active brain was in a turmoil with fresh projects. The failure of Protestantism in Europe worried him terribly. He conceived a scheme for striking a blow against Catholicism by attacking Spanish colonies and Spanish ships. Whatsoever plunder accrued was, there can be no question, to be applied to the furtherance of the sacred cause in Europe, and a series of piratical onslaughts should, he dreamed, serve to humble the pride of the nation whose king was his godfather. In his own words, what he could do or get was to be of "use to the professors of true religion." These words he had used concerning Frobisher's visionary millions; they serve equally well to show the object to which his own acquired wealth must be directed. He saw "our cause withering away, and I am meditating some Indian project." Justice has hardly been done to him in discussing this scheme of his. It is, I think, clear that the Court offered few attractions: his stomach required stronger food than pageantry and flattery.

Ceremonial, however stately, did not crush Spain or help England. Philip's heart, too, was longing for power to strike a blow that should excite emulation among the supine German princes and stimulate the superb courage and devotion of the brave Dutchmen whom he loved. Such wealth as her rich colonies supplied in abundance enabled Spain to pose as mistress of Europe and also to assist with funds that propagator of all false doctrine the Pope. "Unless God powerfully counteract it," he exclaimed with energy, he would do this thing. Languet was, perhaps, the only man in Europe who saw the danger—a danger threatening the successful—of these buccaneering adventures. Pike, in his great work on the History of Crime, very pertinently points out that "booty and adventure . . . were the objects kept steadily in view." These objects were apparent from the beginning. When Henry VII. patronised the Cabots they were charged to discover the countries of the unbelievers, and, whenever they saw fit, they were to set up the English flag and take possession. The doctrine of Colonial Expansion still retains an admixture of its earliest characteristics. Then, as to-day, the opinions and feelings of the aborigines were not much considered. But though the historian of criminal law frankly recognises that such men as Hawkins, Drake, Frobisher, Cavendish, and, one regrets the inclusion, fair though it is, Raleigh, were glorified freebooters and pirates, he recognises that the old feudal spirit was strong enough in them to make them, and willingly, place "themselves at the service of their sovereign in seasons of danger." He adds, however, "the gentlemen to whom England was indebted for such gallant and apparently disinterested conduct had an eye to Spanish merchantmen as well as to Spanish men-of-war, and often brought into port ships laden with plunder." Philip, as we know, would have welcomed an addition to his fortune, and he would have welcomed it the more gladly if the doubloons came from Spanish pockets. In fairness to him, though, it must be remembered that he, at any rate, thought very little of his own profits in comparison with the benefits he sought to gather for his religion, his country, and his Queen. A further point to remember is that piracy was not only an English fashion. From Poole to the Isle of Wight scarcely a harbour was safe, ships dare not sail at times from Southampton Water, and the vessels actually lying in the harbour were threatened on occasion. M. de Ségur in 1574, who intended to embark there, had to journey overland to Plymouth before he could find a ship to carry him in safety. Philip's projected share in the enterprises of adventurers by sea being less for his own advantage than that of others, we can hardly expect him to have realised the doubtful morality of these excursions.

It is not unnecessary to labour this point if one would arrive accurately at Philip's exact position in these affairs. Far in advance of his time in many ways, he was imbued with some of that fever of experiment and exploit that filled the air in the sixteenth century and affected man's passions and desires. But though he could not, as Languet seeing with the calm vision that comes with years, understand all the dangers men and nations were hazarding, the advantages he thought he discerned were of a far-reaching character.

Piracy, to give it its right name, was if not an honourable at least a lucrative and popular employment well into the reign of George III. The Sussex Archæological Collections are full of information.

Man proposes says the proverb ; and Philip's designs were checkmated. One of his temperament, it may be, could not help fretting at the obstacles that blockaded his path. Our piracy is done less blatantly in these days, and more meanly. Reprehensible though Philip's plan was, of justifying "the ways of God to man," it was at least open and courageous and was personally unselfish. Moreover, irksome though life at Court had become, there was much in London to attract him as a scholar and man of letters. These attractions, to which add the society of the friends most dear to him, he was willing to sacrifice. Few in his position would have sought to act so whole-heartedly. Personal profit without personal danger was the maxim adopted, if not spoken, by most. Languet discovered this and commented on Court ways and the decadence of English manhood with severity, after his visit to London. For Philip it was always "the true honour of England," not the weight of his purse, that chiefly concerned him.

Another desire of his, and apparently one more capable of fulfilment, agitated him at this time. Remembering his friend, John Casimir, he rejoiced at the appointment of that prince to a position of importance in the Netherlands and Germany. It was unofficial, but none the less a post requiring tact, insight, and courage. Elizabeth, a year after making him her agent by whom all news in those parts was to be transmitted to her, actually sent him a sum of money, a loan, to be used in raising troops for the Prince of Orange. War was now (1578) being actively waged against John of Austria by the intrepid Stadtholder, who sorely needed men and means. The Queen's religious convictions were no doubt sincere, but even in support of them, and at a crisis, she did not appreciate the necessity of showing her sympathy in hard cash. A lady who disbursed her Christmas gifts by scale and by an arbitrary method of weights and measures could hardly be expected to show great generosity. However, Walsingham, and Leicester especially we may be sure, spurred her to a feigning generosity. She must have known, once she consented, that whatever she advanced would never be repaid, or refunded only after disputes in which she need take no part.

Philip could not, however, go to the Low Countries. Sir Henry, on the suggestion being put before him, wrote a letter to his son at once tender and sensible. He neither recommended him to go, nor did he seek to prevent his going. He said, "this disposition of your virtuous mind I must needs much commend in you. But when I enter into consideration of my own estate, and call to mind what practices, informations, and designs are devised against me, and what an assistance in the defence of those causes your presence would be unto me, reposing myself so much upon your help and judgment, I strive betwixt honour and necessity what allowance I may best give that motion of your going. However, if you think not my matters of that weight and difficulty, as I hopè they be not, but they may well enough by myself, without your assistance or any other, be brought to an honourable end, I will not be against your determination ; yet would wish you, before your departure, that you come to me, about the latter end of this month, to take your leave of me, and so from thence depart towards your intended journey."

Sir Henry was very ill at this time, and dictated the letter, for he could not write with his own hand. Philip was deeply touched by its contents : a true son of so

splendid a father would be ; he felt he must remain by the
side of the sturdy old statesman, and dreams be laid aside
though not necessarily forgotten.  Languet was delighted
at this twist in events.  Casimir was making a mess
of everything.  He was honest, but lacked Philip's valour :
he tried to do right, but had an extraordinary facility
in the perpetration of blunders.  Languet gives a half
humorous and entirely pathetic account of affairs.  Openly
rejoicing that his pupil remained in England, he touches
lightly on his own great sorrow, that thereby a meeting
between the two had been frustrated.  He hints that
he would have had to associate with " men whose society
you could not have enjoyed.  It would have been cheerless
work for you living in a camp where you would have seen
no examples of valour, no tokens of good soldiership—
only troops disobeying their leaders, and acting with
insolence and cowardice."

This description of what was happening contained not
a particle of exaggeration.  Little credit was to be gained
under John Casimir, and some danger courted.

In the same letter the Burgundian ventures on another
sermon, a written discourse " not without merit."  Indeed,
it was a very timely exposition of the real principles
whose absorption can alone insure the right ordering
and solution of this world's problems.  Languet begins
by pointing out that Philip was only justified in regarding
the enemies of the Netherlands as his own private foes
if his own sovereign sanctioned this attitude.  After
laying stress on this point, he comments : " Young gentlemen like you are apt to consider that nothing brings them
more honour than wholesale slaughter.  That is quite
wrong, for if you kill a man against whom you have
no lawful cause of war, you kill one who, so far as
you are concerned, is innocent. . . . Great praise is due
to those who bravely defend their country ; but they
are to be praised not for the number of men they kill, but
for the protection they give their own land."

Palatable these truths have not been to those of our own generation : and they have not been so ably stated as Languet stated them. This reproof was not merely a reproof "of all the volunteer warfare in which men like Gilbert and Raleigh often engaged," it is a reproof that condemns all volunteer warfare unless it be rigidly on the defensive. A later sentence in this letter finally says, speaking of the empty, dreary life at Court, a life beset with every known sort of temptation, "the glory of victory is always great in proportion to the peril undergone." And a compliment closes the epistle, so deftly worded that it was a command : "Will you then, furnished with such weapons [*i.e.*, good gifts of mind and body] refuse to your country the service it demands, and bury in the earth the large talent that God has entrusted to you ?" Talent of this value was not to be wasted in Dutch mud if Languet could help it. The old man's tact and wisdom were not lost on his hearer. Coupled to Henry Sidney's half-veiled pleading, the ardent and genuine enthusiast found them break down his skill of fence. It was fortunate for him that this happened as it did. Henry Sidney was half brokenhearted and needed an advocate, since his fair reputation was attacked, his Herculean labours ignored, though the fruit of them was gladly accepted by those who benefited. He reaped scant reward as his share, but much abuse. Again Philip, in the forced abandonment of his scheme, was luckier than he knew. There was no credit to be won under John Casimir. He was well out of the muddle created by that excellent but not very intelligent prince. Hardly, however, could he be expected to understand this at the time. True he was already famous among his contemporaries, a position that suggests staidness and wisdom ; but he was also barely twenty-four, which goes bail for neither quality. Just at this time, too, Elizabeth made him one of her gentlemen-in-waiting, so he was more her servant than ever, and by no means his own master, though the appointment could add little of dignity and brought nothing to him in the matter of payment. Languet, for once, is somewhat irritating in his letter of congratulation. It may be suggested that he over-acted his part. But his joy at this summary snuffing out of Philip's desires is easily understood. The younger man had to carry his empty and really tiresome honour with all the fortitude he could muster and all the grace at his command.

# CHAPTER VIII

## FAMILY TROUBLES

Lady Pembroke—Her husband—Sir Henry forbidden to attend his
daughter's wedding—Sir Henry abused for ill-success in Ireland
—Philip fights his father's battles—Quarrels with Ormonde—
Philip's letter to the Queen—Sir Henry recalled—Taken ill at
Chester—Philip wrongly accuses Molyneaux of disloyalty—
Molyneaux helps Lady Sidney—The Queen's journeys—Philip
writes a masque—Du Plessis-Mornay arrives in England—Close
friendship with Philip—Philip translates his treatise into English

IN addition to the excitement and unrest which
travellers' tales and Protestant struggles evoked,
much had happened nearer home to interest and
worry Philip. On returning from his mission he found
his sister married to the Earl of Pembroke. The alliance
was in all respects excellent save in disparity of age,
Pembroke being forty and his bride hardly sixteen. As
a husband, however, the Earl was able to show many
advantages. Not without influence with the Queen, he
was far too proud to pay her more than the flattery
that was conventional. A man of serious mind, his
advice could not be despised: nor was he the man to
be afraid of speaking plainly. The great title that he
bore was worthily carried. Nor would his wealth, very
considerable, lessen the esteem in which he was held by
all men. Too powerful to be attacked with impunity,
he was able to befriend and harbour any of the impoverished Sidneys who might incur the Queen's dis-

pleasure. Sensible enough to know that the honour of
such an alliance was equally shared by the contracting
parties, his position made him utterly indifferent to the
prating of either his, if he had any, or Sir Henry's
enemies. The bride herself, whose affection for her
brother, as his for her, was very great, was ready to
wed the man so much her senior, and she had no
reason to regret her decision. Freed from the trammels
of the Court, she was able to employ her sprightly and
sympathetic talents in the channels of her own choosing,
and became the friend of Shakespeare and the great
literary geniuses of her time. The Earl's wealth enabled
her to play the lady bountiful at her pleasure. This
wealth was largely derived from the spoliation of the
religious houses under Henry VIII. The Earl's father
was a brother of Queen Catherine Parr, and therefore
brother-in-law of the King. Deep devotion to the
Reformation inspired him, and paid him, to the end of
Edward VI.'s reign. A politic fervour on behalf of
Catholicism steered him safely through the short crazy
years when Mary sat on the throne. His accommodating
nature made it easy for him to embrace Protestantism
again directly Elizabeth succeeded her unfortunate sister.
Comment is needless on this adroit performance. Many
essayed it with more or less ingenuity, though none quite
so successfully.

Sir Henry was overjoyed at the match. A letter he
wrote to Leicester is too fulsome to afford pleasant
reading, though Leicester was considered all powerful, and
was in high favour, yet it does not sound dignified to say
of a passing favour, "which great honour to me, my mean
lineage and kin, I attribute to my match in your noble
house. So joyfully have I at heart that my dear child
hath so happy an advancement as this is, as, in troth, I
would lie in close prison a year rather than it should break."
Words such as these ill became Sir Henry, especially when

addressed to a nobleman of Leicester's stamp. Before condemning them it is, at the same time, necessary to remember that the son on whose wisdom he relied was abroad, and that his own poverty and pressing necessities were great. He proposes to borrow a sum sufficient to make a respectable dowry, and asks Leicester to lend it to him. " I have it not ; but borrow it I must, and so I will." The amount raised is variously stated at two thousand and three thousand pounds. In either case the sum is not of a figure to have interested the rich bridegroom, who was marrying to please himself. But Sir Henry goes on protesting. He asks that his poverty may be excused : this poverty, brought about by no fault of his own, of which the bridegroom was not ignorant. Further, he promises to present the bride with a goblet worth £500. He declares, too, that if God gave him a choice of all the eligible husbands in the world he would unhesitatingly fix his choice on Pembroke. At the moment of writing, no doubt, he thought he would.

Elizabeth refused to allow him to attend his daughter's wedding. A particular reason for so petulant an insult is not to be discovered. As we shall see, Sir Henry, never in favour, was soon to be abused more abominably than ever. But this marriage of her lady-in-waiting was not opposed by the Queen. It is one of the few ceremonies of this nature to which she lent her countenance ; at least, she withheld her frown. Elizabeth seems to have discovered a rare pleasure in being thoroughly illogical. Pembroke lost none of such influence as he cared for ; the bride was treated with every circumstance of courtesy and consideration ; Philip was advanced in favour and wooed by flattery during the whole summer of 1577. But gracious smiles and words of praise were not the guerdon of Sir Henry. He was always with her " That Sir Henry who doth always put us to charge." Fresh storms, indeed,

were gathering over his devoted head, and this blunt
command that he was not to attend his daughter's
wedding was the first thunderclap of the coming tempest.
So petty an outburst of displeasure, a displeasure only
prompted by covetousness, is not worthy of a queen.
Elizabeth was careful of her dignity as she understood
the word. Few sovereigns have risked it so often or,
at times, lost it so effectually.

Philip regarded the match with equanimity and also
concurred in his father's opinion that it was due to
kinship with the House of Dudley. His own comfort,
and even safety, were greatly influenced by it a year
or two later, when at Wilton he found peace from
his enemies and a cultured leisure very grateful and
beneficial to his health, his studies, and his imagination. What hours he could snatch from attendance on
an exacting mistress he spent in Wiltshire or Baynard's
Castle, his sister's London home. Soon he discovered
that he needed all the comfort he could get from these
pleasant meetings, for at Court, though himself in favour,
he found much to cause him the deepest anxiety. So
badly did his father stand in the Queen's eyes that he
had to reject a proposal to visit him in Ireland.

Mr. Edward Waterhouse, who conducted much of
Sir Henry's private business in England, was greatly
troubled by what he saw. This gentleman was deeply
loyal to his patron, but he knew himself of hardly
sufficient importance to be a successful advocate of
Sir Henry's interests. Scarcely a month after the
marriage he journeyed to Wilton, ostensibly to pay his
respects to the new countess. But the real object of
his journey, as a letter of his tells, was of a less cere-
monious nature. He desired "to have speech with
Mr. Philip concerning your lordship's affairs, and to
understand his advice, what course he would take in
your lordship's defence ; who, because he found such daily

alterations in Court, could advise me none otherwise but
to refer me in discretion to do as I saw cause." This
letter is interesting because it shows how safe and wise
a counsellor Philip was considered by shrewd men who
knew their world. After conversations with Waterhouse
at Wilton, Philip hurried to London and resumed his
palace duties. By so doing, ungrateful though the task
was, he judged that he could the better defend his
father's inteiests.

Here was a difficult task for a young man, requiring
unusual tact and courage. More experienced men than
he could not have managed better. Elizabeth was,
indeed, in a furious and most unreasonable temper with
the unhappy Lord Deputy. His task was difficult even
had his efforts met with her candid approval. That she
did approve his policy cannot be doubted ; for though
she encouraged all sorts of extravagant complaints about
his rule and the measures he adopted, she took care to
keep him relentlessly at his post. Irish problems were
not less difficult of solution then than they are now. Sir
Henry understood them better than any one else could,
but he was not permitted to gain credit or promotion by
reason of his knowledge, his patience, or his honesty.
Plans that he formed for the pacification of the unhappy
country could not be properly realised without adequate
means at his disposal. Also it is obvious that no man
can please all parties, and Sir Henry roused the anger of
those feather-brained members of the Irish nobility who,
by their youth, good looks, and lively manners, were
favourites with the middle-aged Queen. Of these the
impetuous, but not unchivalrous, Earl of Ormonde was
the head. Day in, day out he attacked the Lord Deputy
and the policy he pursued. Philip, who had seen enough
of Ireland to form a just estimate of the wisdom of his
father's actions, quickly showed his determination to do
all that he could to bring the Queen to a saner view

of the situation.  A careful justification of his father's
conduct occupied him for some time.  He committed it
to paper and presented it to the Queen.  Elizabeth based
her annoyance on the ground of the expenses involved
in carrying out the Deputy's schemes for the regeneration
of the island.  " This Sir Henry doth always seek to put
us to charge " we have seen was her constant complaint.

We cannot be astonished at these frequent outbursts of
temper, for Elizabeth was always loath to part with her
money, and expected others to give gladly of their own,
however scanty their resources, for her personal benefit.
Ormonde, and the others like unto him, swelled the chorus
of expostulation, and the first pitiful cry of the Irish land-
lords was now raised and fell on sympathetic ears.  Philip
treated them with open scorn.  " And privileged persons
forsooth be all the rich men of the Pale, the burden only
lying on the poor, who may groan, for their prayer cannot
be heard.  And Lord ! to see how shamefully they will
speak of their country that be indeed the tyrannous
oppressors of their country."  Scathing though the criticism seems, it was true in fact, but not calculated to
advance the speaker's popularity.  Before his memo-
randum was ready for presentation an event happened
which caused considerable sensation in Court circles.
Ormonde and Philip met, and the latter, on the Earl
beginning a conversation, directly turned his back.  On
no consideration would he hold any commerce with the
man who was daily trying to ruin his father.  Not without
reason the onlookers expected a tragic result.  How a
duel was averted is unknown, for neither party lacked
courage.  Sober counsels prevailed, however, and though
there was no attempt made to patch up a reconciliation
hostility, illustrated by sword or pistol, was avoided.
Ormonde said he would not fight a man who was
bound in honour to defend his own father, and he added
some pretty compliments concerning the young man's

virtue and magnanimity. Ormonde quite probably meant what he said, and if he, the insulted one, was satisfied, the affair concerned no one else. Philip, it seems, told the Queen plainly what he thought of the Earl and his compatriots, then he presented his carefully considered letter. In it he proves that Sir Henry's administration was economically conducted and beneficial both to the Queen's interests and those of the people. Taxes, he asserts, were sought to be levied alike, in fair proportions, upon both rich and poor. Money so raised was spent, he declares, for the benefit of all classes, since the wrong-doer was punished and the peasant encouraged and protected. With extreme boldness, but showing himself a fearless and wise statesman, he proved that the real enemies of Ireland and the Queen lived within the Pale, and he roundly calls them robbers, wasters of wealth, and breeders of misery. Proceeding, he points out that his father was never sterner than the occasion fully justified and shows that the nobleman was not, and should not be, freer than the humbly placed if he had done wrong and deserved punishment. Moreover, he claims that severity was needful when the history of the people was taken into account. They had lost their liberty, they engaged in quarrels among themselves, " they choose rather all filthiness than any law." Finally he declares that " there is not a nation that live more tyrannously than they do one over another," roundly asserting that the Queen knows this by the events of her own reign, not forgetting to use the history of the Ormonde clan as an example how inefficient milder measures than those favoured by his father had always proved.

This bold appeal to Elizabeth's common sense had immediate effect. Praises of Philip's ability and statecraft rose on all sides. Tudor princes were not cowards, they appreciated pluck in others, and for a time Philip stood high in the good graces of the sovereign. Lord

Burleigh thought the arguments convincing : despatches from Ireland arrived that confirmed both him and his royal mistress in their belief.   For a time the hard-worked Lord Deputy was kindly treated, pleasant messages and letters from the Queen herself were forwarded to him.  " Let no man compare with Mr. Philip's pen," exclaimed the enthusiastic and devoted Mr. Waterhouse. Certainly a triumph had been won which though not long-lived was very remarkable.

Ormonde and his friends were only temporarily defeated.   In the early days of 1578 they were again plotting Sir Henry's downfall with every prospect of complete success.

About the middle of January, 1578, scarcely four months after victory, the conqueror was again waging his father's battle as vigorously as ever.   Tired of her complacency, Elizabeth was once more in the hands of those who were Sir Henry's traducers.  Walsingham, a keen supporter of his old friend, not liking the look of things, sent private warning to the Lord Deputy. Immediate recall to England might, he hinted, be expected at any moment.  His vigorous measures and constant demands for money were distasteful as they ever had been.  The Secretary of State prophecied correctly, and in March the offender was summoned home.  Prompt obedience to the summons seems to have been Henry's first resolve : that his interests were in willing and capable hands he knew.  But he would naturally wish to exculpate himself at the earliest moment possible.  A high spirit remained to him in spite of the scurvy fortune that attended always on his endeavours.  He could hardly have expected to satisfy the cupidity and selfishness of the Queen when others, better qualified by reason of her personal favour, had failed.  Yet she was not impervious to argument, and at least he could explain his conduct before those whose goodwill he valued.  An opportunity, not unwelcome, presented itself for meeting Ormonde face to face and throwing the lie in the teeth of that arrogant and irresponsible peer of Ireland. Some thoughts of this kind must have buzzed through his brain, for he had evidently determined to leave his work and confront his accusers. His wise son was opposed to any such compliance with the ill humours and clamour of a clique. Writing to his father Philip almost commanded him to stay where he was. He gives little encouragement to Sir Henry of expecting "a happy issue out of all his afflictions." He sensibly remarks that his friends are doing all that can be done to help him. Time may be trusted to alter the situation for the better. Philip and his mother must have discussed together often and intimately. Lady Sidney was in a most difficult position : her husband was maligned, yet she had to attend the Queen, who affected to believe false accusations levelled at the husband she adored. Kindness shown to herself rendered her position still more difficult. Valiantly she fought her "dear lord's" battle, as Philip testifies in a pathetic sentence : "Before God there is none proceeds either so thoroughly or so wisely as your lady, my mother. For my own part I have had only light from her."

September came before the Lord Deputy left Ireland. On his arrival at Chester he was caught in the grip of a serious illness. Notification of this misfortune was forwarded to the proper authorities. Lady Sidney lay ill at Chiswick. Sir Henry sent also his secretary, Mr. Molyneux, to explain the delay. He was a man devoted to his master, and, earlier in the year, had rapped Philip's knuckles severely. The matter has been too harshly dealt with by Philip's biographers. As was to be expected, the Lord Deputy's letters were tampered with. Enemies at Court knew more than they ought to have known, acted on information they could not honestly come by. Who the traitor was Philip had no means of discovering, the results of the treachery he saw daily. Considering the constant state of anxiety, and even danger, in which he lived, it is not wonderful that he was angry. Where he made a blunder was in rushing to the conclusion that his father's confidential secretary was the villain of the piece. Molyneux's long years of faithful and loving service should have made Philip pause before launching so terrible a charge. They availed nothing with him, however, at the moment. He deliberately accuses that worthy gentleman of playing false. In April he writes to Sir Henry :—

"I must needs impute it to some men about you that there is little written from you or to you that is not known to your professed enemies."

Emphatic though the statement was, and no less emphatically true, a definite charge was not made. Some few days later he wrote to Molyneux a letter very foolish, very extravagantly worded, and very unjust.

"Few words are best. My letters to my father have come to the ears of some ; neither can I condemn any but you. If it be so, you have played the very knave with me ; and so I will make you know if I have good proof of it. That for so much as is past. For that is to come, I assure you before God, that if ever I know you do so much as read any letter I write to my father without his commandment or my consent, I will thrust my dagger into you ; and trust to it, for I speak in earnest."

Amazingly silly we may concede this ebullition of anger to be. Languet might, with a show of logic, point out the last sentence as a proof of the evil influence that Italy exercised over youthful minds. Probably Molyneux smiled a little when he read it. Here, none the less, was an epistle that demanded an answer. The accused man kept his temper and his dignity ; his reply is a model :—

"Sir, I have received a letter from you which, as it is the first, so it is the sharpest that I ever received from any ; and therefore it amazeth me to receive such an one from you, since I have (the world can judge) deserved better somewhere, howsoever it pleased you to condemn me now.

But since it is (I protest to God) without cause, or yet just
ground for suspicion, you use me thus, I bear the injury
more patiently for a time, and my innocency I hope in the
end shall try my honesty, and then I trust in the end you
will confess you have done me wrong.  And since your
pleasure so is expressed, that I shall not henceforth read
any of your letters (although I must confess that I have
heretofore taken both great delight and profit in reading
some of them), yet, upon so hard a condition as you seem
to offer, I will not hereafter adventure so great a peril, but
obey you herein.  Howbeit, if it had pleased you, you
might have commanded me in a far greater matter with a
far less penalty.  Yours, when it shall please you better to
conceive of me, humbly to command."

The stately rebuke, at once gentle and forcible, had its
effect.  Friends they must have been, for Molyneux was
ever ardent in Philip's praise ; his letter proves him noble-
minded enough to forgive even so base an injury.  He
knew, also, the troubles and trials that beset every member
of the family whose staunch friend he was, in evil report
and good.  Whether Lady Sidney or her husband suspected
this correspondence is not discoverable.  Molyneux, we
may be certain, would not say anything.  By asserting his
dignity and integrity this modest gentleman had done all
he wished to do.  Philip's feelings before they met, and at
their meeting, are not to be envied.

On his arrival in London this ally of the Sidney family
was not idle.  In the first place he was commissioned to
put Sir Henry's case before the Queen, which he doubtless
did ably and eloquently.  Another and more delicate
affair still demanded his good services.  From her sick-bed
in Chiswick Lady Sidney wrote to him for help in a
matter of urgent importance.  She had been bidden to
Hampton Court, and very narrow accommodation had been
granted to her.  Lord Sussex, the Lord Chamberlain, was
her husband's brother-in-law.  It seems odd that she
should not have addressed herself directly to him.  The
nature of her complaint amounted to this, that though " at

night-time one roof with God's grace shall cover us," an extra room was imperative during the daytime. She pleaded that if an additional chamber were allotted, her husband would be able to do his work free from interruption. Her own chamber, she explains, must always be ready to receive the Queen at any hour the august lady chose to pay her a visit. Sir Henry's presence could be "no impediment" to Her Majesty, she acknowledges; but many people might have business with her husband whose company she wished to avoid. If a second room is granted she offers to defray the cost of furnishing it suitably. Molyneux did his best, but does not appear to have been conspicuously successful. Lady Sidney was grateful, though, and frankly acknowledged his efforts on her behalf. "There are those who will be sorry my Lord should have so sure footing in the Court" is her comment; and there is a wholly delightful touch in her further remark: "When the worst is known, old Lord Harry and his old Moll will do as well as they can in parting [sharing] like good friends, the small portion allotted our long service at Court." Sir Henry does not seem to have busied himself in the matter.

Philip had other services to perform besides defending his father; and other diversions claimed him in addition to the more intellectual ones of his own choosing. By most men of his age the constant progresses which the Queen made to the houses of her greater nobles would have been welcomed eagerly. Entertainments of all kinds were conducted on a lavish scale on these visits, and from the sovereign downwards were joined in by everybody. Philip does not seem to have appreciated them so much as did many of his elders. His mind, even in the midst of revelry, was perpetually turning to graver affairs, politics and religion. He watched events in Germany and Holland more keenly than he watched the dance; his correspondence is of a weighty nature, dealing with the fortunes of nations rather than the witty and idle gossip of the Court.   For the last he cared little.

He contrived, however, on one occasion to exhibit talent in a lighter vein than had been suspected.   It happened in this wise.   The Queen paid a visit to the Earl of Leicester at Wanstead, and Philip, as usual, was of the company in attendance.   A masque was arranged for the entertainment of the royal visitor, and Philip undertook to compose and arrange it.   Entitled " The Lady of the May," it contains some pretty writing, and somewhat too much of the learned foolery that, in various forms in various ages, has passed, and now passes, for wit, especially among headmasters of public schools, who often affect this species of humour. The Queen was a good deal of a pedagogue herself, and appreciated it also.   New and unexpected ability was revealed to the delighted courtiers.   Really it is a pretty trifle, and is not unworthy, as an early venture, of the man who proved himself in a few short years a considerable poet.   A famous critic of recent days speaks of it con- temptuously.   He gives it as his opinion that the lyrics are not tuneful, and carefully refrains from quoting any in support of his assertion.   Mr. Fox Bourne, the historian, quotes one with the kindlier comment, " Philip Sidney was at this time apter as a courtier than a poet."   Some graceful lines are quoted here, and deserve to be remembered :—

" To one whose state is raisèd over all,
    Whose face doth oft the bravest sort enchant,
  Whose mind is such as wisest minds appal,
    Who in oneself these divers gifts can plant ;
  How dare I, wretch, seek there my woes to rest
    Where ears be burnt, eyes dazzled, hearts oppressed ?

  Your state is great ; your greatness is our shield ;
    Your face hurts oft ; but still it doth delight.
  Your mind is wise ; your wisdom makes you mild :
    Such planted gifts enrich e'en beggar's sight.
  So dare I, wretch, my bashful fear subdue,
    And feed mine ears, mine eyes, mine heart in you."

Verses "of occasion" they are, and pretend to no higher quality. Writers of our own day have acquired a quite sober reputation with an infinitely worse performance. More astonishing still, they have managed to keep it. A compliment, and a verse, were required, and both are better than the average of poetry made to order. That these lines convey nothing save the more extravagant fancies of "Astrophel and Stella," yet unborn and undreamt of, is not to be wondered at. They could only have been written by one dowered with a certain gift for rhyme and a pretty taste in metaphor. Were they worse than they are they would be interesting as Philip's first public effort in this medium, setting aside such attempts as he may have ventured on in the Shrewsbury School pageants. He was getting proficient in the handling of metre against the time when love and passion were to demand imperatively the service of his pen.

The story of the masque is really elegant, though it has been laughed at. Briefly put, it recounts how a distracted maiden is compelled to choose between two lovers. "I like both," the lady says, "but I love neither." As was the fashion of the time, the wooers carry mock-classic names. Therion, a forester, is well-to-do by thefts of venison which enable him to be generous in the matter of gifts. His assured income is in the clouds. The method of courtship he adopts might have appealed to the Russian lady who desired a divorce on the ground that her husband could not love her because he did not bea her. Espilus, a shepherd, is well-to-do also, but by honest means. He gives no presents, and shows his affection by reciting verses of a lachrymose character, rhyming upon his lady's name. There is much more of the same fantastic sort. But it amused Elizabeth, and she gave judgment between the rival suitors. A real touch of irony may be observed here, and, oddly enough, it has not been noticed. Elizabeth decides in favour of the careful shepherd, who gave no presents and had no extravagant tastes. She was always willing to receive, but never pleased to give. Careful Espilus was a clever invention on the part of the poet, whom she allowed and commanded to work for her, but whom she never assisted when she could avoid doing so.

An acute and sympathetic German critic finds in the character of the shepherd Espilus something of Philip himself. He suggests that in the constancy and devotion of the Arcadian lover we may see reflected the poet's love for Stella. He looks upon the whole composition as marking a not unimportant stage in its composer's literary career. There is one further merit and peculiarity in this " trifling but very pretty " composition that distinguishes it from other compositions of the kind, a peculiarity very consistent with the whole of Philip's conduct. Not once does he stoop to the obsequious flattery and praise that robs courtly verse of so much of its beauty, and while exalting the subject degrades the author. In paying all the honour due of right to a queen he does not forget his own dignity. Perhaps Elizabeth knew Philip too well to expect from him an exhibition of nauseating servility such as she was accustomed to receive from the mob of versifiers who sang her praises. That, even without this flattery, she liked his masque and praised it, thanking its producer, redounds to her credit, since her appetite for adulation increased by what it fed on. "The Lady of the May," if it reveals, as suggested by the learned German critic, a hint as to the great passion of Philip's life, reveals also, in its restraint and dignity of compliment, a glimpse of the courage that dared to speak out so boldly and authoritatively, if a little impertinently, on a more important occasion.

Serious studies were renewed by the arrival of Plessis du Mornay in England in the summer of 1577. Philip may have met him in Paris at the time of St. Bar-

tholomew, for he, too, had been a witness of its horrors.
His mission was not a hopeful one, for he wanted money
for Henry of Navarre and the French Protestants.
Introduced to Philip by Languet, he was cordially
welcomed and made much of.   Brave, honest, and
intelligent, he deserved to be treated with every courtesy.
The two men loved each other at once.   "You cannot
possibly have such another friend," the old Huguenot
writes, and his praise was not exaggerated.   Among the
many noble men who strove, rightly or wrongly, for the
Huguenots, none was more attractive : well born, straight-
forward, a fine scholar, no mean author, tender hearted,
and in manner conspicuous by reason of his grace and
courtesy, it is small wonder that the two men were close
friends at their first meeting.   They pursued the same
ends in the same unflinching way, and sought not at all
their own prosperity, but ever sunk their ambitions for the
sake of their cause.   Philip in the next year stood godfather to du Mornay's daughter ; and later put into
English a portion of the Frenchman's book, which he
called " A Work concerning the Trueness of the Christian
Religion."   The translation was not wholly of Philip's
making, for he was too busy at the time to give it all that
labour he desired to bestow upon it.   Convinced, however,
that his friend's pages were of incalculable value, he
instructed carefully a Mr. Golding to complete the task
himself had begun.   Faith in Leicester is rather patheti-
cally apparent in the dedication.   Philip to the end of
his life remembered that he was a Dudley.   The Earl
probably accepted the dedication with a show of thanks ;
it may be doubted whether he read the treatise.   A
curious passion for theology is to be noted, though, in
men of all manners of conduct at this time.   The study
seems to have provided a system of mental gymnastics
curiously grateful to the active minded of the period.
Great   political   movements   were   chiefly   stirred   and

animated by the bitterness of theological dispute ; and to be ignorant of the points at issue would have argued ill-breeding and want of education, if nothing worse.

That Philip and Du Mornay took their religion seriously admits of no doubt. Were further proof of Philip's earnestness and their extraordinary knowledge of the points at issue needed, it can be found in the fact that among the Protestants of Europe these two names stood higher than that of the splendid and wealthy Leicester. Philip's counsel was first sought, his advice first heeded, by those who came to England as pleaders for the holy cause they believed in and were willing to die for. As an example of this, may be cited the visit of Baron Henry of Lichtenstein, " an excellent young man," to whom he acted as cicerone.

# CHAPTER IX

## EVENTS AT COURT—LEICESTER'S DISGRACE—LIFE IN LONDON

New Year gifts—John Casimir's visit—Languet arrives—His comments on the Court—Sir Henry commends Philip's example to Robert—Philip's generosity to his brother—The Queen again contemplates marriage—Contending factions—Du Simier—Leicester disgraced—A secret marriage—A quarrel in the tennis court—Philip defends himself before the Queen—He writes an amazing letter about her proposed marriage to the Queen—Leaves the Court—Life in London

O N New Year's Day, 1578, the Queen, as usual on this festival, looked for homage and presents. An amusing account of the ceremony observed comes down to us. Philip, his head and heart worried by serious matters, must have despised and hated the function. It was, moreover, a costly one for all concerned, save the Queen herself, who managed to profit very considerably by the devotion of her courtiers. Philip had his part marked for him, and it is not likely that, publicly, he expressed any of the displeasure that he felt. Such an exhibition of feeling would neither have advanced his father's cause or his own personal ambitions. Naturally he was not expected to give costly ornaments of gold encrusted with diamonds and other rare jewels. But Elizabeth received quantities of diamonds, rubies, and other gems from the Ormondes and Leicesters of the time. The Queen accepted anything good of its kind, so long

as she was not called upon to pay for it. Seemingly Philip
and Fulke Greville took counsel together in the matter
of New Year gifts, as they did in much else. Among
the magnificent presents of jewelry and garments richly
broidered in gold and silver, there is more than one
mention of ruffs and a " pair of perfumed gloves." Philip
and Greville made the same kind of offering, and no one
seems to have thought they offended against good taste.
Their presents were two cambric smocks elaborately embroidered. These somewhat intimate tributes of admiration, coming from two handsome young men, were,
it may be suggested without lack of charity, very flattering
to the lady's not too squeamish vanity. The smocks
were broidered at the edge with gold and silver.

Her Royal Highness did not hesitate to portion out
her thanks to the generous givers. For the most part
he who gave most got most in return. This is certain,
however, that nobody received anything like the value
of his offering. Elizabeth weighed her gifts as carefully
as she weighed men's minds. She found donations of gilt
plate useful on such occasions. Anything between the
four hundred ounces to Sir Christopher Hatton, and the
thirteen ounces to Greville, was doled out in some sort
of ratio to the value of the gift tendered. The expensive
trivialities of the season were concluded by the arrival
of John Casimir in England. The unlucky Prince can
hardly have looked forward to his visit with pleasure,
or even without trepidation. The Queen was exceedingly
angry with him, for at the head of twelve thousand men
he had hindered rather than helped the Prince of Orange.
He was honest enough, but timid and, as are most nervous
men, reckless. Fortunately Languet came with him to
give him courage and advice. Justice is never readily
accorded to a failure ; and Casimir was a very emphatic
failure. But he had tried, to the best of his ability, to
be worthy of the trust reposed on him. Unlike most

of the German Princes he had dared, however feebly the results showed, something for the faith that was in him. He knew, only too well, though, that he had failed. He knew too that the irritable Elizabeth expected an invitation to contribute her share towards the maintenance of the twelve thousand warriors for whose incompetence he was responsible.

Languet was too blind to read, the result of a fever, and his old heart yearned towards Philip. Fears beset him lest he should not be able to accomplish the journey. It is pathetic to think of this resolute old man, kinless and kithless, longing to rest his sight on the young man he loved passionately, in whom he recognised the champion of the good cause which he knew his own humble efforts had done something to further. " I shall come if I possibly can," he writes. He did come, and if his reading was limited and done with difficulty, he has left at least one letter which points to keen observation.

The illustrious visitor and his suite were met at Canterbury by Sir Henry Sidney ; from thence they proceeded to London. Arriving at the Tower, his movements marked by every sign of honour, Casimir was conducted to the house of Sir Thomas Gresham, a great merchant of the City. We read that good entertainment was afforded the foreigners, bands played, and there was plenty to eat and drink. Two days of civic hospitality, dispensed by the man who was, indisputably, the greatest of the London merchant princes, helped Casimir to face the ordeal when, after the banqueting, he went to Whitehall to pay his respects, and make his apologies, to the Queen. Nervous the Prince must have been on his journey to the Palace. Neither Sir John's wine nor his lavish hospitality can have altogether comforted the heart of the apologist. His conduct, however, was so contrary to every rule of Court etiquette that he saved himself, and considerably embarrassed the royal lady. When the Queen, as Queen,

and we may guess very much as woman too, offered
to kiss him, the sturdy German refused the compliment.
She must have felt anger though she did not show any.
Here, indeed, was a novel experience for one whose kisses
were so notoriously chaste. Elizabeth behaved cleverly, and
did not allow her annoyance to be observed. But her
temper must have been considerably stirred when, fearful
that a draught in the passage might cause him inconvenience on the way to the audience chamber, she bade him
wear his hat. He plumply refused. Protesting that he
was her servant, the clumsy fellow remained hatless.
Elizabeth's chance came, "As you are my servant I
command you to put on your hat," was her unanswerable
answer. Bluffness of the sort he evinced, not unmixed
with dignity and courage, made a favourable impression
on the Queen. She did not treat him hardly or rate
him too soundly, and his stay in England was made
pleasant for him.

Casimir was dependent, mainly, on the Queen's private
table for his meat and drink. But she was a Tudor, and
had a Tudor stomach. At Somerset House his wants in
both respects were very carefully seen to by her commands.
Others, however, were forward to assuage his thirst and
minister to his hunger. History was repeating itself in
Casimir's day, as . it is now ; for we read of a great
banquet given to him by the Lord Mayor and Corporation.
Various nobles extended their hospitality ; at Hampton
Court he hunted ; in Hyde Park he shot deer. On the
whole an unsuccessful man had a cordial greeting from
all classes and, conceivably, was sorry to return to
Germany.

More important than the headpiece of the mission was
the quiet scholar whose notes formed the gist of a pithy
sentence in a most wise letter. What Languet did with
his time, save observe with his still shrewd eyes, is not
known. He did not hunt the stag in Hyde Park, he

did not jam his hat more firmly on his head in the presence of the Queen. But he had seen, as sometimes an old hound sees, even with the film of death crawling over its eyes, further than a puppy whose eyes are full of life, merriment, and fire. Languet's letter is not greatly commented on: it is among the wisest of the very wise ones he wrote. Other influences, which he could not have foreseen, made his prophecy or suggestion futile, and probably some who did see it only regarded him as a stupid old man. He, like Philip, was forced into the position of getting what satisfaction he could from his own self-approval. But Languet was watching the times shrewdly.

The hope of Protestantism lay in an English cradle, and that hope was known to the world as his beloved pupil Philip Sidney. What he observed at the Court was not likely to inspire him either with hope or satisfaction. From this experience his words take on another meaning. He saw for himself that Philip was not wholly wrong in fretting at the apology, the tiresome apology, for work, he was called upon to get through. The Court was brilliant enough as Courts went, but the master felt it was a sphere beneath his pupil's consideration. " I was glad "—he writes on his return—"to see you in high favour with your Queen, and so well thought of by your countrymen. But, to tell the truth, the ways of your Court, seemed to me less manly than I could have wished. Most of the courtiers seemed to win applause by an affected courtesy rather than by those virtues which are healthful to the State, and which are the chief ornaments of generous minds—of high-born men." And then, for Languet knew little of Drake and the others, he adds regretfully : " I was much grieved, and so were your other friends with me, because you seemed to be wasting the flower of your life upon such things. I fear lest your nature should be warped." Hardly can this be true : the

master knew his pupil well enough not to fear that
calamity.  Events were rapid and decisive ; Languet had
only to observe and rejoice.  Rapid as they were, they
required all the pluck that Philip could muster, and
bravely he faced and dared, going out to meet every
difficulty.  Philip is too often unsympathetic, but no
man has ever confronted more unflinchingly the great
trials.

Languet was no surly, albeit perhaps an over-anxious,
mentor.  In his letter it is easy to read that he was happy
about his pupil's conduct.  Indeed, the younger man must
have welcomed it, not only for the writer's sake, but also
for its general tenour.  He had in his mind those letters,
received not long before, wherein he was so sternly
reproved for his desire to change his position and to
busy himself in matters of more public importance.  At
last Languet retires from the position he had adopted,
for he declared: "If your Queen had been bound by
treaty to send troops to the Low Countries, and had
ordered you to go with them there, it would have been
your duty to regard the army of the Netherlands as your
foes.  But from a mere desire for praise and glory, and
that you might give public proof of your courage, you
determined to treat as your personal enemies those who
seem to be taking the wrong side in the war.  It is
not your business, it is not for any private person, to pass
judgment on a question of this kind.  It belongs to the
magistrate (by magistrate I mean the prince), who should
decide with the help of counsellors he believes to be wise
and just."

Little has been said about this curious epistle: yet it
is remarkable as coming from Languet to Sidney.  In
it there is more than a suggestion that the writer was not
wholly conversant with his pupil's character.  Nothing
was further from Sidney's desire than to advertise his own
merits.  Pride he had, often an undue pride: but it was

the pride that prompted him to feel he could advance
the cause he held at heart, not a conceit suggesting that
by his advocacy of one cause he would advance his own
value in the eyes of the combatants. When he read
the old man's words it is impossible to think that he
was not angry, though there is no proof that he showed
even a passing irritation. This doctrine of fighting, these
strange references to magistrates and the wrong side
of the war, is a little confusing coming from such a pen.
At Oxford Philip must have learnt logic enough to confute
so specious an argument. For hereby he is directly told
that he must obey his Prince without question on whichever side of the dispute he was bidden to draw his sword.
So literal an interpretation Languet can hardly have expected should be put on his words. No other, however,
is possible without equivocation and casuistry. Both
esteemed themselves too honest to resort to either. The
scholar was using an argument that was unanswerable
had Philip been bidden by his Queen to fight for the
Inquisition and Spain. This he would have absolutely
refused to do, howsoever strong the persuasion and terrible
the punishment following upon wilful disobedience. Conscience was a greater king to either of these men than the
occupant of an earthly throne.

To any one but Sidney it would not have been a wise
letter to write. He himself must have been hurt at its
reading. Interpreted by the light of it, this recent letter
must have been as grateful to con as the former was
unpleasant. He had been seen in person among his daily
companions, his bearing had been noted, judgment from
one whom he revered had been given. That his father
was constant in approval of all he did and said came
as no surprise to him ; nor, if he saw the letter Sir Henry
wrote to his son Robert, then starting on his travels,
can he have felt the parental tribute undeserved. The
advice Sir Henry gives may be summed up in four words :

"Do as Philip did." Less colloquially, but at no unpleasing length, it runs as follows : "One thing I warn you
of, arrogate no precedency, neither of your countrymen
nor of strangers ; but take your place, promiscuously with
others, according to your degree and birthright, with
aliens. Follow your discreet and worthy brother's rule,
who, with great discretion, to his commendation, won love,
and could variously ply ceremony with ceremony." This
was not the only occasion on which the father wrote
shrewd and affectionate monition to his son. But the
burden is the same : "Follow your loving brother, who
in loving you is comparable with me and exceedeth me.
Imitate his virtues, exercises, studies, and actions. He
is a rare ornament of this age, the very formula that all
well-disposed young gentlemen of our Court do form also
their manners and life by. In truth—I speak it without
flattery of him or of myself—he hath the most rare virtues
that ever I found in any man." Robert took the advice
with a good deal better grace from a younger son than
might reasonably have been expected. Philip, however, was kind and generous to his brother, though his
letters to Robert, one may guess, were provocative of some
impatience. They are far too near akin to sermons for
an eager young man to have wholly welcomed them. An
accompanying allowance of £200 a year, with a promise
of more should it be needed, no doubt did something
to make them more pleasant than otherwise they would
have seemed. At least when lectured about the "virtue,
passion, and vices" that he must observe swaying the
peoples of foreign States, he may have reflected that
though Philip had never been so seriously warned his
brother only drew one allowance, while he, more fortunate,
could count on two sources from which to derive an
income. It is not easy, or quite natural, for a very young
man to accept such a maxim as that of the great Boileau,
"*Aimez qu'on vous conseille, et non pas qu'on vous loue,*"

especially when the preacher is himself scarcely more than a youth. He knew enough of the classics to agree with Juvenal, *Omnia Romae Cum pretio.*

Even the golden solace of guineas must have made it hard for a boy to accept with equanimity or, if he had a sense of humour, which Philip had not, without a smile such a sentence as "have a care of your diet, and consequently of your complexion ; remember *Gratior est veniens in pulchro corpore virtus.*" Robert could not at that date reflect *Point d'argent, point de Suisse :* nor would the phrase exactly suit his circumstances. But it was eminently a case of no advice, no money. And few there are who would not willingly listen to a lecture if well paid to do so.

Somewhat clamorous authority would have us believe that a man is the architect of his own fortunes. A modern poet reminded us that he rejoiced because he was the master of his own fate. Philip anticipated the boast of the modern singer. He knew the doctrine, though he did not praise it. Other students knew it, too, and there were more students proportionately in his day than ours. He was deliberately the master of his own fate during the months that immediately followed on Languet's departure from London. Bold as was his conduct in dangerous circumstances, however, it must be remembered that from his own family whatever he did would win applause, no matter how uncomfortable to him or them the consequences of his actions. Elizabeth once more was considering, or pretending to consider, the necessity of allying herself by marriage to a foreign prince. The chosen suitor was the French King's brother, the Duke of Anjou, already an unsuccessful suitor when as Duke of Alençon he had aspired to so conspicuous an honour. It is customary for historians to copy the manners of his relatives and say impolite things about him. Of a truth there is little to be urged in his favour. He was ugly,

he was cruel, he was unscrupulous.  His person, Elizabeth
knew, was unpleasing.  That she was flattered at the
suggestion that she should wed him no one can reasonably
deny.  That she ever meant to marry the Duke, or any-
one else, I doubt.  But an elderly lady may be supposed
to swallow flattery easily, and the Queen for her own purposes was not at all unwilling to pose before Europe as a
coy maiden whose hand was sought by a wealthy and high-
born prince.  Mean as she was, she had some feeling, though
even Miss Strickland cannot make her attractive ; and she
hated Spain, with reason, and the Catholics also without.

Now Anjou was crafty.  His brother had thought
" Paris worth a mass," so rumour went; and it was at
least certain that the Duke had won considerable credit
in the Netherlands.  It is not accurate to say that the
match was unpopular.  A great many people of "importance in their day" supported it.  A "lewd and
seditious" pamphlet was published, couched in violent
language ; and though both author and printer were
ruthlessly punished by having their right hands chopped
off by the common hangman, there seems to have been
small anxiety among "the English people" concerning
the matter.  "The English people" it may be conjectured,
knew nothing at all about the whole affair.  Modern
historians are apt to write as though telephones and
telegrams were not nuisances of recent invention.  At
Court there was no necessity to place confidence in these
ingenious contrivances, for at Court whispers conveyed
news far faster than electricity can.  Two factions immediately ranged themselves in order for a struggle.  Lord
Oxford was enthusiastically in favour of the match.  He
stood high in the Queen's favour so many followed the
Earl.  One may reasonably suppose that royal favours
would become less irksome, and no whit less valuable,
when their donor was provided with a consort.  Anjou,
also, had a good Protestant record, no matter for what

particular reason he had chosen to obtain it. For the moment they who were desirous of the match seemed to hold the winning cards. Political and religious freedom was in danger, not in England only, but in the Netherlands and elsewhere. A prince, mightily backed, would help the workers and instruct them in the building of the bridge that should span the "Gaping Gulf," more effectually than the lopped-off hands of Stubb and Page, though one had cried "God save the Queen!" and the other "There lies the hand of a true Englishman!"

During all the negotiations, necessarily prolonged in so delicate an affair, Du Simier acted as the Duke's agent in London. Now Du Simier was like a weasel, he never slept. He very soon, within a few months of his arrival in England, discovered that Leicester, the chiefest opponent of the marriage, was himself married. The clever Frenchman knew perfectly well that Elizabeth would not have been angry with the Earl in that he opposed her wishes, if that opposition had been a cloak to conceal his own devotion to herself: that it was prompted more by a lover's devotion and jealousy than by religious zeal. Leicester had been married for a year, and married to no other than the Countess of Essex. Having witnessed what evils the marriage of Essex had brought about, a reigning favourite must needs go and marry that deceased favourite's widow. The Queen, so soon as the information was given her, was furious. Leicester was disgraced and had to leave the Court, or was forcibly removed therefrom. There are two stories, one that he was placed in a fortress in Greenwich Park, with a warning that if he attempted to leave he would be committed to the Tower; the other, that he retired hastily to his country house and gave out that he was seriously ill. Anyhow, he disappeared from the scene, willingly or unwillingly, shielded by an excuse, often used by statesmen, and others, when awkward happenings seem to call for explanation.

Leicester's disgrace cannot have been of happy augury to those who were antagonistic to the French marriage. Least of all can it have been cheerful news for Philip, who knew that his own pedestal of favour was by no means securely based. He did not have to wait long before he found himself in a most uncomfortable quandary. There is no fault attaching to him; the most censorious will praise his conduct. That great events, or the menace of them, spring from small causes, a foolish quarrel in the tennis court was soon to prove. One day in September, 1580, he was engaged in a game of tennis when the brutal Earl of Oxford happened to approach the court. Not too civilly he proposed to join the game. At first Philip took not the slightest notice of the suggestion, but continued playing. The Earl repeating his request, was answered by a reproof that startled and angered him. With the arbitrary insolence of a Jack-in-office, or at least of a pampered friend, he told the players to leave the court. This they most properly refused to do. Philip kept his temper well, explaining with the grave courtesy that really became him, how he and his friends would have retired had they been asked to do so with some show of courtesy. The only answer he got was the contemptuous retort "Puppy!" Philip's rejoinder was not so happy as Fulke Greville would have us believe. The incident is important enough to refer fully to Greville's lengthy account of the squabble, but his narrative is not lucid enough to stand by itself. The vulgar affront was overheard, as intended, by the loungers and onlookers, Frenchmen mostly, of the Duke's following, and they rushed to the galleries, expecting, and hoping for, trouble. Philip, having said what he had to say, left the court, and Oxford proceeded to play tennis. The onlookers, we read, were amazed at this peaceful conclusion of the incident. At this point the incident did not terminate. There was a second chapter, and the voluntarily evicted player is still more to be congratulated on his courage and the dignity of his demeanour.

A duel was expected as the natural and logical result of this encounter. Duelling was no uncommon pastime in England, though less usual than in France. There, a hundred years later, the direct authority of so mighty a King as Louis XIV. could not prevent, though he did prohibit more than once, this absurd resort to arms in private quarrels. In this particular dispute Philip fully expected a challenge from the man who had insulted him. The inequality of rank prevented his being the challenger. But Oxford made no move in the matter. For him it was enough that he had obtained possession of the tennis court and sent Sidney and his friends packing. He boasted that he was "rid of the fellow," and with that boast thought the episode might be considered closed. Philip was less easily disposed of. It was as little in his nature to receive an insult as to give one. The Earl sending no messengers to the outraged knight, that aggrieved gentleman despatched a trusted friend to interview the Earl. This messenger was instructed to say that a communication from his lordship was expected, and a taunt was added that if Oxford was ignorant what course to pursue his French friends might be relied on to give him the necessary instruction. Even a bully could hardly ignore so pertinent a sarcasm, and a duel was arranged. Nothing came of the matter. Philip had the supreme satisfaction, as he put it in a letter to Hatton, of knowing that he was in the right, for he declares : " I should never have forgiven myself, if I had lain under so proud an injury as he would have laid upon me. Neither can anything under the sun make me repent it, nor any misery make me go one half word back from it. Let him, therefore, if he will, digest it."

Honourable and brave words these were, for the man who used them was not a braggart. Hatton, it is not unlikely, showed them to the Queen. Oxford was willing to digest anything so long as Elizabeth shielded his cowardice by forbidding him to fight. So serious was the wrangle considered that the Privy Council met and entreated the Sovereign herself to make the peace. She consented to do so, and summoned Philip to her presence. He faced the interview as calmly and determinedly as he would have parried Oxford's sword-thrusts. He was most unkindly treated though, somewhat as a naughty schoolboy might have been. He was reminded that in the matter of precedency Oxford was his superior. As a gentleman, he was told, he was the Earl's equal, but that becoming deference was due from him to a peer of the realm. To this correction he gave fitting and bold reply. Acknowledging the superiority of Oxford's rank " by birth, alliance, and grace "—here was a clever but quite courteous hit at Cecil and the Queen herself—he refused to consider himself one whit the Earl's inferior. Then most ingeniously and with supreme courage, he reminded the Queen that her illustrious father always sided with the gentry against the nobility to prevent the undue aggression and usurpation of power affected often by the great lords. Elizabeth could not deny that his reading of history was correct; and for the moment, it would seem, liked him none the less for daring to be outspoken. Peace was patched up, but the honours were all on Philip's side. Even Languet, to whom a full account of the proceedings was sent, is forced to write : " I think you were unfortunate to be drawn into this contention ; but I see that no blame can be attached to you for your share in it." Oxford was probably glad of so happy an issue out of the trouble. It has been said he had a design to poison Philip. Wicked enough to contemplate any kind of villainy, he was no fool : there is not the slightest evidence of any such intention

But Philip's friends had reason to feel uneasy concerning

their hero's safety. Philip himself, though, not Oxford, gave them serious cause for anxiety. He felt that now he could openly despise Oxford's meditated insults and even laugh at his insolence. Neither his rank nor his favour with the Queen sufficed to justify his blustering nor his cowardice in the eyes of sensible onlookers. But Philip, and not Philip only, saw in this tennis court broil and its sequel a hint of wider-spread evil to come. To them it was not only that an arrogant lordling had affronted a noble gentleman whom good men loved and admired; it was that the manner and place of the drama had been deliberately chosen with the express intention of amusing and edifying the French courtiers who were its chief spectators. The story could not be kept secret, and wherever it was told must have provoked angry comment. Oxford had intended to throw scorn on the upholders of Protestantism who opposed the suggested marriage of Elizabeth and Anjou. Philip, it was contended, was the fittest person to attack for this purpose. That he himself regarded the manœuvre in this light is certain from his own words and immediate conduct. He understood fully the duty now, though unsought, necessarily cast upon him. No man in England was so little likely to flinch. Determination and courage such as he possessed are rare, and, while the anxiety of his friends grew greater than ever, he was quite ready, even eager, to risk his own safety and suffer gladly for his cause.

Allowing the Christmas and New Year festivities to be celebrated with the peace appropriate to the season, he, within the month of January, showed the nature of that "peace to men of goodwill" he contemplated. Anjou and his Frenchmen were not dowered with goodwill; rather they cherished the most devilish projects and went about seeking to do evil. So when the Queen received her customary gift there was put into her hands also a letter from the giver. The opening sentences can hardly have

prepared the imperious lady for the grip and vigour of
the composition, though she was not so foolish as to
think it would be exactly delicate reading. This letter
has been finely described as " the grave but modest
warning of a faithful squire to his liege lady in the
hour of danger." Such commendation, noble indeed,
it deserves; though the modesty, other than that due
when a subject addresses his prince, is not blatantly
obvious. One is not tempted to look for unnecessary
humility on this occasion. Rather must it be regarded as
a stern, outspoken reminder of what the Queen owed to
England and her people, and of the attitude that people
had a right to assume towards her should she shirk her
obligations.

To be aroused from her debauch of Gallic flattery was
not at all agreeable, especially to be aroused by so young
a monitor. Her anger is easy to understand, and the
knowledge that she had little right to be angry probably
increased her fury. It cannot, therefore, be reasonably
urged that she visited the offence of her outspoken
courtier with a harsh severity. She showed the wound her
haughty spirit had suffered by banishing the writer from
the Court. For two years longer she dallied with the
project of the hateful marriage, heedless of the advancing
age that menaced her, and apparently enjoying the fulsome compliments of those about her. It was supposed
that Philip's life was in danger. That imprisonment was
the least penalty he could expect to be called upon to
suffer was a generally diffused opinion both at home and
abroad. The culprit seems to have ignored whatever
warnings were conveyed to him. One, an urgent one,
came from Languet. The old Huguenot can see no
safety for him, if forced to leave England, but in Germany.
He points out, though Philip would not need to be reminded, that France was no abode for the exile, that his
religion prevented his sojourn in Italy or Spain; he is

even compelled to write : " You will hardly find safety in Flanders." Languet's ideas as to the advantages to be gained from Court favour had, as we have seen, undergone an emphatic change. Now was the time come, he thought, when Philip might properly join the camp of William of Orange. Indeed, on first hearing of his pupil's quarrel with Oxford, he had declared : " If the Earl of Oxford's arrogance and insolence have awakened you from your sleep"—a sleep, be it noted, the old man had once deliberately encouraged—" he will have wronged you less than they who have been so indulgent to you." Provided that Philip's parents raise no objections he can only assert baldly, " I think you ought to come." So direct and unhesitating a statement of opinion did not on this occasion persuade or convince its hearer. The quiet of Wilton and his sister's company made a joint appeal too strong for him to resist, and he retired, with relief, and it may be also gratitude, to the pleasant place of exile, where the Countess of Pembroke gave him a noble and hearty welcome.

Of the letter compelling his retirement much has been written, and though its merits as a piece of sound reasoning are not far to seek, it perhaps is well to summarise its contents briefly. From " Most Feared and Beloved, Most Sweet and Gracious Sovereign " to its dutiful close the points are admirably argued in language often eloquent and always worthy the occasion. There is not one hasty sentence, not one phrase of nebulous or halting meaning. Custom of the time was not our custom in the matter of composition; Elizabethan prose was not the prose of to-day. The great masters, the very founders of English prose, had yet to begin their labours. It is difficult to imagine, so much do we owe to it, a man attempting to write at all unless supported by adequate knowledge of the English Bible. From thence comes chiefly all that is best in our prose literature, from the

grave splendour and subtlety of phrase in Browne to the
resounding rhetoric of John Bright.

Yet Philip, too early born to rely on the support that
later authors may use at will, has here managed to
produce something not easily equalled by the most
famous and skilful who succeeded him. Limit must be
set to our praise, however, in that one or two phrases are
more forcible than fortunate. They are sentences easily
remembered and, by some at any rate, cannot be readily
forgiven. The marriage he pleaded against could scarcely
have been a happy or a wise one. Violence of language,
a narrowness of outlook, a noisy bigotry allied to a complete inability to see both sides in a religious dispute, are
unpleasantly obvious. Herein he sins with more excuse
than his successors, who even in our own day delight in
proving that *Disputandi prioritus fit Ecclesiarum scabies.*
None the less may we regret his frequent lapse from charity
in this connection ; nor can we cease to wonder at the
spectacle of so cultured and noble a mind being so
distraught. If Dr. Johnson was right, and he was not
often wrong, the man who busies himself not at all on the
subject of religion is either a fool or a knave. The pity
is that so many falsely flatter themselves that they are
very zealous in its cause, whereas they are in reality
mere sowers of strife or conceited and ignorant fanatics.

Doubtless as affairs in Europe then shaped themselves,
and as the temper of the English people showed, any
alliance between princes of the Catholic and Reformed
Churches in marriage was certain to give an unhappy
result. Politically Philip had a very strong case, a case
so unanswerable that it had been wiser to state it with
more serenity. There is not much reason to believe
that the majority of Elizabeth's Catholic subjects looked
on the debated marriage as other than a blunder, if not
worse. Their loyalty must have been strained during the
first moment of irritation on reading " How their " (Pro-

testant hearts) "will be galled, if not aliened, when they shall see you take for husband a Frenchman and a Papist, in whom (howsoever fine wits may find further dealings or painted excuses) the very common people well know this, that he is the son of a Jezebel of our age—that his brother made oblation of his sister's marriage the easier to make massacres of our brethren in belief; that he himself, contrary to his promise and to all gratefulness, having his liberty and estate by Huguenots means, did sack La Charité and utterly spoil them with fire and sword!"

Presenting so strenuously such facts as these, for unhappily their truth is established, fairness might have prompted him to add that they were equally deplored by those who could not honestly accept the Christianity of the Reformers. Something too much, it seems, is made of Anjou's nominal adhesion to the Catholic faith. His type is the type that discredits whatever creed it affects. And even here it is well to reflect that many a struggling Protestant abroad rather encouraged than discouraged the consummation of the match. Philip's second argument is quite unanswerable. He points out that Anjou is next heir to the French throne. Many of those Reformers who favoured his suit had reckoned on this as an asset. An alliance between the two kingdoms, supposing the Duke to have been anything but the scoundrel he was, would at first sight have been an impregnable fortress against Spanish and Papal attack. A moment's consideration should have shown them how unreal such protection must of necessity have been. Of all forms of speculation the rashest and most futile is concerned with the might-have-beens of history. It is interesting but useless to draw a probable map of the world as it would have shown to-day had Napoleon won at Waterloo or the Germans failed at Sedan, or if Cortez had never stood " Silent upon a peak in Darien," and steamers and telegraphy were no more realities than Northcote's beloved Jack the Giant-killer.

But if any speculation approaches certainty it may fairly
be adjudged certain that Anjou would have deceived their
hopes and betrayed their confidence.

As the letter shows, the very position of the bridegroom,
his then title, his future magnificence, made it impossible
for him to play a secondary part.   As a set-off to this
inconvenient tangle he suggests bluntly that she desires
to be a mother.   This laudable purpose, he shows, could
be achieved more worthily and at less risk.   Her isolated
position in the councils of Europe, he conceives, may
frighten her into making this false step.   Why should
so proud an isolation intimidate one who has the love
of her people for a bulwark, which love, he intimates
plainly, would be jeopardised should she insist on the
marriage : the ambitions of her counsellors was her greatness, they left "the study of their souls in your hands."
That France must be great would of course be Anjou's
guiding motive in all his acts, and he urges that this
ambition clashes with hers who, being English, would
rather see France "not great."   Again he refers to the
questions of children and religion.   Quaintly, but not
without logic on his side, he protests that he does not
deny the bliss of children, but only seeks to show that
religion and equity are in themselves sufficient stays.
Coming from a young man to a middle-aged woman,
the remainder of this truism is not devoid of pathos.   It
is difficult to believe that religion brought the Queen
much consolation, the fervour and sustained faith of a
Sidney were strangers to her soul, though she knew their
value as weapons by which she might hope to see won
her worldly aspirations.   Equity her staunchest admirers
cannot praise her for showing ; she had little notion of
a justice that could in any way interfere with her own
conduct or limit her desires.   When reminded that gossip
made free with her name, she was only being told what
she must have known for many years.   How little she

heeded "the barking of a few curs" may be estimated accurately by noting her conduct during the remainder of her reign. The finish of the letter is composed in a lofty strain with its reference to "the singular honour God hath done you, to be indeed the only protector of His Church." Unfortunately the Queen's piety was on a level with her "liberality," a compliment so deftly introduced into the closing sentences ; yet she must have experienced a thrill of pride as she realised the superb position her truest friends believed she had been chosen by Providence to occupy. Be this as it may, the punishment was not permitted to press heavily on the audacious author, though the offence was not one she could allow to go wholly without a decided token of the royal displeasure.

Philip could not have been sorry to leave London. All that was most mentally alive belonged to the Court and attended the Queen on her processions. She carried the literary and artistic elements of the nation in her train. Their function was mainly to supply her with entertainments at the various houses where she rested. The theatre, so soon to become famous, was little better than a cock-pit. Dismal masques, and morality plays scarcely less dismal, enticed the uninitiated on serious occasions. "Gammer Gurton's Needle," stupid though it be, is above the average of the usual fare provided. The tradition is to praise this masterpiece, the antidote is to read it. To men of sense and fancy its fatuity must have been obvious. Philip's views on the drama were naturally influenced by his surroundings. He cannot be blamed for his lack of prophetic instinct. The door that was to reveal a new and dazzling world had not been opened. He could not see through the barrier. Therefore, in despair at what he did see, he turned to the old writers and made comparisons not to be wondered at. He had an undue reverence for Aristotle, and he saw that when Aris-

totle was passed over and his theories ignored the result
was signally unhappy. That Shakespeare, and others only
less great, would successfully rid themselves of Aristo-
telian shackles it was not given to him to foresee. Therefore he was all for the unities of time and place. Æscylus,
Sophocles, and one hopes a greater than either, Euripides,
had in him an attentive listener. But the modernity and
the hints of Euripides he did not understand. Had he
half apprehended them he would not have railed against
a blending of tragedy and comedy, such as we have in the
" Alcestis " in the scene between the foolish old servant
and Hercules. The necessity for a moment of respite, as
in " Macbeth " just after the murder, was a lesson he had
not learnt. What plays he did see, however, fulfilled one
of his requirements, they were written with a purpose.
This dogma that " poetry is a deep thing, a teaching thing,
the most surely and wisely elevating of human things,"
was in a measure the dogma of those who wrote for
the stage. Certainly their efforts were not contrived for
the glorification of Art, or to satisfy the vanity of a particular performer. These tasks were left for Shakespeare
to accomplish. The masque, in its more graceful moments,
evolved a laboured compliment; the play, such as it was,
abounded in dreary platitudes. For Philip there was no
Mermaid Tavern, and he had no chance of burnishing his
wit by a discussion with Ben Jonson. Except by the
text of the " Apologie " we have little means of guessing
correctly what latent dramatic instinct Philip had. *Arcadia*
suggests that in this quality he was absolutely deficient.

There were, it would appear, certain performers whom
he must have seen often enough. From them he would
not acquire the seer's familiarity with the unrevealed
future. Some of them gained a pleasant notoriety, and
one we may feel confident that Philip knew and liked.

This gentleman, Robert Langham, claimed as patron
the Earl of Leicester. He was a keen observer, preluding,

as it were, some of the clever and witty society entertainers
familiar to us and popular to-day. Skilled in music, a
singer of some distinction, he seems to have delighted
his hearers and won for himself a position well worth
having. Minute details of his success are wanting, but
to some extent he was his own historian. As is the habit
of biographers, he was not blind to his own merits : he
rated them very highly. His official position was that
of an usher to the Privy Council and he, if we may believe
him, was assiduous in his duties. " If the Council sit,
I am at hand. If any make babbling, ' Peace,' say I, ' wot
ye where ye are ? ' If I take a listener, or a prier in at the
chinks or at the lock-hole, I am by and by in the bones
of him. But now they keep good order ; they know me
well enough." As though this passage were not sufficiently
amusing, he gives us a complacent account of his performances, both as master of musical instruments and as a
vocalist. If we are to believe him it cannot be urged
against him, as the great modern poet urges against
Galuppi, " In you step with your cold music." Langham's
songs were not frigid, whatever else they were. " For
dinner and supper I have twenty places to go, and heartily
prayed too. In afternoons and a' nights, sometimes I am
with the right-worshipful Sir George Howard, as good
a gentleman as ever lives ; and sometimes at my good
Lady Sidney's chamber, a noblewoman that I am much
bound unto as any poor man may be unto so gracious
a lady ; and sometimes in some other places ; but always
among the gentlewomen by my good will. Sometimes
I foot it with dancing ; now with gittern, or else with my
cithern, then at the virginals—ye know nothing comes
amiss to me. Then carol I up a song withal ; then by
and by they come flocking about me like bees to honey ;
and ever they cry, ' Another, good Langham, another ! '
And to say truth, what with mine eyes, as I can amorously
gloat it, with my Spanish *sospires*, my French heighes,

my Italian dulcets, my Dutch hoves, by double release, my high reaches, my fine feigning, my deep diapason, my wanton warbles, my running, my timing, my tuning, and my twinkling, I can gratify the masters as well as the proudest of them. By my troth, it is sometimes high midnight e'er I can get from them."

Mr. Langham was, we may feel assured, never a martyr to stage fright. Seldom, indeed, can there have lived a man so frankly pleased with himself. Vanity of this sort if it does not excite our respect, does not arouse our anger. Good-natured conceit helps to make the world go round. Mr. Fox Bourne suggests that this boudoir artist was a near relative, perhaps a brother, of the John Langham who also stood in some favour with persons in high places. To him, with Richard Burbage, John Perkyn, William Johnson, and Robert Wylson was given the first royal patent that any company of players received, as "well for the recreation of our loyal subjects as for our solace and pleasure when we shall think good to see them."

Elizabeth often did "think good" to see them. In her reign, as in the reign of her sister before her, actors, even in the bad plays provided for them, were most seriously thought of. The powers they possessed of influencing public opinion was recognised to the full. Hamlet was exercising the prerogative and copying the example of English princes when he bade Polonius treat the players well; he expressed an opinion, not disputed, when he dubbed them "chroniclers" and "recorders." The players, not the plays, were what people came to see. The play was important only so far as it was apposite.

This is beyond controversy, for Hamlet alters without compunction another man's work to fit in with a contemporary event. The comedian who gags does no more than Hamlet told his leading player to do. The freedom given to, and consideration shown for, the players, is emphasised by the Prince's injunction to the actors not to mock Polonius: "See that you do not mock him." When Queen Mary wanted the people to denounce the Reformation, it was to the players that she turned. "Respublicæ," says Doran, "exemplified her inestimable qualities, by making all the Virtues follow in her train as Maids of Honour." Bishop Bale's "John, King of England," was a violent party pamphlet, spoken, not read. Hooted and applauded by rival parties, the sentiments of the audience, not the merits of the play, moved the hearers. The restrictions put on the actor were due to fear more than contempt. He was the savage house-dog, whose chain must only be unloosed in cases of necessity. The history of Shakespeare's "Richard II.," and the use Essex made of it is well known, and may be read in Doran's instructive, and here accurate, pages.

The greatest, after Burbage, of the players was Tarleton, to whom, as Yorrick, Hamlet pays so great an eulogy.

Tarleton was very humbly born, and his wife, of whom it seems he was frightened, kept a public-house. The meagre accounts we have of her do not commend her to our favour. But if Tarleton could not control his wife's temper he had power over Queen Elizabeth. Fuller, a shrewd observer, says, "He could undumpish her at his pleasure." The excellence of the Shakesperian clowns is owing, probably, to this, that their speeches and antics are a faithful record of what Tarleton did and said. The Queen rejoiced in him, and men of mark had to seek audience with her through his good graces: "In a word, he told the Queen more of her faults than most of her chaplains, and cured her melancholy better than all her physicians." He was given wages and livery as a groom of the chamber. So neither his occupation nor his plebeian origin were reckoned up against him. His child was named, after his godfather, Philip; it was to Walsingham he appealed on his death-bed, fearing lest his widow and child should suffer want. That Philip should have officiated as sponsor to the player's infant is evidence that Tarleton was a man of importance and consideration. The evil days of the players began some years after Tarleton's death.

Two others whom Philip first met at Kenilworth were George Gascoigne, author of *The Steele Glasse*, and Thomas Sackville, successively Lord Buckhurst and Earl of Dorset. They were both poets of real power and distinction. Each left behind him a permanent gift to English literature. Their interest in the drama was at once sincere and practical. Gascoigne, whom Webbe calls "a witty gentleman and the very chief of our late rimers," made from Ariosto's *Suppositi* the first, perhaps, of our English prose comedies. The name he chose for it was not a happy example of his wit. *The Supposes* is not an attractive or suggestive title. It is distinctive, however, in an age when poets loved to grace their compositions with such elaborate legends as a modern author may only regard with wonder and envy. His next play was *Jocasta*, a paraphrase of the *Phoinissai* of Euripides. He tried his hand, not with success, on blank verse. His performances in this style, ingenious in fancy, are most unequal in manner. An educational value may be claimed for them, since they encouraged further efforts by others who had better fortune. His lyrics are of a very high order, nimble, witty, and abounding in graceful fancy and whimsical conceit. Well, though not nobly, born, he early gained a hearing for his muse, and was much thought of by the gentlemen of the Inns of Court. Their advocacy and applause were eagerly coveted and worth having. They seem to have preferred literature to Lyttleton, and their verdict often made or marred an author's reputation. Gascoigne, endowed with "a good metre and a plentiful wit," quickly became a favourite. Such merits as these smoothed his way at Court. He was a soldier of some

distinction, too, and had seen service in Holland.  Nash
sums up his importance in a single sentence : "Whoever
my private opinion condemns as faulty, Master Gascoigne
is not to be abridged of his deserved esteem, who first beat
the path to that perfection which our best poets have
aspired to since his departure ; whereto he did ascend by
comparing the Italian with the English, as Tully did
' *Graeca cum Latinis.*' "

This devotion to Italian literature and Italian devices
is even more evident in Sackville's output.  He was the
finer poet of the two, though less prolific : at any rate
less of his verse has come down to us.  There are passages
in it that transcend anything Gascoigne ever did.
The magnificent lines inspired by Dante, from *The
Induction*, are of exalted and ascetic beauty.  In Sackville's poem it is Sorrow, not Virgil, who leads him to the
regions of the dead.

> " Lo here, quoth Sorrow, princes of renown,
>   That whilom sat on top of fortune's wheel,
>   Now laid full low, like wretches whirled down,
>   Ev'n with one frown, that stayed but with a smile :
>   And now behold the thing that thou, ere while,
>   Saw only in thought : and what thou now shalt hear
>   Recount the same to Kesar, King and peer."

The writer of this impressive and splendid stanza, and
others not less noble, had not the leisure one less highly
born might have controlled.  The Queen commanded his
services in many ways, and praised or blamed as the
fancy moved her.  Had he been asked, he would probably
have told us that he had been best content to write.  His
muse was austere, solemn, but not fickle.  Elizabeth was
fickle, not at all austere, and only solemn when defending
her own vanity.  Sackville was present officially at the
three great State trials of the reign, those of Norfolk,
the Queen of Scots, and Essex.  He died while seated
"at the Council table."  There it was that came to him

> " The body's rest, the quiet of the heart,
>   The travail's ease " ;

there that his soul answered to the touch of one

> " Without respect, esteeming equally
>   King Crœsus' pomp, and Irus' poverty."

The blight of Euphuism, as it was afterwards called, seems to have but little affected the vines that Gascoigne and Sackville tended.  In spite of the Queen's perverse and disgusting affection for an affectation, the disease was bound to perish within a few years of its birth. Lyly was not a man of sufficient genius to found a permanent style ; with all his conceit he cannot have regarded himself as the high priest in any school of thought.  But the influences that he absorbed scarcely touched his immediate predecessors, though they, like he, wandered in the infected Italian marshes.  Their reputations were firmly established before Lyly, with his *Euphues*, set courtiers agape.  To read *Euphues* now is a trial and a perplexity.  All that is good and worthy of imitation in the Italian masters is ignored, everything decadent and futile is imitated, cleverly and ingeniously to be sure, with heartbreaking fidelity.  Words are used, not to conceal thought, but to hide the absence of thought. Nor is this to be wondered at.  The Euphuists would seem to have considered that men should write not because they had something to say, but because they had studied how to express an inanity elaborately.  When Languet, and others like him, so strenuously opposed the submission of English boys to Italian influence, a possible menace to the language of the country was not among the dangers they feared.  None the less it was a more formidable danger than the one they so especially dreaded.  Philip escaped the contagion in part, but only in part, for *Eupheses* doubtless suggested *Arcadia*, and

*Arcadia,* a result of conscientious imitation, is decidedly
tedious. It is not, one opines, altogether wise to laugh at a
literary habit because it is an ephemeral whim or fashion.
In the last two decades there have been a dozen, none
of permanent value. But in every case something of
importance, something that can be usefully employed
for definite ends, has been saved from the wreckage of
reputations that have foundered.

The employment of unusual words, used wrongly and
absurdly, has reminded us of their merit when used
rightly. From twenty conceits one strong infant may
be reared. As Green says, "The quickness and vivacity
of English prose was first developed in the school of
Italian imitators who appeared in Elizabeth's later years."
This quickness and vivacity, noticed by the historian,
though his own work escapes cleverly the just application
of both epithets, is kept alive by every effort, however
fantastic, to contrive a new sensation in the use and
arrangement of words. Greene boasted that printers
would pay largely for the " dregs of his wit," and think
these dregs cheaply procured. He and Nash could supply
plenty of dregs to their wit. As with Falstaff's, there was
always in their tavern bills "a pennyworth of bread to
an intolerable deal of sack." None the less they were
popular authors and not in the least original. They stole
much that was virile from the Italians : they also appropriated a great deal that was hardly worth their labour.
But their efforts were immensely popular. And work
of the kind they, who made no pretence at artistry, were
doing, demanded a drag. This check Euphuism gave ;
the value of a story, the value of a word properly used,
a phrase properly placed, were at length understood to
be one value. Then Shakespeare welded "fire-new
words" into their right places, and Armado would have
discovered that his fine periods, however carefully invented,
were not an example of *Love's Labour Lost.*

The modern writer who has best understood the importance of a word, as a word, is Browning. He misused his knowledge at times, we know ; but in *A Grammarian's Funeral* he suggests to us not a little of the intense delight Philip Sidney and others derived from a sudden realisation of words and phrases ; what meanings they did imply, what, deftly handled, they might be made to convey. To have " a mint of phrases in his brain " set up a man as a poet at once. These phrases proved useful when men had time to think. The glitter of a coin attracts first : the purchasing value is learnt later. Lyly had more of the glitter than Gascoigne or Sutcliffe, and Philip was attracted by it. Most young writers would have been. Unconsciously he followed, I think, the example of worthier masters. Whoso, at and after his day, could not " parly with Euphuism " passed as more ignorant even than the dullards who lacked knowledge of French. And this toying with a sentence, this playing with a word, putting a jewel in the sun so as to catch the particular sparkle from each separate facet, was no merely idle amusement.

We have here the first instance in English of an appreciation of the subtlety of a language, and that language the English, hitherto unkempt and untrammelled. Without Lyly, neither our Bible nor the Book of Common Prayer could have been contrived. John Bright, likely enough, had never heard of, certainly had never read, the effusions of this young pedant. But the best of his speeches owe something to him. For from the Court the humour spread downwards, and common men played with words and felt themselves suddenly enriched. And as the power of mere words became apparent, the tinsel was abandoned. "The street was ready to receive it," says Green ; that is this new dowry, the knowledge of words and " popular literature " had a virile beginning. At last men could express themselves, men of all ranks. When the mob has learned to speak, the result is that tyranny and despotism can for brief intervals only assert their divine pre-eminence. Then tyranny and despotism, after such a revelation, change sides. Elizabeth found a few scholars near her throne, and she encouraged them. At her death there were many printers and more books than the most generous dreamer had dared to contemplate : though the printers and the purchasers as yet did not understand a tithe of what their newly acquired powers were capable of accomplishing. They were not long in understanding and using their wealth. Temporarily, that is till the Restoration of Charles II., in many branches the arts and letters suffered. But in the rhodomontades of the strictest and most bigoted of Puritans—and none could be so narrow and unjust—there is ever a stately eloquence not observable before. This eloquence comes not merely from enthusiasm, however rightly or wrongly inspired, but from a reverent, awesome feeling that the right word used in the right place had the force of volumes. Cromwell's preachers little thought that the resounding sentences they thundered forth so glibly owed their origin in large measure to the finicking and dandy poet, Italian tourist, and febrile playright, Lyly. " How far this little candle spreads its beams, So shines a good deed in a naughty world." Lyly's candle was tallow of the worst, those who carelessly handled it got besmirched with the drippings. But it gave a light, and from it others have illuminated braver torches.

Lyly is a man whose vanities we must forgive. Though vacant of thought himself, he showed us how those who can think may accurately use the intricate machine by which alone thoughts may be expounded and disseminated. This tawdriest of writers, who did so much, unwittingly, to stifle the genius of his immediate neighbours, achieved something greater than he knew. But for his work our struggles after fit expression would be even more hopeless than they now are. For though the temple Lyly built unto himself has crumbled, modern architects still utilise his bricks in the fashioning of buildings that shall prove more permanent.

The eccentric in literature, as in all forms of art, carries in itself a disease that spells death. This we see even in the work of quite modern writers, sometimes men of genius, almost always of unusual talent. After the first curiosity has begun to languish, and pupils of smaller merit have imitated the tricks too often, the new school perishes in dust and ashes. In the short course of one decade these elaborate triflers taste of a fleeting fame before sinking into eternal oblivion. For them—and their work, as I have suggested, is of real value when the gold is sifted—Fortune smiles less fairly than she did for Lyly. They do not stand at the cradle of English prose, and their uses are less perceptible. However mistaken in their methods, such men as Lyly and his successors preach and practise a certain reverence for their art, though one cannot help wondering how far their creed is the orthodox doctrine of *Euphues*. " Far more seemly," he says, " were it for thee to have thy Studie full of Bookes, than thy Purses full of Mony." This sentence recalls that saying of Seneca's: " He that is well employed in his study, though he may seem to do nothing, yet does the greatest things of all others." Lyly, born a year earlier than Philip, survived him fifteen years, dying in 1601.

# CHAPTER X

## AT WILTON

AT Wilton House, that beautiful house Holbein created and fire destroyed, Philip lived for seven months. He was not idle, however, for his active brain was never still. For him rest was always merely a change of occupation. He could not say, nor wish to say, with Thomas à Kempis that he had sought rest everywhere but had only found it in quiet corners and tiny volumes. For him it was no part of a man's duty to God to play the anchorite and shun the world. There were things to be done while life lasted, and mere dreaming was not an honourable or a satisfactory vocation; though he could dream beautiful dreams too when so minded, as all real poets can. Intercourse with friends of his own choosing, correspondence with Languet and others, spent some of his leisure. But this was not all. At the suggestion of his sister he began, for her pleasure, his *Arcadia*, on which much of his fame rests. Horace Walpole, indeed, did not think much of what he had read of it, saying that the patience of "a young maiden in love" was quite unequal to the task of reading so involved a mass of sentiment and adventure. Walpole is not a safe guide in literary matters though, to do him justice, he is always a witty and amusing one. Pleasant is it to remember that he could contradict Voltaire's assertions about the merits of Shakespeare in the most fearless manner possible, only avoiding a prolonged controversy because no good could come of it, since all France would be on one side and all England on the other. Years afterwards he proclaims his faith to Sir Horace Mann, asserting that Shakespeare "was superior to all mankind"; which profession of faith is adroitly wedded to a sweeping condemnation of contemporary dramatists. His taste was not always, or indeed often, so sound. However, it is on record that, as an antiquary, he respected Philip. He connects him with Houghton, and describes the knight's crest carefully. Others than Walpole, it must be conceded, have found *Arcadia* something less than exhilarating. Be its virtues or defects what they may, their detailed examination demands a place in this volume ; the book marks an important episode in the history of English prose and the evolution from chaos of the English novel.

While Philip was at Wilton his friend Edmund Spenser left for Ireland, as the Viceroy's secretary, a country where he was unhappy and discontented. This is not to be wondered at, for even sterner spirits than his, unless mere adventurers, were not eager for exile, however dignified, in that troubled and troublesome kingdom.

An event happened in March more pleasant to contemplate. The Countess of Pembroke gave birth to a son, William. In his turn this William became a famous man and the friend of Shakespeare. So much has been written of the sonnets to *Mr. W. H.*, that the riddle of the dedication is, likely as not, more undecipherable than ever. It is, however, frequently contended that their " only begetter " was this same nephew of Philip's. A poet's nephew certainly was more than merely the patron of the greatest of all poets. Were there less reason than is forthcoming for the truth of the tradition, one would willingly vouch for it as truth, on sentimental grounds. As Macready was proud of a blessing that made him, as it were, the spiritual grandson of Keane ; so though the greater poet, Shakespeare may well have been proud to find himself linked thus by friendship with one whose sonnets were, till then, but second to his own.

Considering the condition of affairs at Court the choice made of sponsors is at first sight a curious one. Against the suitability of the Earl of Warwick nothing can be urged : but that Leicester should have been asked, and consented to stand, is strange. That Elizabeth should have swallowed her resentment caused by the Earl's marriage and completed the trio is stranger still. Leicester was not yet forgiven, and the child's grandfather was, as so often happened, passing through a period of marked disfavour. The Queen seems to have been fond of Lady Pembroke, and was willing to show good feeling. Her conduct towards the Sidney family displayed on every conceivable occasion an amazing mixture of kindness, pique, anger, and condescension.

Sir Henry had flattered himself that in Wales he might live in peace among people he liked and there try to forget the story of his Irish wrongs and difficulties. These hopes seemed not ill-founded, and he visited Wilton with delight several times in the early part of 1580. Elizabeth, aware of these journeyings of the Lord President, chose to be annoyed. According to her wont she made no secret of her displeasure. Walsingham had the painful task of advising his old friend " to walk warily." What the Queen did not see other eyes saw for her, and other ears besides hers itched for news of his doings. Everything he said or did at length was known to his Sovereign, who was an adept,

when the whim moved her, in the fashioning of mountains
out of mole-hills. At first the complaint was that he
neglected his post, that the Principality was threatened,
that the defences were neglected. He was told that in the
hours of danger a Lord President should be always at his
post. Unfair and irritating as these grumblings were, the
unlucky gentleman does not seem to have regarded them
so seriously as past experience should have taught him
to do. August brought with it a more petulant and
explicit censure. The royal anger was aroused in the
royal zeal for the true religion. As is the case with most
people who are conspicuous rather for a lack of religious
principle, she was more bitter when differences of faith
were in dispute than on any other subject of controversy.
Catholics, we hear, were not being hunted down in
sufficient numbers, "recusants and other obstinate persons"
went about their daily business in comparative comfort.
Deplorable indeed was the state of Wales according to the
Queen's account. This outburst is doubly ridiculous,
because the most obstinate person in the kingdom was
the Queen herself. The projected French, and therefore
Catholic, match had not been abandoned, and Sir Henry
Sidney, worn out in her service, was rapped over the
knuckles for not rigorously and systematically ill-using
members of that same Church whose pretentions, represented by Anjou and his French followers, had brought
about the opposition and consequent disgrace of Philip
Sidney. "You cannot blow hot and cold" is a wise old
saw ; the dexterity of the Queen was equal even to showing
that the maxim does not admit of universal application.
She proved her superiority to all rules of logic in yet
another way. At the identical moment Sir Henry was
digesting, as indifferently as he could, this last affront
Leicester, and Philip with him, was summoned to the
Court. The Earl seems to have patched up a kind of
peace with his arrogant mistress by promising to voice

his dislike of the French match. What were the terms on which Philip returned I do not know. His uncle probably talked him into a reluctant consent, and Languet wrote a plausible enough letter of mingled warning, encouragement, and advice.

That Philip himself felt little enthusiasm at his restoration to favour is certain. He hated the noise and glitter of a Court after the peace of Wilton. His essays in poetry and prose had become truly serious and of moment to him, though Languet may be readily pardoned if he did not understand this. "I supposed," he writes, "that your thoughts would change as you grew older, and that your duty to your country would keep you in public life." Duty, patriotism, in the writer's eyes could have only one meaning, the furtherance of Protestant hopes in England and abroad. Weaving romances and inditing sonnets were not accounted to their author for righteousness. Listlessness, which the old man believed had fallen on him and was increasing, was not to be feared ; nor was his vigour, if needed, likely to relax. An adroit reference to Philip's "famous embassage to the Emperor" could only have provoked a smile. What, we cannot hesitate to believe, did weigh with him was that his master had chosen the Netherlands to live in that his anxiety for the favourite pupil's welfare might more easily be lessened. There is eloquence and reason too in this appeal : " Ask yourself, I do beseech you, how far it is honourable for you to lurk where you are, while your country is claiming help from all her sons. If the advice you offered to your Queen, thinking it helpful to the nation, was not taken as it deserved to be, you ought not on that account to be angry with your country or to desist from seeking its safety. When Themistocles proposed measures beneficial to the State, and Eurybiades threatened to strike him unless he held his peace, he answered, ' Strike, but hear.' Imitate Themistocles ! "

It was rather gratuitous to remind Philip of history, for by presenting his letter he had literally adopted the "strike, but hear" attitude. Blame cannot be levelled at him if he thought he had already said what had to be said, and was chary of destroying or hurting his first protest by repeating it again, possibly more feebly. Back to London he went, whoever persuaded him. A further letter from Languet, very gentle, grave, and tender, greeted him in October. " I am glad that you have abandoned your retirement and returned to the daylight of the Court. But I am afraid that you will soon get weary of it. I see that its honours and dignities are given to age and wealth, rather than to virtue and prudence, so that you, who are yet young and without property of your own, will not easily reap any advantage. It will be dreary work for you, wasting the springtime of your life amid the formalities and indolence of a Court ; for the occupation of courtiers does not often advance the public good, and are very seldom concerned with the better part of life. I think there are not many men among you who would prefer the welfare of the State to their own interests. I forsee many troubles, a future when your noblemen will be separated into factions, and at strife with one another, when the neighbouring nations will throw fuel on the fire which is to be kindled among you. Believe me, there are storms brewing which are not to be dispelled by fallacies that have well-nigh driven all noblemindedness and simplicity of thought out of the Christian world."

A sad picture truly is drawn here, and lugubrious was the outlook in fact. To Philip, fortified as he was by youth, the prospect was menacing towards which he turned his face. Reading the words of his venerable friend, he was permitted to console himself with the reflection that he was thought worthy in an unworthy age ; that in the day of disaster and tribulation his nerve might be relied upon, his honesty of purpose and zeal for all that was of good report would be needed to fire the waverers and strengthen those of a fearful heart. Eleven months later the old man died, glad to quit a life that had given him few pleasures and many disappointments. Striving ever loyally for all he believed to be good and true the miasma of failure wove his shroud. Hope for the future of Europe, and the great cause, seems scarcely to have flickered in his breast. Worse and still worse appeared the condition of the world to him with each succeeding year. It was as "if the diseases of Valdichiana, between July and September, and of Maremma and Sardinia, were all together in one ditch." Du Plessis-Mornay, a Philip also, aided by his wife, sought to soothe the remaining days, to give what comfort they could. He was, however, more than content to go. The "faithful heart, clean hands, and mouth as true," could perform their offices no more. This much, at least, may have given a touch of solace to the last dreary agony, the knowledge that a Philip of France and a Philip of England were willing to receive the torch from the failing hands of one who had taught them to have

> "A feeling taste of Him that sits
> Beyond the heavens, far more beyond our wits."

The Prince of Orange followed Languet to the tomb, a third and powerful witness to a scholar's integrity. Whatever his limitations, there have not lived many men who loved truth and justice more. Amidst those few we discern clearly the faces of William Prince of Orange, du Plessis-Mornay, and Philip Sidney. Were it only for the encouragement and advice he tendered to them Languet had not lived in vain. His death happed during the darkest hour that heralds in the dawn. He did not for all his wisdom understand that

> "Not by Eastern windows only when morning comes comes in the light,
> In front the sun climbs slow, how slowly, but westward, see, the land is bright."

It is not astonishing that the old scholar was unhappy and only glad to leave the world, for he had lingered just long enough to learn strange and disquieting news. That the Protestant princes should choose Anjou as their leader against the Spaniards, that Leicester and other English nobles should so completely fulfil a promise not to oppose the Queen's marriage with Anjou as actually to encourage her design, must have made a broken and disillusioned man feel that all was lost. The shadow world of Death was midsummer daylight to the darkness he was leaving.

Philip, when he arrived at Court, after a slight delay, owing to a bad cold, found Leicester busied with plans for obtaining and perpetuating the safety of the Dutch Provinces. Spanish influence, engineered by the Duke of Parma, was making appreciable headway. It was felt that a decided step must be taken to stem the inflowing tide effectually. Direct opposition, it would seem, was regarded for the moment as hopeless. English influence was desired and relied upon. This William thought might be obtained if Leicester were to accept the sovereignty of the North. Should the Earl receive the proposition favourably the active sympathy, he felt, of Elizabeth would be firmly secured. The proposition must have flattered Leicester, but if his vanity was tickled his good sense came to the rescue. Not only was the fickle caprice of the Queen well known to him, for he had basked in her smiles and scarcely yet recovered from her displeasure ; but his own capacity to rule, as he must have realised very well, was mediocre. The Prince, on the other hand, had too exalted an opinion of the Earl's administrative ability, and he was not alone in nursing this delusion. Putting their wits together, they hit upon the plan of raising Anjou to the position which they both hesitated to accept. Neither of them had any doubts as to the kind of man Anjou was ; they would easily have agreed to Margaret of Navarre's verdict, " If

fraud and cruelty were banished from the earth, there was
in him sufficient stock from which it could be replenished."
The Duke was already chief of the Catholic provinces, and
many of the Catholics had small veneration for Spain. A
scheme by which Spanish domination would be opposed
by a Prince round whose standard those of the old and the
new faiths could decently rally had much to be said in its
favour. Anjou was quite eloquent when he explained and
asserted how fairly and honestly he would treat the adherents
of both religions. As the husband of Queen Elizabeth
he would be doubly able to put his good intentions into
practice. Reasoning of this or a similar nature must have
persuaded many. At first sight one inclines to the belief
that it was sound and was calculated to thwart Spanish
aggression successfully and sink the differences of the two
religious factions, in that averting a common danger they
might contrive to live at peace with one another. This
alliance with Elizabeth led them to a sensible theory enough,
namely, that the Duke would have to do as he was told.
The Virgin Queen of fiction was a most masculine prince
in fact. Hence, while the Catholics would be mollified, the
Protestants would have in reality the power they affected
to relinquish in a measure. Of a surety the Queen would
allow no partner to her throne. Her accepted suitors had
invariably been her courtiers, the importunities of the lover
were tolerated and encouraged, but a thick wall separated
the boudoir from the council chamber. Credit came to her
as the acknowledged champion of the Protestant cause
and, much as she averred her inclination towards the
Duke, she was shrewd enough to have it made fixed and
certain that he would join her in a league against Spain.
Neither Leicester nor Orange had misread her character in
this particular. Sir Francis Walsingham was despatched to
Paris and instructed to make the situation quite clear to all
whom it concerned. His was not an enviable task. Tasks
that the Queen gave her emissaries seldom were. On this

occasion she chose to play the *rôle* of the nursery heroine
with " A then she would and then she wouldn't" policy
that bothered her representative to the edge of distraction.
" When her Majesty is pressed to the marriage," he complains, " then she seemeth to affect a league ; and when a
league is yielded to, then she liketh better a marriage ;
and when thereupon she is moved to assent to marriage,
then she hath recourse to the league ; and when the
motion for the league or any request for money is made,
then her Majesty returneth to the marriage."

Negotiations in Paris were merely useless, or dangerous,
or amusing, according to the several dispositions of the
onlookers. Anjou's advisers persuaded him to visit
London, and on November 1, 1581, he arrived there
and stayed three months. Philip went to Wilton for
Christmas, but made his holiday a short one. His attendance was needed among the train of nobles and
gentlemen whose presence added lustre to the Duke's
departure as an accepted suitor. Such, at any rate, he
was supposed to be.

Before the Duke came in person a bold attempt had
been made by the French Court to force the Queen to
declare herself. In April a splendid embassy had arrived
from Paris with the view of settling this difficult matter
of the marriage of the French King's brother with the
English Queen. The reception accorded was magnificent,
the result was absolutely to seek. Philip, however, played
a conspicuous part in the organising of entertainments
contrived to please the illustrious visitors. Leicester was
of those chosen to discuss and arrange the more prosaic
and vastly more important part of the business. How far
Philip prompted Leicester is not known ; probably the
uncle was greatly influenced by the nephew. A very full
account is extant of a tournament held at Whitehall in
which he took part as one of the " Four Foster Children
of Desire," who took it upon themselves to gain access

to "the Fortress of Perfect Beauty." The fortress was
erected in front of the Queen's window at Whitehall.
Philip wore armour of blue and gold ; his lack of humour
prevented his feeling in the least ridiculous.  This consideration is not very important; his participations in
these heavy junkettings is.  For it proves beyond cavil
that he was decided in his own mind that the Anjou
match was necessary.  Hateful though the conclusion was
to him, he never for a moment wavered in his allegiance
to the Protestant faith.  It cannot be suggested, however,
with any show of authority that his antics in this panto-
mime increased his dignity.  Nor could the thirty gentlemen
and yeomen, attended by trumpeters, and gorgeous in lace
of silver and Venetian hose, have added one whit of merit
to his performance.  It is a rather feeble excuse to make,
yet it is made, that Philip's delight in fencing and such-
like exercises led him to take part in this unworthy Tom
Fool's play.  Better is it to remember that he was a young
man, that the " Fortress of Perfect Beauty " was absurdly
pleased by a clumsy compliment, which had little foundation in fact, and forget as readily as we can the whole
foolish performance.  That the " Fortress of Beauty " was
not to be taken easily by impetuous assault seems to have
been the conclusion of the whole matter.  Therefore the
Duke of Anjou thought he had better come over himself
and test the efficacy of a more protracted siege.

That he was successful, though little detailed knowledge is to hand, appears certain.  When he left for
Flushing a famous company of lords and gentlemen
accompanied him.  The Queen herself rode with him
on horseback as far as Canterbury, Lord Hunsdon,
Leicester, Walter Raleigh, Fulke Greville, Dyer, and
Philip Sidney went even farther.  At Flushing they
were all greeted by the great Prince of Orange himself,
whose conduct in the whole proceeding must have gone
far to persuade Philip that he was acting rightly, and

brought him to believe, as William did firmly believe, that the saviour of Holland was the miserable scoundrel whom they were now anxious to honour. At Antwerp follies not dissimilar to those performed at Whitehall were repeated. In a large theatre the French impostor was hailed Duke of Brabant. Inflated with his new dignity he swore that he would rule sagely and fairly, that no customary laws should be broken, no privileges ignored. Easily enough he took the necessary oaths, easily as he put on his head the crimson bonnet and threw over his shoulders the crimson cloak. Allegorical side-shows were provided when the more austere preliminaries were come to a close. The "Maid of Antwerp" laid the city keys at his feet, Religion and Justice walked on either hand of her. Ahead paced Concord, supported by Wisdom and Force; Samuel, Saul, Jonathan, and David were not forgotten in the motley show. Heroes of mythology, Scripture, and tradition were drawn into the pageant to prove that Brabant triumphed over Spain at last.

It would be worth all the knowledge we have to know what Elizabeth pondered over when she took her leave of the Duke and rode back from Canterbury to London. For she was clever enough to understand the folly of the wooing, and far-sighted enough to see that, in spite of pageants and tourneys—

"The earth hath bubbles as the water hath
And these were of them."

# CHAPTER XI

## FINANCIAL TROUBLES—ROBBERY AND PLANS

Sir Henry's financial troubles—Philip in need of money—He enters
Parliament—His work there—A sidelight on Elizabeth—Robbery of Papists—Philip claims his share—Secures substantial
benefits—Is callous how he comes by them—A very lame
excuse—Is knighted—Not for personal merit, but to expedite
a delayed Court function—Sir Henry demands a peerage—His
reasons—A refusal—Philip gives a golden flower-pot to the
Queen—He marries—Simulated anger of the Queen—The
Queen as godmother—Her munificent gift—Languet's advice
and Philip's real character—Bruno, how far Philip helped
him—How far Philip helped du Mornay—Philip's impatience
of caution—American plans revived—Spain to be humiliated
on the Spanish Main—Humphrey Gilbert wrecked—Philip's
charter—Ralph Lane

IN addition to the French marriage complications,
there was much to trouble Philip and his family.
Habitually short of money, they were at this time
more hard put to it than ever. Sir Henry was spending
double his salary retaining a post in his conduct of
which he only reaped most plentiful abuse. In Ireland
his expenses had come to sixty pounds a week; a
niggard mistress allowed him thirty. He was not, of
course, the only sufferer. Every one who served the
Queen competently had to fill the vacancy in their
purses with the wind of her abuse. She was too shrewd
to dismiss her servants, too mean to pay them, and they

were too loyal to resign their offices.  Elizabeth has
become a myth, "Good Queen Bess" and many other
untruthful compliments are repeated, and believed in,
by the unthinking.  She was mean, had no sense of
honour, though some of dignity, and with a vanity quite
beyond human measurement expected as a right the
immolation even of decent comfort on her altar steps.
There have been good women whose names are hardly
remembered ; a thoroughly ᵥad woman has grasped, as
she always did grasp everything within her reach, a
reputation for virtue.  The shrew is always feared, and
Elizabeth was playing the part on a grand scale.

However, in this essay it only concerns us to know
how the Sidneys fared at her hands.  They fared badly.
Sir Henry as Lord President of Wales received twenty
pounds a week "to keep an honourable house," and "a
hundred marks a year to bear foreign charges."  In 1583
he protests, and with much reason, "what house I keep,
I dare stand to the report of any indifferent man.  True
books shall be shown to you that I spend above £30
a week.  Here some may object that upon the same I
keep my wife and her followers.  True it is, she is now
with me, and hath been this half year ; but before not in
many years.  And if both she and I had our food and
house room free, as we have not, in conscience we have
deserved it.  For my part I am not idle, but every day
I work in my function ; and she, for her old service, and
marks yet remaining in her face, taken in the same,
meriteth her meat."  So all Philip's parents had received
by way of payment for their devotion were, "the one an
emptied pocket, the other a pock-marked face."  Men
with an eye on what is elegantly called "the main
chance," could have answered Sir Henry's complaint
had they heard it.  The office he was holding, it would
seem, was in reality a gold mine if properly understood.
The Queen thoroughly appreciated the nature of a bribe,

and thought no ill of him who took one.   Her representatives were, if not actually encouraged, not prevented from
increasing their incomes and making a profit out of their
positions.   This royal complacency was not at all to Sir
Henry's liking.   " I sell no justice, I trust you do not hear
of any order taken by me ever reversed, nor my name or
doings in any courts—as courts there be whereto by appeal
I might be called—ever brought in question.   And if my
mind were so base and corruptible as I would take money
of the people whom I command for my labour, yet could
they give me none or very little ; for the causes that come
before me are causes of people mean, base, and very many
beggars."   One must understand how highly Sir Henry
considered of his position.   A full third of the whole
kingdom was under his jurisdiction, and he accepts the
responsibility because every day brings him an opportunity of doing good.   That satisfaction, to solace the
suffering and protect the weak, was the only salary he
received.

While this most noble gentleman grew more and more
poor, Philip too was in a dilemma.   He may have saved
a little during his stay at Wilton, but if he did his economies
can have totalled but a small sum.   He was not able, in
1580, to forward a New Year's present to the Queen, which
is a significant fact ; he still clung to his Flintshire living,
and he accepted from his uncle the office of steward to the
Bishop of Winchester.   Perhaps this promotion, though
the salary attaching to the office is not on record, enabled
him to repair the omission of the former year.   On New
Year's Day, 1581, he did present the Queen with tokens of
his loyalty.   They do not seem to have been expensive
gifts, but they might have furnished him with sufficient
material for a sonnet.   They were a gold-headed whip, a
chain of the same metal, and a heart of gold.   If he sent
with them the verses they pertinently suggest, we have no
mention of them by his biographers.

Almost indigent though he was, he entered Parliament on the 16th of January of this year. His election expenses cost exactly nothing, and probably he never saw his constituents. Local authorities chose their member, who graciously condescended to accept the favour. But in this instance the local magnates concerned displayed considerable acumen. Reports of debates, if there were any reports, have not come down to us. During his two months' attendance in the House he evidently made his mark. This is beyond controversy, for he was nominated to a committee deputed to consider the machinations of the Papists and help to devise methods of punishing these wicked and malicious people. In addition to this congenial employment he was called upon to suggest how best by sea and land all possible enemies could be most expeditiously circumvented. This particular portion of his duty reads like a paragraph from an alarmist newspaper of our own day. He fulfilled his duty most vigorously. The result of the committee's deliberations are very unpleasant reading, although he was in sore need of money. He could not, like the character in Moliére's play, apostrophise "*les beaux yeux de ma cassette.*"

Unfortunately Philip had a keen eye for the money-boxes of other people, and a most vague notion of the difference between *meum* and *tuum* decidedly eccentric in a man who was a skilled scholar. His laudators say little of his feverish energy at this time ; it is as well to state, with absolute calm, what the facts are. The value of knowing them is not merely that they debase Philip in our estimation—they do that—but in the strange light they throw on the public morality of the day. By the standard of any age Philip, pardoning occasional lapses, would take a conspicuous place. He stood absolutely first among his own contemporaries, and they were eager to make way for him. Even a modern historian catches something of their enthusiasm when, in the preface to his book, he says : " I have endeavoured to draw a true and not incomplete picture of him as a type of English chivalry in the Elizabethan age." Had Philip done nothing more than shine among his fellows, he would hardly have become a national hero. Morality was at a low ebb, whether Puritan or Catholic. A pretty story goes that Elizabeth, in public, placed the Bible next her heart, thereby assuring her cheering subjects how deeply she valued the foundation-stone of the greatness of England. It would have been wiser of her to read the Sermon on the Mount. Of Elizabeth herself, however, the best-natured burrower in archives quickly realises little good can be found. The shock on making so lamentable a discovery is overwhelming, it is so utterly unexpected : what one learns is so pointedly at variance with all most of us have been trained to believe. To find an excuse for Philip's conduct is difficult. We learn that the Queen, with frugal generosity, distributed among her courtiers the spoils seized from those Papists who had, in one way or another, offended her. Rank robbery, one would have supposed, was not a feat that was likely to appeal to Philip, however dexterous the knavery. Contrary to all expectation, he plunges gaily into the game of grab, and plays it without a shadow of shame. With engaging frankness he writes : "Truly I like not their persons, and much worse their religion : but I think my fortune very hard that it must be built on other men's punishments." It does not for a moment occur to him that the penalties were unjust, and that a decent man should have taken shame to himself for benefiting by them. So far from experiencing shame, he first of all boldly asks for £100 a year " in impropriations"; and two months later, in December, 1582, asks casually, as a man might borrow an umbrella, at least £3,000 from the Papist penalties. A letter of thanks to his uncle seems to show that he got all he asked for. His demands scarcely erred on the side of moderation, for he also secured a sinecure of £120 a year directly from the Queen. It is to be regretted that these transactions should be so casually referred to and treated as a matter of course. This spoliation was disgraceful, and it is as well to acknowledge that Philip did more than acquiesce in the robbery. He clamoured for, and obtained, a quite considerable amount of the booty. To blame him unduly would be ridiculous ; to pretend there is nothing to blame is wicked. The best of men are not saints ; even the gods have club-feet sometimes. To emphasise the halo is not good art and is bad history.

There are plenty of human excuses for Philip acting as Philip did, he was poor and his family were harassed with pecuniary troubles ; but this lapse from virtue should not be condoned by a silence that nearly amounts to positive praise. A great difficulty that besets the man who would write the history of this period fairly is that he perpetually finds himself on the side that he had always believed did not even possess the elements of the most primitive virtue. Philip deserves his halo, but in this particular instance he behaved badly and greedily. I do not think a proper estimation of his exalted merit is easier conceived by the veiling of a considerable fault. Not only did he look after his own interests; he was set equally on the interests of his friends. Fulke Greville, saying nothing of the transaction, profited substantially through Philip's endeavours.

No doubt we must take into consideration the fact that this relentless system of plundering those of whom the authorities disapproved was no new device. Henry VIII. set an evil example at the Reformation when he sacked the monasteries and distributed their lands, buildings, and possessions among his courtiers. Many a noble family supports its nobility on this foundation of robbery. Indirectly the despoiled monks were paying for the lavish splendour of Elizabeth and her courtiers.

It is, possibly, some excuse for Philip's conduct that he
had been reared in an age of robbery and violence; that
he had been accustomed to hear theft spoken of with
approval by men of repute. But if this may be urged
in extenuation, it cannot be put forward as a satisfactory excuse in his case. He saw and acted more cleanly
than most men; he was often inspired by motives of
unusual excellence. In the matter of ruining his religious
opponents he was as base and greedy as his neighbours.
His very merits and virtues make his lapse from austere
goodness and rightness of conduct the more lamentable.
How he reconciled his conduct with his conscience
we are not told. We do know that his conscience
was a mentor whom he listened to and obeyed. There
must have been something even subtler than Jesuit
casuistry in his reasoning when he could not merely
take gladly, but clamour for, an adequate portion of the
goods of another. Unfortunately the Reformation is not
only a period of religious ferment, it is a period also of
villainy and plunder. It may be that, sagacious and
level-headed though he was, robbery was not robbery to
him if sanctified by zeal for the true faith. Of course,
it must not be forgotten that quite sensible people affected
to regard every Catholic as an enemy to his Queen and
country. The belief was a comfortable one, though like
many comfortable beliefs there was little truth in it.
Supposing these much-wronged people to have been
traitors, it was easily argued that money in their pockets
added dangerously to their power for evil. When their
pockets were emptied they became comparatively harmless. Such an argument, based on a fallacy, naturally
had in it the seeds of popularity, and it is remarkable that
they who profited were very staunch Protestants. Philip,
however, does not condescend to consider this train of
thought. Perhaps he saw its weakness. Reluctantly one

is forced to the conclusion that he saw no harm in robbing
a Catholic if the plunder was directed by law, and he
openly declares that he wants his share for the alleviation
of his private necessities, a declaration in which it is difficult
to trace the influence either of patriotism or religion.

A curiously perverted sense of both patriotism and
religion did possess men at this time, and from this time
to the end of Elizabeth's reign. Nor was robbery by any
means the only injustice suffered by the party out of
favour. Laws against the Catholics after 1581 were
stricter and more savage than ever they had been before.
It was not altogether zeal for a purer religion that
prompted them. Fear of Spain, troubles of Scottish
invention, rumours of popish plots combined to shake the
public nerve, and often danger was suspected when no
danger threatened. It was believed, and in some instances
with reason, that Elizabeth's throne was in peril whenever
Catholics met together. Any idea of toleration could not
be entertained for a moment. That great patriots had been
Catholics was conveniently forgotten. Save among bigots
on both sides there was, probably, little interest taken
in religious bickerings. Sensible men wanted peace : and
many were of opinion that the difference between the
hostile sects was not worth a quarrel. As has been well
said : " The Tudors committed many tyrannical acts.
But in their ordinary dealings with the people they were
not, and could not be, tyrants. It cannot be supposed
that a people who had in their own hands the means
of checking their princes would suffer any prince to impose
on them a religion generally detested."

The Protestantism of Elizabeth was distinctly of an
elastic quality. The children of the clergy were accounted,
by her, illegitimate. Though she forbade the elevation of
the Host, she favoured ritual and observances that would
have awakened the angry thunder of the Protestant Alli-

ance.  Politics were inextricably mixed up with religion, and however we may condemn, and should condemn, the atrocities of Mary's reign, there was an excuse for them. Judges and executioners were sincere in their terrible creed that by torturing and destroying the body a soul might be saved from perdition.  But the honesty inspiring this dreadful theory had no counterpart in the tenets of the Reformers.  Elizabeth was both "indifferent and intolerant" : Mary was intolerant, but she was zealous and faithful to the truth as she misunderstood it.

That Philip, and others scarcely less sensitive than he, could persuade themselves to witness with approval the diabolical policy of Burleigh and the Queen's advisers, makes a very unpleasant chapter in their histories.  Not merely do we find Philip and his friends eager to share the spoils accruing through fire and robbery, but we discover him absolutely dumb when hideous and sickening atrocities were committed.  He was not once eloquent on behalf of Maine, he raised no protest when Campion was put to the rack and then executed with twelve other priests, less famous but not less unfortunate than himself. Campion had put forth his case boldly and challenged the Universities.  This chivalrous daring stirred no sentiment of chivalry in Philip and others accounted brave and generous.  Yet Philip must have known that all Catholics were not implicated, and that the doctrines of Parsons were most keenly opposed by many loyal men who still clung to the old religion.

It may be urged, perhaps, that the very diversity of Philip's studies made it difficult for him to attain absolute pre-eminence in any.  The speculations of Giordano Bruno attracted his attention as we have seen, and he was willing enough to discuss the Italian's philosophy of doubt.  From this it has been argued that he was open · to new ideas, and there is a certain specious persuasiveness in the suggestion.  On reflection, the nugacity of such reasoning must be quickly seen. Doctrines of the Reformed Churches were not immediately menaced by the theory that the earth moved round the sun. Nor was the stability of the Catholic Church threatened by any such teaching, though unwise Catholics thought it was. Bruno had to pay the penalty too often inflicted on men who are in advance of their time. The penalty was cruel, ridiculous, and has been universally condemned. On the other hand neither Bruno nor Philip when discussing their high philosophies gave a thought to the unhappy men who were being disfigured, tortured, and executed near by them in the Tower. Assertions that Philip was tolerant underscore a real truth too deeply. Bruno's negative attitude towards Christianity interested him and he was tolerant towards the philosopher; towards those who stood for the Pope he was never even decently polite. To condemn, as he did, more than half the civilised world, and the head of that majority whom he spoke of always bitterly, is not a desirable performance on the part of a man who claims our admiration because of his tolerance. Still less is it agreeable evidence on behalf of such a quality that the candidate was un-moved to pity by the anguish of the martyrs, and showed an unbecoming readiness to enrich himself at their expense.

Grateful as were these rewards, they by no means satisfied Philip. He wanted money, and he wanted it very badly. The three years from 1582 to 1585 are not in the least interesting except episodically. I shall not attempt to deal with them in chronological order. A dignity was conferred upon him, which he certainly deserved, which, also, must have made his expenses considerably higher. Then, as now, the untitled made the decorated pay for their honours. There are a hundred and one reasons why Philip should have received the honour of knighthood.

For one thing his father could not afford to accept

the peerage offered to him, so Philip had no hereditary distinction to expect. His work had always been well done and was generally worth doing. Even when he was a bigot and a thief, neither character was suspected by himself nor his contemporaries. He was a fine poet; though his work was not printed it was already discussed and passed from hand to hand. The Queen had declared that knighthood was the highest honour she could bestow. So Philip became a knight, and succeeding ages have taken pleasure in emphasising his title. In fact, the barren honour was accorded him, not as a high-sounding and cheap reward for what he had done, but for the performance of a part assigned to him in a most silly ceremony.

The Queen had decided in 1579 to create Prince John Casimir a Knight of the Garter. The ceremony of installation having been delayed for four years she, or her ministers, thought it well to settle the matter. Therefore on January 13, 1583, the final details of the ceremony were arranged. The anniversary of the Queen's Coronation provided a suitable date. Prince John not being in England, a proxy had to be found for him, so his "Very dear friend" Philip was promptly chosen. It being necessary that a Knight of the Garter should be personated, on these auspicious occasions, by one who is himself a Knight, Philip was promptly accorded the requisite qualification. He could not evade the honour; it did him no good, it probably embarrassed him, and he had not sought it or desired it. The poet Dyer earned his knighthood in a similar manner.

A few months before this empty distinction was conferred, there had been grave discussion as to the wisdom of sending Sir Henry Sidney back to Ireland. Had he gone it would have made his fourth term of office. Lord Grey of Wilton, the retiring Viceroy, friend and patron of Edmund Spenser, had not added to his reputation. He meant well, he worked hard, he was no fool, and he was not unpopular. He lacked, however, some sort of quality, indefinable but necessary, to make his conscientious endeavours successful. Sir Henry appeared to be the only man fit for the post and was, in fact "the only man wished for here by the country people." A greater compliment than this wish, voiced by the Governor of Connaught, can hardly be desired or imagined. Sir Henry was not at all inclined to accept the offer. He was growing old, he was ill, and he felt he had been abominably used. Having duly weighed the suggestion he did not reject it immediately. Enthusiasm and alacrity he can hardly have been expected to evince; a blunt refusal would not have been astonishing. The position, however, seems to have presented itself to his mind as one giving him an opportunity to further his son's fortune. Cherishing this idea he expressed himself quite ready to undertake the arduous duties of Viceroy on certain conditions. These conditions he stated very frankly, as was always his wont, for he hated subterfuge, and if they were thought unreasonable he said he should refuse the distinction and continue his "quiet and contented life at home." First and most important of his stipulations, was an entreaty that Philip should accompany him to Ireland and eventually succeed him as Lord Deputy. If this request was granted he promised to go at once: if it were refused he could not be tempted by any bribe however glittering. A second demand was that his title should be no longer Lord Deputy, which he thought mean, but Lord Lieutenant. A third was a point-blank intimation that he expected a peerage, which he could have had before, together with a grant of land or a fee farm sufficient to enable him to maintain the proper dignity of so exalted a rank. To put forward these points required no ordinary courage. Probably Philip himself formulated them. The Queen was invited to consider a fourth proposition, more daring than any of the above. She was told in one simple

direct sentence that she must publicly acknowledge he
had done "as good service as any other rulers before
or since." Brave as these demands were, their acceptance would not have gone far towards paying off the
immeasurable debt Elizabeth owed to her illustrious
servant. She, with the meanness that always distinguished her conduct, ignored the whole letter, so neither
Henry nor Philip went to Ireland. The son found plenty
to do in Wales and in the general supervision of his
father's affairs.

Philip, doubtless, was not disappointed at the decision.
Ireland would have suited him as little as it suited
Spenser. How far he would have succeeded is one of
those amiable but useless speculations to which we have
before referred. It is not, however, too much to say that
he would have imperilled the reputation he now has had
he gone. Even had he continued his father's policy the
results would not have been satisfactory. A most curious
phenomenon presents itself to us. With all his chivalrous
courtesy and usual high motives, he was incapable of being
sympathetic or just to the Irish. He neither understood
them nor did he wish to understand them. Just he would
have been, his writings concerning his father's rule over
them show that; but sympathetic he could not be, many
scornful expressions prove his incapacity. Never so brutal
in his language concerning this unhappy people as, to his
eternal shame, was Spenser, it is yet of a nature to call
forth reproof and some disgust. He was far better fitted,
both by temperament and inclination, for the management
of Sir Henry's business and the unravelling of his complicated difficulties.

Of these filial labours, admirable and engrossing as
they must have been, it is not necessary to say anything. That he was eager and perturbed and unwell
is certain. More than one allusion is made to his health
in contemporary correspondence. He refers to it himself

in a letter to Lord Leicester in the December of 1582. He wished to be excused from all the Court festivities, and writes, just as a schoolboy might, to ask "whether I may remain absent from the Court this Christmastide." The Queen, of course, knew better than Philip or his doctors, and graciously refused leave of absence.

Her grateful subject presented the Queen's Majesty on the following New Year's Day with a golden flower-pot encrusted with diamonds, purchased by a portion of his ill-gotten three thousand pounds. A certain amount of correspondence occurred at this time (January, 1582), in which it seems that Philip expected to be joined with the Earl of Warwick, his uncle, as Master of the Ordnance. What the position exactly was, or what salary was forthcoming from it, is not very clear. That Philip was anxious to get the post is shown by his letters. Some mystery, too, is ingeniously invented as, " I pray you withal that for some considerations you will keep the matter secret." What the considerations were, why the matter had to be kept secret, and what the matter actually was are still respectable conundrums. An infinity of space has been occupied in discussing them ; so writers have been pleased, critics annoyed, and the average reader left wondering

Philip was anxious to obtain a position which carried a lucrative salary. He was, for example, a candidate for the post of Captain of the Isle of Wight. I have not been able to discover what increase of fortune he would have won by his nomination. The distinction sounds an empty one, but it must have possessed solid advantages, otherwise it is impossible to account for Philip's anxiety. He consulted his friend Dyer. Dyer writes to some purpose, and in view of Philip succeeding Sir Edward de Horsey, suggests that certain amendments in the patent should be seen to forthwith. One is led thus to think that the position must have been of real value, which belief is strengthened by the fact that he was not appointed. In-

stead he was made a General of Horse, a position no doubt
dignified but not remunerative.  He did, however, manage
to reap some reward in hard cash for his labours.  They
who most revere his memory can but wish such recompense had neither been offered or accepted.  Recusant
clergymen, of blameless life and spotless morals, were
driven to ignominious poverty, and their fortunes, such as
they were, a complacent Queen and Government ladled
out to a parcel of hungry favourites.  One historian
actually rubs his hands and talks of " this advancement,"
and chuckles the startling comment, " His merits as something more than a courtier were at length beginning to be
recognised."  Most people, we believe, on reflection, will
wish that Philip had not allowed his merits to be recognised in this way, and would feel happier in some proof that
he found his ill-gotten gains considerably more of a nuisance
than a benefit.

The year 1583 was important to Philip in another
serious matter.  He took unto himself a wife.  His choice
fell on a lady of marriageable age ; that is to say, were she
now living she would touch the mature period when a girl
leaves the nursery for the schoolroom.  The whole affair is
commonplace and prosaic and exasperating in its lack of
romance.  Why Philip wanted to marry is an impenetrable
mystery, which worthy writers have rendered still more
unfathomable by their explanations and apologies.  Money
was not the bait that attracted him, poor though he was,
for the lady was penniless.  Her father, the noble Walsingham, was poor in all but honour.  He and Sir Henry could
cry quits on pay-day, for their beloved Sovereign treated
them both with exemplary impartiality.  Philip had, it can
hardly be disputed, a genuine affection for the girl, whom
he had known most of the years that totalled up her short
life.  But he makes no pretence of overwhelming passion.
The lover and the poet are as calm as an ice block, and
decidedly less interesting.  Besides, Philip had been in love,

was in love, and remained in love.  The true object of his affections was not Miss Frances Walsingham, but Lady Rich.  A great deal has been written on this subject, and none of it to much purpose.  Commentators seem to have thought it their duty to prove, with irritating iteration, that on the whole he would have preferred the gatepost to Lady Rich.  It is necessary to speak out, because, for the most part, all the comments are so obsequiously tarred with humbug.  The matter will be dealt with in detail in the chapter devoted to a consideration of the sonnets.  Here it is only needful to say that Philip, like many another good man, loved a worthless woman.  In short, he was not an anchorite, and he could not have become so great a man had he been one.

How much Miss Walsingham knew, or considering her age understood, about Philip's liaison with Lady Rich might be interesting, is not revealed, and is not important. Let us remember Walsingham was not an insignificant father-in-law.  He was as poor, if not poorer, than the Sidneys.  But he had great power.  Considering that he was a very honest man the Queen was rather kind to him. A lively sense of favours to come, in consequence, probably figured most brilliantly amongst Philip's wedding presents. Any promotion Walsingham obtained quite certainly would mean a step for his son-in-law.  Even a hysterically importunate schoolgirl could not have wished for a more romantic husband.  Unfortunately for her, the husband was not romantic as regards his wife.  He treated her admirably; she seems to have been happy.  The real touch of romance is furnished by the Queen.  Having shown her appreciation of the Sidney family by a series of almost unparalleled insults, she decided to be offended because Philip wished to get married.  She was, or chose to pretend she was, engaged herself: Philip had never made love to her, nor she to him.  Philip's dislike of Anjou was emphatically expressed, but the hatred was the wholesome hatred of an Englishman, and not the puling imbecility of a rejected lover. Elizabeth, to feed her own silly vanity, chose to be disagreeable. Uncommonly disagreeable she was, too. She knew, no one knew better, that the marriage was likely to be a happy one, at least in the sense that it would not be unhappy. She knew, further, that it was an alliance smiled on by the two fathers, for both Sir Francis and Sir Henry were of " one heart." She knew the contracting parties had obeyed the sound advice not " to carry their love in their purses." Very good care had been taken to prevent a Sidney or a Walsingham amassing even moderate wealth. If the Queen had any inkling of Philip's affection for Lady Rich she could have shown her jealousy sooner. In any case, whatever sins the poet and his mistress may have committed, the "Virgin Queen" was the last person in the world who had the right to sit in judgment upon them. Elizabeth elected to be angry, and made herself cleverly disagreeable. Even the recollection of a gold flower-pot, studded with diamonds, if she remembered it, could not mollify her. She eventually forgave the offence, after giving as much trouble as afforded her amusement, and two and a half years after rode to London from Richmond, quite eight miles, to officiate as godmother to Philip's daughter. The child was called Elizabeth, a fine name, and the Queen gave the nurse and midwife five pounds between them. She does not seem to have given her god-child more than the customary blessing, and even that is not recorded.

Philip lived at Barne Elms with his wife's parents, but of what he did, read, thought, wrote, or dreamed not a single word comes to us. Information regarding his life severed from the domestic circle we have. It is not derogatory, and it does not call for praise. He seems to have lived very much the life of the barrister who leaves his breakfast to find a brief, or the stockbroker who discovers at the same meal that the postman has presented him with a gold mine. Over the more frequent days when these discoveries are only anticipated, I draw down the curtain. The Greeks would not permit murder on the stage; more convenient receptacles were provided for the performance in the bye streets of Athens or Corinth : and I most emphatically refuse to reveal the shifts some of us are put to. So the whole matter can be arranged in a common-sense sentence : " Sidney was ill, was very poor ; he was in love with a lady he could not marry, but quite prepared to wed some one else at the call of duty, and he was certain they would respect each other. The fathers of the contracting parties were excellent friends." That really is Philip's contract boiled down to intelligible terms. There is a vast amount of literature I could quote, on this period, but it does not help one either to understand Philip or his age. As a great historian once said, " Why quote what other people can read for themselves? You don't want to dispute facts, and if they make blunders it's quite cheap to be sorry."

During this period of Philip's life it is imperative to be sorry. No evidence is tendered that he made the faintest attempt to back that eminent Italian savant, Giordano Bruno. He got the " Trueness of the Christian Religion " twisted into some sort of English, but towards anything he could not understand he was always a very narrow-minded and petulant young gentleman. As public approval puts him in a place quite conveniently near to St. Matthew, St. Mark, St. Luke, and St. John— and if one is to believe rumour, he is rather better than any of them—it is just as well to say, frankly, what he was. Two lines convey the verdict ; it is this : " He was not a saint, and did not seek to be one ; he was a God-fearing, proud, imaginative, and unbusiness-like English gentleman." Such an epitaph is a fine one, and worth dying for. Philip's death brought him a better one. By it he was ranked above kings.

It is very silly to disguise all Philip's faults. They were not altogether bad ones; they are very intelligible and pardonable. But to present him as a hero who was, like the traditional Bayard, as "*sans peur et sans reproche*" is to coquet with folly. Nobody has ever yet been all this, and if the world is to continue fairly healthy we may hope nobody ever will be so immaculate. Why it should have been considered necessary to make Philip ridiculous, it is not for me to suggest. This I do know, that the earnest endeavours of somewhat rashly inspired enthusiasts do not make a historian's task very easy. Incidentally one may add that it makes his labour really distasteful because his verdict cannot, if honest, be popular. Philip was a great man, a good man, and a man who sometimes erred. We may rejoice that he was not the good boy of the Sunday School, or that he early went to heaven because the bullet of a kindly enemy sent him there.

Languet, when Philip judged a man harshly, remonstrated in this wise: "I am accustomed to judge of men otherwise than most persons; unless they are utterly depraved (for I do not think such men's vices ought to be concealed) I cull out their good qualities if they have any; and if through error or weakness they fail in any point, I put it out of sight as far as I can." He says that he learnt this lesson from Melancthon. Whoever was his tutor had wisely instructed him. Panegyrists should take to heart this temperate utterance. To "put it out of sight as far as I can" is a fair thing to do; but it is the extreme of folly to deny the existence of the probable and possible. By this attitude they convert into an epic what, at worst, was only an episode. In one matter, referred to elsewhere, Philip has scant reason for gratitude towards those who deny he committed what, harshly judged, was one fault and reasonably considered only an indiscretion.

I have written that there is no evidence that Philip attempted to back, or support, Bruno. The two were, however, frequently together, and there was acquaintanceship between them. Philip, however, was firmly convinced that Protestantism could alone save the world. No other solution of the mysteries that play with our lives and deaths, or reconcile or estrange the soul from God, was possible for him. Bruno was a free-thinker, and as such, better than a Catholic : more Philip would not have advanced in his favour. At the same time the Italian's scientific theories and expositions attracted him, and he knew enough of science to understand them. Meetings were held at the house of Fulke Greville " to discuss moral, metaphysical, mathematical, and natural speculations."

A demonstration was there given, on one occasion, of the startling truth that the earth moves. Bruno must have been deeply impressed with the part Philip took in these discussions, for to him were dedicated *Spaccio de la Bastia Trionfante* and his *Degli Heroici Furori*. "There is," he wrote in the dedication to the latter, "none more proper to receive the dedications of these discourses, excellent sir." Nor was there, great as was the compliment. In it one may read an implied disapproval of the learned men at Oxford, to whom he had lectured on the immortality of the soul and other great matters. Although patronised by the Earl of Leicester, these discourses were a failure. Professors and students showed themselves hostile, and the great man of science was justified in declaring them to be men of bad manners, bigots, and pedants. After the reception accorded to him by these ignorant people he must have rejoiced in the more liberally conceived courtesies of Fulke Greville and his friends. No detailed reports have come down to us of the debates on Ash Wednesday, 1584, and on other evenings. This is unfortunate, and a distinguished example of the truth that only the least vital facts of history are fully reported. Sixteen years later a crueller fate than inattention and contumely was Bruno's, than ever Oxford pedants devised. In that year his words were punished by worse than laughter and indifference. To the lasting disgrace of his judges and executioners he was burned to death for uttering speculations that are to-day recognised on all sides as crystallised truths.

But greater work than Bruno's was, in Philip's estimation, crying for his attention and active support. Du Plessis du Mornay had composed a volume which he entitled a "Work concerning the Trueness of the Christian Religion." Here was a subject that interested him more than a dissertation on the movement of the earth and the laws that might be supposed to control and direct that movement. This work, too, echoed, nay emphasised, the contempt and horror with which all Catholic claims should be regarded by every decent man.

So Philip, as we have seen, was not at all content merely to read the book and express, in a private letter to the author, his approval and congratulations. Mornay was a few years older than his English friend, yet he was the recognised leader of the Huguenots. It has been said, with no touch of exaggeration, that he was "already distinguished for his high Christian principles, his learning and his judgment." The friendship of the two men was deeply rooted in an unalterable affection. Their natures were singularly akin, their fortunes not dissimilar, their rank equal. Both had escaped the Bartholomew massacre, both were scholars of repute, both were trained courtiers, both eager in the Protestant cause. The treatise is nobly written and sincerely felt. Therefore his English comrade set about the translation of it into the English tongue, or, when his own could not be used employing the pens of others whose labours he edited. He was, indeed, at this time very busy and full of schemes. To him it was amazing that older statesmen should act with so much caution. His own idea was that active operations should be begun against Spain. A blow swiftly given was, in his eyes, a blow twice given. The power of Spain had to be destroyed : he did not live to see how effectually it was shattered by the stealthy policy his quick spirit condemned. He made no secret of his opinions, and never had sought to conceal them. If Spain could not be humiliated in one way he would attempt another. America offered a ,vast field for his activity. Spaniards might be ousted from their colonies, and their power weakened in Europe by loss of supplies. British colonies were to be founded, " so as either to stop his springs of gold and so dry up the torrent which carried his subduing arms and armies everywhere, or else, by the wakeful providence of threatened neighbours, force home that conquering metal with infinite charge." The sentence is somewhat involved, but its meaning is clear. On this occasion he, at any rate, cannot be charged with concocting a plan whereby he should enrich himself. When Languet had reproached him for being idle he was not idle, as a letter to his brother shows, dated 1580 : " Portugal we say is lost ; and to conclude, my eyes are almost closed up, overwatched with tedious business." His heart was with the Belgians in their struggle. Disgust and anguish at the apparent want of sympathy of his countrymen rendered him miserable. Whatever could be done by the activity of private persons to assist them, however indirectly, he was determined to bear a hand in. " Her Majesty," he wrote to Sir Edward Stafford, " seems affected to deal in Low Country matters, but I think nothing will come of it. We are half persuaded to enter into the journey of Sir Humphrey Gilbert very eagerly." Fulke Greville quaintly says,

"There were but two ways left to penetrate the ambitious monarch's designs" (Philip of Spain's designs),
"the one, that which diverted Hannibal, and by setting fire
on his own house, made him draw in his spirits to comfort
his heart ; the other, that of Jason, by fetching away his
golden fleece."

Gentlemen adventurers are not always quite so public
spirited as enthusiasts are disposed to believe.    They
are not fonder of empty pockets than their less courageous
contemporaries, no matter in how early or how modern
a period they seek to dazzle the spectator.   That Philip
had personal desire to replenish his purse is certain.   At
this particular date (1583) others were of a like mind.
Storms were gathering that would have to be faced ; these
expeditions might break their force, perhaps dissipate
them.   No doubt Philip talked matters over with his
brother-in-law, Christopher Carleill, and Humphrey Gilbert.   In the summer of 1583 Gilbert sailed for New-
foundland, where he was wrecked two months later,
leaving us the immortal phrase, " Courage, my friends,
we are as near to heaven by sea as on the land."

Philip had obtained a charter, somewhat earlier than the
setting out of this ill-fated expedition, by which he became
possessed of "thirty hundred thousand acres of ground
and wood, with all commodities, jurisdictions and royalties
both by sea and land, with full power and authority," for
himself and his heirs to do practically anything they
chose.   A delightful proviso in this stupendous deed
of gift is that it refers in explicit terms only to "certain
parts of America not yet discovered."   I suppose that
Philip had persuaded the Queen to make over this vast
empire, the better to show her contempt for the sovereigns
who, by boastful proclamations, were in the habit of
appropriating to their own uses any portions of the New
World that chance discovered, and denying the right of
others to so much as mention the existence of such places.

A solid value attached to the charter, for if it meant anything it meant that Elizabeth was, by witness of her own sign and seal, willing to help the explorer if his proceedings were interfered with. Had it not this meaning it is difficult to understand why Philip took such trouble to get the document prepared. However, no sooner were these nebulous regions granted to him, than he made them over, in some part, to Sir George Peckham "for the more speedy execution of her Majesty's grant and the enlargement of her Majesty's dominions and governments, for the better encouragement of Sir George Peckham and his associates in so worthy and commendable an enterprise, as also for divers other causes specially moving him." "Divers other causes" is as sufficiently clear a phrase as it is a cleverly vague one. What it means is simply that Spanish wings were to be clipped whenever a Spanish bird could be successfully netted. The deed invested him with an arguable authority to act as he chose, or to compel his representatives to act according to the instructions he gave them.

Philip was about to be married at this time, so was wise in obtaining his piece of parchment before the ceremony. Had he tried to sail for America the Queen would have peremptorily stopped him. Other work was at hand; it was becoming every day more clear that his good fight would be on a battlefield nearer home. His interest in colonisation was not restricted, for he helped Raleigh considerably with advice and had a fair word to say for Ralph Lane, an honest, impoverished, but somewhat incompetent person who accompanied the expedition to "take office as governor on land." The early history of Virginia presents the case for and against Lane; it is too long to tell here. His own words do not pronounce for his wisdom, but they redound to the Queen's discredit: "Having served her Majesty these twenty years, spent my patrimony, bruised my limbs, and yet nevertheless at this day not worth one groat by her Majesty's gift towards a living." This pitiable plea cannot be laughed at : that a worn-out and ruined man should be humiliated, that only by petition could he obtain such scurvy recognition as the promotion to the governorship of a wild province, after twenty years of adequate service, is far more disgraceful to the Queen and the cheerful historians of his failure, English and American, than it is to Lane.

# CHAPTER XII

## ZUTPHEN

Anjou's death—Orange murdered—Description of the Prince by a contemporary—English activity—The King of France shirks his responsibilities—Parliament adjourns for Christmas—Philip attacks the Jesuits—Is deceived by Gray—Master of Ordnance—Burleigh angry—Delegates from Holland visit the Queen—Philip would join Drake—Drake's treachery—The Queen's anger—Philip goes to Holland under Leicester—His difficulties—Troops not paid—His officers troublesome—Count Hohenlo—Rowdyism in camp—Leicester inefficient—Philip's rashness—His gallantry—His death—World-wide grief

TWO events happened in the summer of 1584 of great consequence to Europe. In June Anjou died, in July the noble Prince of Orange was foully murdered. Their deaths made instant change in the aspect of European affairs. Events pass very rapidly now for two years, and then Philip also died and the story ends. Anjou and Orange had been closely associated for a time, the unequal partnership having only been abandoned, to William's relief, a year before the Duke's death. High politics had appeared to demand the ill-assorted union. The noble Dutchman must have chafed under a yoke that bound him to a prince whose abilities were of the meanest and whose moral character shocked even those most willing to overlook a lapse from not too strict a standard of virtue. His falsehood and his folly were such that Henry IV. says of him : " Il a si peu de courage, le cœur si double et si malin, le corps si mal bâti, si peu de graces dans son maintien, tant d'inhabilité à toutes sort d'exercise, que je sçaurois me persuader qu'il fasse jamais rien de grand." Fortunately for Europe this objectionable mockery of royalty died in his twenty-ninth year. His aspirations to the English Queen's hand were discussed and debated to the last days of his life. Death prevented Elizabeth from further contemplating the possibility of a loathsome marriage. William's death was a calamity, the other's a grimly designed blessing. The whole hope of the Netherlands was centred in the person of the strong, wise, silent hero, who accepted defeat with equanimity and victory without boasting. Wise and brave in the council chamber, he was adroit and unflinching on the battlefield. Absolutely honest, his own welfare was as nothing compared to the good of his country. There have been few greater men in history. He cheered himself by some such motto as that of Rasselas : " When we pursue our end by lawful means, we may always console our miscarriage by the hope of future recompense." Ostentation of all sorts he abominated. Success he seldom had, but he often twisted a failure into a valuable semblance of victory, for he possessed in a marked degree a quality which Greville noted of the Germans, " that long breathed nation, where many strokes hardly leave any print." Strokes, however adverse, left him still feared, imperturbable and silently determined. We have a description of his dress when Philip first met him. " His uppermost garment was a gown, yet such as (I dare confidently affirm) a mean-born student in our Inns of Court would not have been well pleased to walk the streets in. Unbuttoned his doublet was, and of like precious matter and form to the other. His waistcoat, which showed itself under it, not unlike the best sort of those woollen knit ones, which our ordinary watermen row in ; his company about him, the burgesses of the beer-brewing town

(Delft)." Philip delighted in pageants, often proclaiming
the pleasure he derived from them. He was becomingly
splendid himself in demeanour and dress when a chance
occurred. But for these vanities William cared not, and
his simple, almost untidy, garments must have struck the
young visitor as strange wearing apparel for so great a
prince. Many a young courtier would have laughed at
and despised the homely figure. Philip, to his credit,
found his hero no less a hero because he wore, like his
faithful Delft brewers, the garments of an honest citizen.
He learned, too, that the simple Dutch brewers among
whom William moved so familiarly, were in reality sturdier
courtiers, fitter to attend on a great ruler than the elegant
Osrics of the Courts whom he had also seen. Polonius
advised Laertes admirably enough, but his words must be
taken to convey a meaning rather different to that the
chamberlain intended when he declared

"The apparel oft betrays the man."

Apathetic German princes could not be brought to understand the majesty of mind, the cautious courage, that
knew danger and avoided it if possible, yet faced it without
a tremor whenever necessary ; any more than they could,
or cared to, understand, that the biggest heart in Christendom beat beneath the rough fustian of the rather shabby
gentleman who could be seen daily, in peace time, strolling
up and down the decent streets of one or other of his
harassed cities.

William was not afraid of death, though his desire was
to live. Again and yet again attempts had been made to
kill him. He knew, none better indeed than he, that his
own would be a violent ending. Serenely at peace with
God, he pursued unswervingly and without complaint the
task allotted to him. It must have seemed a hopeless one
often enough, but if he thought it hopeless he kept his
thoughts to himself. He had signed his own death-

warrant when he proclaimed his belief in mutual tolerance and equal justice for men of differing faiths. The chances were all against a long life for a man daring to hold such liberal views. The story of his heroism cannot be told too often. His title of " Silent " was well chosen, for he never told what he knew and seldom confessed how much he suffered. He knew this, that he suffered chiefly because he was immeasurably in advance of his age. He had discovered that his attitude made him the target for attacks from all sides and all parties. In the words of Mr. Frederic Harrison: " Some Catholics could be brought to abstain from persecuting heretics ; but none could be brought to surrender the exclusive prerogatives of their own Church. Calvinists clamoured for protection and freedom, but they all used both as an engine to suppress Catholicism. Catholics could only endure Protestant worship in private, and provided it did not menace the Church ; and in like manner Protestants, where they were in a clear majority, strove to get rid of the Church altogether." William was an atheist, a Catholic a godless man in the eyes of all. Scarcely a sect or a person had a good word for him. His charity and tolerant sense were despised and calumniated. Then come the *Treaty of Arras*, by which the Southern provinces declared themselves irrevocably Catholic, followed by the *Union of Utrecht* binding the Northern States to Protestant creeds. Doubtless he had learnt what these treaties prove, and modern history has substantiated the proof, that the peoples of Belgium and Holland are as the poles asunder in ideas and aspirations. There can be no union between them. A kind of madness seems to have seized on the people. The cause and the man whom Philip loved were, indeed, *in extremis*. But the Prince stood superior to his perils. Vilest accusations of treachery, stories afloat and believed that he sought only his own welfare and aggrandisement, left him un-

moved. He brushed them aside as men do flies, and
with less show of temper. He could not be beaten by
any means, fair or foul. Yet Cardinal Granville, who had
made fervent protestations of friendship, devised a plan
whereby to silence him, "the very fear of it will paralyse
or destroy him." William was not to be paralysed; it was
less easy than it seemed to destroy him. This plan was
the offer of a vast sum of money to whomsoever should
take the Prince "dead or alive," and it was a plan that
won the King of Spain's adherence. Indeed, he was
enthusiastic, and published from Maestricht in 1580 his
Ban, at once famous and infamous. By this iniquitous
decree: "We interdict all our subjects from holding
converse with him." As though this were not enough,
the savage and morose Spaniard swore: "On the word of
a King and as minister of God we promise to any one who
has the heart to rid us of this pest and who will deliver
him dead or alive," no less than 25,000 crowns, a full
pardon for any offences the assassin may have hitherto
committed, and, above all, a patent of nobility. To this
abominable composition the Prince returned an answer so
scathing and dignified that its parallel is hard to find in all
history. "Adulterer, he calls me, who am united in holy
matrimony by the ordinances of God's Church to my
lawful wife—Philip, who married his own niece, who
murdered his wife, murdered his own son, and many
more, who is notorious for his mistresses and amours, if he
did not instigate Cardinal Granville to poison the late
Emperor Maximilian!" The tone of the reply is well
exemplified by this extract. From every charge in the
Ban he categorically and conclusively clears himself. He
says, and the words ring sincerely indeed, that he would
gladly die if his death spelt freedom for his people.
"These locusts of Spain," he declares, made him a Protestant, for he was bred a Catholic, and he adds: " I
confess that I sought my friends and nobles of the land

to resist these horrors, and I glory in that deed." Further he boasts : " He accuses me of being a demagogue, a flatterer of the people. I confess that I am, and whilst life remains, shall ever be on the popular side, in the sense that I shall maintain your freedom and your privileges." Such an answer, and there is much of it to the same effect, was not the kind of reply to pacify Philip of Spain and his Council. Let it be war and no quarter was its real meaning, while also it is a complete justification of everything the Prince had done. Moreover, it was a potent call to arms, and led almost immediately to a declaration of Independence by the States General. The Prince would take no ostentatious title himself, though he would face all risks accruing from his answer. His conduct at this time is a complete refutation of the charge that he sought out his own power and glory. The choice of Anjou, which he supported, was a hopeless one, but he hoped to be the shadow behind the throne and bring about a reconciliation between Catholic and Protestant. Neither his conduct nor his speech could be forgiven. For a reward of 80,000 franks, a Spanish merchant, who was insolvent, persuaded two of his clerks to attempt a murder. A foolish and fanatic youth, one Jagueray, protected by an Agnus Dei, a Jesuit catechism, and a toad skin, took a pistol and attended mass in Antwerp. When William was at dinner the murderer presented himself with a petition and, as he took it, shot him in the face and neck. When the unfortunate, deluded boy fell, for a dozen spears pinned him to the ground, the wounded hero cried aloud, " Do not kill him ; I forgive him my death." But the Prince recovered, and repented not a jot of deed or word. For many weeks his life hung on a thread. He would not allow his assassin, or the more cowardly accomplice, to be tortured. The Princess died of anxiety and fright. A second attempt, by one Balthasar, a Burgundian, was more successful. This man seems to have been a madman, but certainly not the less dangerous on that account.  He was a fanatic, and honest in his hideous folly.  On reaching Delft, under the name of Guion, he made ardent proclamation of his adherence to the Protestant cause and said he was the bearer of a despatch touching the Duke of Anjou's death. He must have acted his part with really consummate skill, for he was believed implicitly.  On being ushered into the Prince's bedroom, he discovered William in bed.  The two were alone, but the rascal had no weapon.  Foiled in his endeavour, his wits, such as they were, unhappily didnot desert him.  He procured a Bible, hung round the palace, and stoutly boasted of his Calvinism to all who would listen.  That he had suffered grievously and become a beggar for the cause was the gist of his story.  The tale reached William's ears, whereupon he ordered that Guion should be given twelve crowns.  Thus suddenly, and from so unexpected a quarter, possessed of money, he persuaded one of the guard to sell him some pistols.  The man stupidly, his suspicion not aroused, amazing though it seems, complied and a bargain was struck.  On July 10, 1584 the Prince dined, as he always did when he could, with his family.  As he left the hall and was proceeding to the staircase he received three shots in his breast, and fell mortally wounded.  His last words were, "God have mercy on my soul.  God save my people."  The murderer was seized, and soon after put to tortures as unnecessary, inhuman, and revolting as any the Inquisition contrived. William's horror of such punishment was forgotten or ignored.

When the Prince was made away with Philip forgot his promises.  He reaped what benefit he could from Guion's conduct, but shrank from handing over the promised reward.  The boy's family were, it is true, given a patent of nobility and were exempted from taxes.  Money to support the dignity was actually found on the victim's estate.  The murderer's relatives were rewarded by the gift of some property that had belonged to the Prince. Later these demesnes were restored to William's son, but they were charged with an annuity to be paid to the murderer's family. The foolish guardsman who sold Balthasar the pistols shot himself in despair when he heard the dreadful news. Incredibly stupid as was his conduct, his loyalty was not doubted. The ease with which the culprit gained weapons and access to the Prince is a striking, in this case a melancholy, proof of the simple and honest arrangements of the Dutch Court.

The deaths of William and Anjou stirred the English statesmen, of whom the Queen was not the least clever, for all her vanity, to unusual activity. Elizabeth felt that a mission should be sent to Paris to express the magnitude of her sorrow at Anjou's demise. What could be more natural and proper than an expression of grief and condolence from a bereaved queen? "The loss of so noble and worthy a friend," she felt, must plunge her into abyssmal woe. But there was a real, as well as theatrical, aspect to be considered. No harm could possibly be done by expressions of sorrow, however counterfeited, and Elizabeth had been regarded in Europe, with how much certainty and terror we know, as the future bride of the dead duke. Behind the ostensible reason for the suggested embassy of etiquette there lay a much more important consideration, and one that she had considered quite as carefully as her conduct during a most prematurely anticipated widowhood. Mr. Fox-Bourne suggests—and I think he is right, as he generally is—that Philip himself had drafted the form his instructions should take. Philip had been appointed to head the embassage of woe, about the most unpleasing duty he could have been asked to perform. Elizabeth had so ingenious a sense of humour and so retentive a memory that, reflecting his outspoken letter, her ready wit assigned him a position he could not refuse.

There was another reason which confirmed her view that
Philip was the right man for the office of spokesman to the
royal grief. William's death had advanced the Queen to
the position of undisputed head in Protestant Christendom. A Fabian policy could not be adopted much longer.
Henry III. of France, her expectant and woebegone royal
brother-in-law, was committed, by traditional hatred of
Spain, Anjou's partnership with William, the definite
anticipations of Holland and England, and his sympathy
with the sorrowing lady in her cruel affliction, to explain
his future policy with regard to the Low Countries. Also
he was asked to say precisely how much he was anxious
to spend. He was reminded that " those poor afflicted
people of the Low Country " needed assurance of most
prompt assistance, and that if this assistance was not given
the Dutch would perish, gloriously but certainly, along
with true religion, virtue, and liberty. Henry, a foolish
man, incapable of decisive action or a connected train of
thought, was rapped over the knuckles for lethargy in
that he had not prevented Spanish impertinence, and was
told bluntly that once Flanders and the Low Countries
were in his hands, Philip of Spain would appear as the
most potent king Europe had ever known, and that, with
the advent of his power, the danger to France, too late,
would be fully understood. With a message couched in
these terms to deliver, Philip was quite willing to perform
the ceremonial part of his duties. Considerable preparations were completed and a beginning of the journey was
made. He was an adept in bearding personages, an adept
in uttering wholesome truths ; it is just possible that, on
second thoughts, he enjoyed the prospect of his journey.
Henry III. did not, and showed so emphatic a dislike of the
whole performance, that he retreated to Lyons, and from
this fine city courteously offered to receive the deputation
on his return to Paris two months later. Here was an
impossible suggestion. The members of the embassage

returned to London, each member considerably out of pocket. Philip must have been appreciably poorer. This starveling creature, Henry, has been once and for all pertinently described by Walsingham as "a king who seeketh nothing but to impoverish his poor people and to enrich a couple, who careth not what cometh after his death so that he may roam about while he liveth." It is not too much to say that he was frightened of the responsibility that had fallen on his shoulders, that he did not care to tackle truths uncompromisingly stated, refused to hear them, and therefore retired hastily to Lyons. All of his career that concerned Philip is summed up in Walsingham's sentence. It would have been well for others had it ended for them so suddenly; but he managed to drag through a few miserable years. His life was not long in the land. He was a passing inconvenience.

Meanwhile a general of undoubted capacity was taking further advantage of the tribulation that beset his opponents. Philip's new viceroy, Alexander Farnese, Duke of Parma, was a general of real ability, and knew how to plant a bribe skilfully. His successes at Ghent, Dendermonde, and a dozen other places showed that he was a man to be reckoned with. Who should be his antagonist was a difficulty less easily solved. Spain was in the ascendant again, forming the first person in the unholy trinity that comprised Rome and "the Jesuitical faction of France."

Parliament met late in November, 1584, and talked for nearly a month. Then six weeks' holiday was taken to tide over the Christmas festivities and allow time for a becoming recovery. The House met again on February 4th, and dissolved on the 29th of March for an indefinite holiday. A better comment on the absurdity of Parliamentary proceedings it would be difficult to find. Every man had in his mind the gravity of the situation in Europe, every man knew Philip was earnest to unravel or, if need

be, cut the knot.   So he was employed on evasive committees to decide as to the best way of preserving timber
in Kent and Sussex, to give a common juryman's opinion
as to how Rochester bridge should be preserved, and to
take a friendly interest in the local woes of the carriers
whose Company's complaints called for examination.

There were, none the less, debates of supreme importance.   He could leave a committee-room to join in them
with fervour, and probably did.   The ardour of the orators
in these debates was directed against the Jesuits.   This
unfortunate Order has been more misunderstood and more
maligned, through ignorance, than any communion of men
known to modern history.   I am not a Jesuit, but I find
nothing in any evidence against them much more substantial than a soap bubble.   They were, as they always
have been, amazingly clever.   I have seen them at work
in Eastern countries.   I have heard from eye-witnesses the
dangers the fathers ran, and these without a complaint.
But Philip, and there was excuse for him, believed, as
people believe now, for whom there is no excuse, that there
is nothing so bad but that it belongs to them by a devilish
system of primogeniture, with Satan as the founder of the
family.   The abuse hurled at them consists of a perversion
of doctrines they never held.   No historian can pretend
that they have not committed mistakes ; on the other
hand no historian, who values evidence, can suggest that
they sought only their own advancement.   But historians,
like " even the youngest among us," are not infallible.   No
set of men can show so splendid an army who stood up for
all that was good and right ; the one true accusation
against them is, that they meddled in politics.   Herein
they shared a blunder with Calvin.   The weapons they
faced in Sidney's day were, as now, misrepresentations of
their sayings, which have become recognised beliefs among
the common people.   Though founded by a man who sat
lowest on the lowest form in a village school, among dirty

village children, eager to be taught, they have continued to teach, and to teach with unequalled success. So much must honestly be accorded to the credit of an Order which any outsider, not wholly ignorant of history, must, at least, respect.

Philip took a very active part in the House of Commons in support of a Bill against the Jesuits. So violent were the provisions of this measure that the Lower House passed it almost unanimously, thereby giving the Upper House a chance of asserting itself and sending it back to the Queen's "faithful Commons." The decision at last arrived at by both Houses was sufficiently stringent. "Excessive Puritanism" was advanced as a reason for the rejection of the first Bill; its extreme moderation when amended is scarcely obvious from a careful study of each detail in the Act approved by both Houses. Within forty days all Jesuits, seminary and other priests, were required to leave England ; if they refused to do so they became traitors. The penalty inflicted on men adjudged traitors was well understood. Harbouring or helping a felon, if the delinquent in an act of mercy was discovered, meant barbarous treatment. Finally, those gentlemen who had gone abroad to study must return to England within six months, make submission humbly, or be deprived of every penny they possessed.

Philip gave this wicked Bill his unflagging support. To those who hold no brief for the men attacked, it is monstrous as an example of what Protestantism, when in power, thinks it may do with impunity. To the unbiassed student it proves how easily men may make a better cause appear the worse. The reasons for the hastening forward of the Bill are amusing. Affairs in Scotland were advanced as an argument, and it was an argument believed in by the people who advanced it. Mary, Queen of Scots, had been in prison for eighteen years. Her son reigned in her stead, and was even then the silly tool of the favourite

who flattered him most adroitly. It was a very unpleasant, very self-satisfied, very learned, and very absurd
man who adorned the Scotch throne. His learning got
him some distinction, even in an age when men and
women knew their Greek and Latin. Walsingham had
summed him up : to do him a favour was to earn his
ingratitude ; he never told the truth, though he always
declared he spoke nothing else ; he dallied with his
religion, and he was a bully and a coward. This
miserable person was next heir to the throne of England.
He was clever enough, however, to employ a pleasant-
spoken gentleman as his ambassador. An idea was abroad
that the Spanish plotters, who hoped for England's overthrow, were to get their work done through a Scotch
agency. There does not seem to have been much truth
in the rumour. That, probably, is why it was believed.
Anyhow, Gray, an arch-hypocrite, was sent to England
to lie, and he lied splendidly. He seems to have impressed
Sir Philip Sidney greatly. Philip cannot be blamed ; he
could not know that Gray was playing for his own hand,
was a grandly titled adventurer, and regarded as fish all
that came into his net, whether Pope, Emperors, Kings, or
Queens. One of the first things he did on his arrival in
London was to announce his abhorrence of the Catholics,
or, as he called them, Papists. That he was a Papist he
kept to himself. His mission was to hoodwink everybody
and get the best terms he could for his master, whom he
must have laughed at in his dissolute sleeve. There is but
little evidence, if any, to show that James was even
cognisant of any Catholic plot ; on the other hand, there
is all probability to show that he would have disliked a
successful one. He could hardly remember his mother, if
he remembered her at all. He posed as King of Scotland
while the Queen was still alive. Had she been released
his vanity would hardly have made a secondary place
endurable. However, he was shrewd enough to see, he

was always shrewd in money matters, that something might be made out of convenient rumour. The master of Gray was his efficient ambassador. How well this Scottish nobleman did his work there is plenty of evidence to show. He made a long stay in London and saw Philip often. When he returned north of the Tweed he writes : " I commend me heartily unto you, and will you do to all my friends in my name, but chiefly to Sir Philip Sidney." What Gray got for himself is not on record. It was probably considerable. He got for his master the offer of a very substantial pension, on the trivial consideration that he would not support the Spanish King's leagues. He acquired, also, a present of horses, which James clumsily endeavoured to ride and manage, " to the great contentment of himself and his courtiers." His courtiers no doubt laughed consumedly in secret.

Official worries were also Sir Philip's lot at this date. For some time he had virtually been, as we have seen, and was now duly accredited as, Master of the Ordnance. The appointment dates from July 21, 1585. Only two months before he obtained the position he had been compelled to speak out plainly concerning the impoverished condition of the stores. He made his complaint, it would seem, directly to the Queen. That it was based on solid foundation is demonstrated by the fact that the great Lord Burleigh himself had to bear the brunt of the royal anger. Lord Burleigh did not relish censure ; he was too accustomed to abusing others to take a reprimand kindly. From Sir Philip, who was now a person of authority, yet at one time merely his suggested son-in-law, this snub was additionally unpleasant. The old man became very angry ; in his opinion a Lord Treasurer was too great a personage to accept a scolding. Sir Philip received a curt letter, in which he was reminded how sacred a person a Lord Treasurer was and how far removed from menial criticism and human error. Philip answered the letter when he was obviously in a hurry.    An immediate answer, there can be no doubt, was expected, and a prompt reply was sent.    This reply is a note written or dictated under pressure of affairs requiring more careful consideration than the composition of a letter intended to pacify an irate old gentleman.    For once a scholar who knew so well how to write put his signature to a document almost devoid alike of grammar and of style.    Burleigh is told that somebody must be blamed " for faults in the office," that no imputation was necessarily cast on Cecil himself, that the faults were grave and required immediate attention, that the Earl of Warwick and the writer of the letter had done no more than their duty in revealing to an august lady the shortcomings of the Ordnance Department, for which they themselves were nominally responsible.    Such, I take it, translated into the best English at my command, is the meaning of Philip's reply to his powerful kinsman.

The moment was not happily chosen for Burleigh's outburst of anger.    Philip did not feel called upon to treat it with more than a hasty civility.    Fulfilment of all he had hoped and prayed seemed at hand ; for the realisation of his dreams a well-found arsenal was an essential.    A Dutchman's safety at this moment was of more importance than the dignity of a Lord Treasurer.

Early in the spring of this year, sacred to Burleigh's anger, certain deputies from the Low Countries visited Paris.    They had a petition to present to the King of France and the Queen Mother.    Honest men, as they were, sensible business men too, such as we know delighted William, they could not expect much help from a fool and a bad woman.    Henry not long before had retreated to Lyons, the better to evade unpleasant questions.    On this occasion he was called to face his accusers, for their entreaty was an accusation, and answer their minatory question.    Antwerp, so these stolid Lowlanders declared, was undergoing a siege, now many months old. The city could hold out no longer unless prompt help was vouchsafed. Further, they declared that they looked to France for help, and had a right to look to France. French help not being forthcoming, they would look elsewhere. Henry did not approve of these plain-speaking brewers from Delft. The Florentine woman abetted his resentment and showed her own. Disgracefully treated by the descendant of a moneylender and a puny King, the stolid burghers left Paris for London. They had arrived not long before Philip Sidney saw fit to brush aside the anger of Lord Burleigh. With their great concerns he was concerned when he wrote his ungrammatical letter to the omnipotent Cecil.

On the 29th of June the Queen received the delegates at Greenwich. In her they had a sympathetic audience. They were lucky in their spokesman, who at once caught the royal ear, for he was an orator, and also in his way a clever flatterer. He described the awful danger that threatened the Dutch States, explained how brave a fight was being made for their liberty and the liberty of all Protestants. Then he told her that an afflicted people looked confidently to her in the hour of need. Should she help them, all Christendom, immortal fame, and the approval of God Himself, she was assured, would contribute to her reward. In addition to these sufficient honours the sovereignty of the Netherlands was laid at her feet. After listening carefully, and with the courtesy she could splendidly exhibit on occasions, and occasions such as this became her greatly, she gave a dignified and right royal answer. She could not, she said, accept the crown offered to her; she was pleased at the offer and did not disguise her pleasure, and she promised immediate help in men and money. As soon as possible arrangements were made by which an army of six thousand men was

to be despatched to the Netherlands; the cost of maintenance was to be borne by England. Care was taken
that the English general should be granted a place in the
Council of the States, and it was agreed that Flushing,
Rammekins, and Brielle should belong to the Queen until
such time as the Spaniards were beaten and the necessary
expenses of the war liquidated. To many it must have
seemed the dawn of a new era. The Dutch were popular,
their cause was felt to be the cause of all freedom-loving
men, their heroism was the talk of the world. Unfortunately a bad choice was made in the appointment of
the Earl of Leicester to command the English contingent.
The Earl has been frequently abused, sometimes unfairly.
He was vain and not a martyr to conscience; what
scruples he had he could swallow comfortably when
necessary; his religion was more fashionable than
serious. He would have changed it as readily as his
doublet for a pecuniary consideration. "A bird in the
hand is worth two in the bush" would have suited him
for a motto, and he considered the privileges of heaven
might be prepared for by filling a comfortable seat on
earth. He was worse, but not much worse, than the
majority of men. It was against him that he held a high
rank, with the result that his defects have at times been
made to seem bigger than they were. There can, however, be no doubt that he was shockingly incompetent as
a general. Personal valour he had, but in military skill
he was a dunce and a conceited dunce. Philip was to
go with his uncle and take up his duties as Governor of
Flushing. Apparently he somewhat disliked the task;
at any rate, he does not appear to have exhibited much
enthusiasm. Firmly convinced as he was that Spain
should be attacked through her colonies, he seems to
have concluded that operations in Holland were a waste
of men and money. Fulke Greville says of him at this
time, " He found greatness of worth and place counter-

poised by the arts of power and favour ; the stirring
spirits sent abroad as fuel to keep the flames far off, and
the effeminate made judges of danger which they feared,
and honour which they understood not." To whom or to
what this passage refers is a little uncertain. When Fulke
Greville becomes eloquent he is apt to be obscure. But
it is clear that Philip objected to the policy and to the
men chosen to advance it. He had, too, schemed out and
settled a West Indian project, which he was very unwilling
to abandon. He had learned from Lane a glowing account
of St. John and Hispaniola, and was quite willing to undertake an expedition in which, Lane assured him, only he
was fit to be leader. Flattery, however, though he was
probably no more averse to it than other men, to move
him had to be backed by solid reasons. These reasons,
the humbling of Spain, the destruction of the Catholics,
were a powerful incentive. Poor man though he was,
he had subscribed largely towards the building of a fleet
to attack the Spaniards wherever they could be found.
Thirty gentlemen, influenced by his pleading, joined him
in the enterprise. Sir Francis Drake was chosen leader
of the expedition.

Some apology seems to be needed for his conduct in
the matter. Philip thought the Queen would object to
his participation in the adventure. A secret contract was
therefore entered into with Drake by which, once the fleet
had set sail, he and Sir Francis became co-admirals. Fulke
Greville also was to be assigned a high position of trust.
Absolute secrecy as to Philip's and Greville's movements
was to be observed. Towards the end of August the ships
were ready, and Drake sent word to Philip and Greville
that they were to join him at Plymouth. A certain Don
Antonio, a claimant to the Portuguese throne, but otherwise of no importance, was due in Plymouth about this
time. Being the friend of Philip and Greville his arrival
offered the necessary excuse for their departure from

London. Drake was in no hurry to sail, and does not seem to have wanted the two friends aboard his ships. His motives are difficult to fathom, but whatever they were he acted very unscrupulously. The younger men were eager and full of hope. " As we lay abed together," Greville tells us, he and his friend discussed their scheme and rearranged the world according to matured plans of their own drawing. Drake was also arranging plans, and in their execution the two men who had so generously supplied him with money were not needed. He sailed away without them, having first carefully warned Elizabeth of the intentions of the truants. The Queen was furious and sent three letters. In one she told Drake that he was not to allow Philip to sail ; in a second she warned the Mayor of Plymouth that it would be well for him to keep the runaways within sight ; Philip she treated as a naughty schoolboy, and ordered him to return to her without delay. It is not on record what Philip said when he made his peace with the offended Queen. On September 21, 1585, peace was signed between them, and in the following November he was taken into such exalted favour that he was created Governor of Flushing and called upon to serve under Lord Leicester who, with no qualifications, but considerable pluck, took up the responsibilities of a Commander-in-chief.

Philip followed his uncle to Holland and did his duty as best he could. He was very young, and he had faced disappointment often enough to anticipate Burns's verdict on the best laid schemes of mice and men. The work he was called upon to do required neither initiative nor conspicuous talent. The last chapter in Philip's life is a very sad one—not because it is the last chapter, there is a last chapter in every one's life, but because he was employed on work a haphazard handful of men could have done as well or better. Limited opportunities sufficed to provide material for a record of his dignity, courage, and ability. But all his energy was quite uselessly spent: Spain was being fought in the wrong way. He knew this.

We have some memorials of his movements, and proof enough that he was a valiant soldier and a great captain. Although he could not pay his men their wages, his followers loved him. He could not, as he complains, "command by authority," but he managed to command by love. His behaviour at Axel not only won for him the generous applause of friend and foe, it stamped him as the most chivalrous and fearless man in Europe. Moreover, his plans in the action won the applause of men of experience, and men opposed both to him and the cause he was supporting.

Various bickerings agitating the Netherlands were, if unavoidable, at any rate rather foolish. Leicester, in safety, played the general, and Philip, who knew his time was being wasted, was killed. It should always be remembered that Philip was little more than a boy when he died. He was very often wrong, and therefore often delightful, as most boys are. But it must be recognised that he risked everything for what he conceived to be right, and if sometimes his judgment failed him he was never mean and never did a paltry action. His contemporaries might be angry with him, they could not despise him; they had to respect him; even the Catholics, with Philip and Mendoza at their head, led the pæan of subdued applause that followed a most noble gentleman to his grave. A characteristic touch is that those who helped him most he paid out of his own pocket. Elizabeth with wordy generosity had made fine promises to the stalwart burghers. She had not the slightest intention of spending sixpence on helping one of them. She had great qualities, for which she has been overpraised; she had contemptible faults which have been overlooked. Philip found himself in the Low Countries, where he did not wish to be, with no money in his pocket and an army to support. There is only one letter of his, I find, in which he even so much as hints at his troubles. There were a few skirmishes to get through, and the Protestant cause was just about as much advanced as if he had gone to Virginia. He was sent to Flushing and was expected, he tried to believe it, to understand that Elizabeth was a woman honest people could respect. She was a very wicked and vain old person, and one of her most splendid victims was Sir Philip Sidney. She never read the Bible herself; Philip did, and translated the Psalms into decent English. Moreover, he built his life on the precepts he found there. Elizabeth found the Bible a convenience, hugged the book to her heart on a processional occasion, and on the whole played her part cleverly. It is rather sad that such a woman was the indirect murderess of such a man. There is no difficulty in the finding of this opinion; public libraries are free and disseminate diseases without opposition. With all the proofs in their hands historians choose, for their own purposes, to apologise for a thoroughly bad woman, who by paying tribute to her vanity killed a good man. That is really the summing up of the whole matter. Philip's death at Zutphen has passed into history, and what is truer than history, into poetry. The details are sordid enough; for the sake of historical accuracy the few dates may be given.

Philip could not look to Leicester for help in money, and was greatly distressed, for he feared that his soldiers would mutiny. His personality, however, impressed them so powerfully that they followed him gladly, and understood their lack of pence was not due to his neglect of their interests. He felt that even their loyalty might be unduly tested, and wrote bitterly, "We are now four months behind, a thing unsupportable in this place."

The society of his fellow-officers was uncongenial. Their cruelty was as wanton as ever that of the Spaniards

had been. We learn of the useless destruction of a defence-
less and peaceable village, and the brutal butchery of some
rough peasants. These brilliant feats of arms alienated his
sympathy, and sickened him of a war conducted on such
unchivalrous lines.

Moreover, he not only had to defend himself from a
declared and honest enemy, he found himself called upon
to interfere in drunken quarrels amongst his friends, men
of high birth, whose conduct must have deeply edified the
common soldiers. One of these disputes, though nothing
came of it but a broken head, has been as much related as
the battle of Agincourt, certainly as much as one of Cæsar's
campaigns, save when the distinguished Roman decided to
celebrate his successes through the powerful trumpet of his
own pen. Schoolboys would prefer to read about the
quarrel ; it is more dramatic. Like many of the apparently
trivial episodes of history, it throws a powerful light on the
manners of the times, and proves once again that an anec-
dote is better worth possessing than the most learned treatise.
A certain Mrs. Horley, so that delightful and strangely
neglected author, the late Rev. Mr. Pyecroft, assures us,
once annoyed her husband beyond endurance, and he
threw a teacup at her. Mrs. Horley, not to be outdone in
a sensible argument, responded promptly and accurately
with a saucer. By the aid of this simple story we are permitted to understand Mr. and Mrs. Horley. The pages of
careful, and very witty and entertaining criticism, which
this very witty and entertaining author devotes to a minute
study of the Horley characteristics, are not nearly so
illuminating as the bare recital of a cup and saucer
comedy.

Historians, like others, have their failings, but it is incumbent on them, even as is the case with other poor
though genteel individuals, to keep up appearances.
Therefore it will be noticed that they seize on a likely anec-
dote eagerly, as a drowning man exhibits unexpected but

emphatic affection for a straw.  Dr. Johnson called these
trivialities "airy gratifications."  It is comforting to know
that so noble a man consoled his self-respect by abusing
the particular vices his own compositions show he most
superbly patronised.  He declared, with all the authority of
a pope, " The general and rapid narratives of history, which
involve a thousand fortunes in the business of a day, and
complicate innumerable incidents in one great transaction,
afford few lessons applicable to private life "; he proceeds
to quote Pliny : but he evidently thought private life more
important and instructive than public life, which is, after
all, a clumsy way of touching pitch."  Unfortunately, most
historians are less honest than the genial dictator whose
worth Boswell first discovered and students of to-day
begin to understand.  The doctor would have said to Count
Hohenloe : " Sir, you are drunk," and having silenced that
exalted personage would have proceeded to explain how
inebriated he himself could become if occasion offered, and
had therefore decided that thirteen cups of tea should, at
one sitting, be the limit of his excesses.  Beyond these
narrow bounds he never strayed.

Count Hohenloe murdered a few people, whose names he
did not know : this daring feat accomplished, he returned
to camp for supper.  He drank a good deal of wine, it
travelled to his head and he became abusive.  Unluckily a
Pelham and a Norris were supping with the Count, and
their respective relatives were not on visiting terms.  What
the quarrel was has long ago been forgotten.  The claret
was sound and generously distributed.  The three men
lost their tempers, and the Count swore to some purpose.
He came to the conclusion that his oaths were not so effec-
tive as the gilt top of a decanter : with this elegant weapon
he tapped Norris on the head ; then a dagger was drawn,
and the combatants, at Philip's orders, were removed to
their respective tents or quarters.  In essentials the quarrel
reads like one between angry and not quite responsible

undergraduates. What is not sufficiently understood is that Count Hohenloe committed a folly, but was a man of worth no less noble than his breeding, which ranked him beside princes. Norris and Pelham were silly, but they were gentlemen. In our own day they would have still been at Pembroke, Trinity, or the House, a kindly dean would have told them of their folly, and sent them " down " for the benefit of their college and themselves for one term. But these were the men who led the Protestant cause, and whom Philip had to rely upon in his struggle with Spain.

Flushing was a prison. What Philip would do he could not, even in his own jurisdiction. His limited powers were still further limited by the means to exercise them. " Bad begins, but worse remains behind," was his continual lament. He had no power to direct the course of events, and his heart was sad because he saw that those who had the power were wickedly incompetent. Once he managed to escape from his captivity with Prince Maurice, who was worthy to be his father's son, and attacked the near town of Axel. The result of this expedition was brilliantly successful. Perhaps their elders disliked the achievement, for they had not been consulted. Within the walls of Flushing he won a more difficult victory by reconciling Count Hohenloe and Leicester. Hohenloe was a much greater man than the English Earl, and as high, if not higher, in rank. But he was a bluff soldier, and could not endure fopperies and make-believe. To neither man can the word "genius" be applied, yet it was vitally necessary to make them friends. Leicester, however inadequately, stood for England ; the Count was Lieutenant-General to Prince Maurice. Hohenloe was at least in earnest and by all accounts a fine soldier; Leicester knew nothing, and had accomplished less. Philip managed, by some gentle persuasion of which he had the secret, to reconcile the two men. " A brilliant career was now opening before Sir Philip Sidney, but it was to be a brief one." The career suggested was so brief

that it did not exist. At thirty-two he was called
upon to bid farewell to a life that had been brilliant.
The sentence of the Oxford historian is curious, the end of
his preface to Languet's letters is more curious. Here it
is: " And if he must needs fall in battle, though Zutphen
was truly a brave affair, and long remembered for the
obstinacy of the contest, Philip Sidney would have found
a more worthy termination of his honourable life by the
side of Gustavus on the plain of Lutzen." If Philip had
to fall, no better field than Zutphen could have been
chosen. It gave him distinction. On a field where no great
heroes were employed, one great hero died. A small battle
and a small victory kept an apparently invincible enemy
at bay. And Zutphen, by the glamour it threw over
Philip's heroic death, did more for his cause than if he
died as one only of many gallant gentlemen fighting by
the side of the King of Sweden. His efforts proved, if
proof were needed, that in the worst hour of defeat and
terror brave men and convinced men neither lost their
courage nor their convictions, be the enemy never so
mighty, so long as they could still hold sword and shield.
The fatal affray was chiefly due to Leicester's incompetence
and a lazy appreciation of his duties as commander-in-
chief. But Philip, by an action chivalrously foolish
contributed to his own death.

There seemed every prospect that Zutphen would soon
fall into the hands of the besiegers. On the 21st of September, however, news came to the camp of the allies that a
large stock of provision was being sent to the town, and
would be smuggled within the walls under cover of darkness. The messengers of these tidings may have been
thanked, but were certainly not cross-examined. How
much they knew, or on which side their sympathies lay, is
not known. Leicester, however, must have been most
childishly simple if he thought that the astute and brilliant
Parma would neglect to assure the reasonable safety of

the convoy, though he understood the extreme incom-
petency of his adversary. Expecting to find Leicester
napping, the Spanish general found his expectations
realised. The food-carriers were protected by nearly three
thousand picked men, the most tried and dangerous
soldiers in Europe. So ignorant was the English courtier
that he fondly thought a body of two hundred horsemen
and three hundred pikemen was a force sufficient to
prevent those who would relieve the town. This meagre
army was augmented at the last moment, without orders it
would seem, by some fifty men of rank who wished, with
youthful enthusiasm, to be in the fighting-line. Amongst
the eager Philip was conspicuous. Any peril these people
ran was voluntary and hasty. Sir William Pelham, in his
hurry, could not find his leg armour, or did not trouble to.
Philip very absurdly thereupon discarded his own. It is
difficult to understand or apologise for such folly. He
knew, and Languet had always told him, how valuable his
life was to the cause. With reasonable luck he could have
lived for it, foolishly he died for it. His absurdity was
splendid, none the less it was absurdity. Moreover, it was
not kind to his reputation for sobriety of conduct. At
thirty-two Sir Philip Sidney became for a moment a
schoolboy. An impetuous and silly freak cost him his life.
The actual fight was not of long duration. On either side
was valour, but on one side only was discipline and fore-
thought. These qualities were not Philip's allies.

While it lasted the fighting was of a desperate character.
But the Protestant allies, individually brave, seem to have
fought without a leader, and followed no general plan of
battle. Hurling themselves promiscuously against a
superior and well-disciplined army, admirably led, they
courted disaster. Philip, though insufficiently armed, was
no wiser than his fellows. Without definite plan to guide
him he plunged into the thick of the fight. His "very
friend, and indeed a valiant and frank gentlemen," was

discovered by him in sore straits. Surrounded by the
enemy, the young lord appeared to have little chance of
escaping with his life. Philip called a few gentlemen to
him, and at the third charge they extricated their friend
from his dangers. Philip, however, in one of those curious
and not frequent fits of impulse that made drunk his judgment, rode too near the walls of the town. The risk he
ran was unnecessary, the consequence of his bravado was
fatal. Stow, in the then language of universal eulogy, says
that his conduct was " a wonder to see." This is probably
no overstatement, but a battlefield is not the proper setting
for ill-directed deeds of daring. The wound was in the
left thigh, and does not at first seem to have been considered necessarily fatal. That it was very serious, however, was at once recognised. Leicester, it is solemnly
reported, said, " Oh ! Philip, I am sorry for thy hurt," and
the wounded man answered bravely, " This have I done
to do you honour and her Majesty service." These
heroics do not blind us to the fatuity evinced by Philip
and others in attempting, without sufficient consideration,
a dangerous task, one not worth a tenth of the risks they
so carelessly ran. That Sir William Russell was moved to
tears is to his credit, but his eulogy of Philip's exploit, when
coldly considered, must be accounted exaggeration. " Oh,
noble Sir Philip, there was never man attained hurt more
honourably than ye have done, or any served like unto
you." Noble and honourable beyond the common the
dying man was, but he had by imprudence sacrificed a
noble and an honourable life.

An immortal passage in Greville has made a glorious
episode immortal : " The horse he rode on was rather
furiously choleric than bravely proud, and so forced him to
forsake the field but not his back, as the noblest and fittest
bier to carry a martial commander to his grave. In which
sad progress passing along by the rest of the army, where
his uncle the general was, and being thirsty with excess of

bleeding, he called for drink, which was presently brought him, but as he was putting the bottle to his mouth he saw a poor soldier carried along who had eaten his last at the same feast, ghastly casting up his eyes at the bottle; which Sir Philip perceiving, took it from his head before he drank, and delivered it to the poor man with these words, 'Thy necessity is greater than mine.' And when he had pledged this poor soldier, he was presently carried to Arnheim."

There are several accounts of the sixteen days during which Philip lingered. Perhaps that of Dr. Zouch is the best. From this narrative we read that he was grateful to God in that the mischievous bullets had not fulfilled their mission more expeditiously. God, he declared, chastised him, "with a loving and fatherly coercion." He accused himself of having walked in "a vague course": some men, he contended, would face death happily full of the knowledge that they had served God well. He refused to console himself by any such reflection. "It is not so in me," he exclaimed. "I have no comfort that way; all things in my former life have been vain, vain." These are the ravings of fever, as also was his description of himself as a poor worm. But the pitiful sentences have been preserved. He cared for music to the last, and hearkened to it with pleasure. When many thought that he was dead Mr. Giffard spoke to him as follows: "Sir, if you hear what I say, let us by some means know it, and if you have still your inward joy and consolation in God, hold up your hand; with that he did lift up his hand and stretched it forth on high, which caused the beholders to cry out with joy, and so at last he yielded up his spirit into the hands of God unto his most happy comfort."

Philip died, as he had lived, an honourable Christian gentleman. The minute accounts of his last hours add little to his dignity or our edification. His body was carried to England and was buried in the Abbey at West-

minster.  Christendom was profuse in lamentation, but no
monument was placed over his grave.  He was in no need
of eulogy or bust.  Mr. Pears, in an eloquent passage,
says : " We fancy that, had he lived half a century later, he
might have found a sphere of action more congenial to his
disposition ; not fretting and idling at home, not serving
in a country where he was vexed daily by the intrigues of
parties, and the supineness of all in the cause which
he had so much at heart ; not acting under the cold and
selfish Leicester, who scarcely knew how to value his
talents, and only smiled at his enthusiasm.  He might
have met with a leader such as his spirit looked for in
vain in his own times : a man whose genius was large
enough to embrace all those designs which he had but
faintly imagined, and whose heart was bold enough to
carry them out."  Fulke Greville is even more eloquent :
" He was a true model of worth ; a man fit for conquest,
plantation, reformation, or what action soever is greatest
and hardest among men ; withal such a lover of mankind
and goodness, that whosoever had any real parts in him
found comfort, participation, and protection to the utter-
most of his power ; like Zephyrus, he giving life where he
blew.  The universities abroad and at home accounted
him a general Mæcenas of learning, dedicated their books
to him, and communicated every invention or improve-
ment of knowledge with him.  Soldiers honoured him,
and were so honoured by him, as no man thought he
marched under the true banner of Mars that had not
obtained Sir Philip Sidney's approbation.  Men of affairs,
in most parts of Christendom, entertained correspondency
with him.  But what speak I of these, with whom his own
ways and ends did concur?  Since to descend, his heart
and capacity were so large that there was not a cunning
painter, a skilful engineer, an excellent musician, or any
other artificer of extraordinary fame, that made not
himself known to this famous spirit, and found him his

true friend without hire, and the common rendezvous of worth in his time."

Some latitude must be allowed to Greville, whose affection was so great that his enthusiasm rather than discretion guided his pen. Yet, due allowance made, we have here an absolutely true summary and estimation of Philip's virtues. The picture was accounted an exact likeness by those among whom he had lived.

Probably his only equal was du Mornay, whose death occurred much later. He, too, was hero and scholar. Officious people must decide for themselves which was the superior. Simpler folk will be content to thank God for both. They each tried, not always wisely but always fearlessly, to fit Christ's maxims and example to the politics of their day. When death came to them no two men stepped more bravely into the darkness ; none more surely, we may believe, stepped out into the light. Whether or not their conduct was invariably perfect or commendable matters little, since to *Truth* and *Justice*, as they understood *Justice* and *Truth*, they were willing slaves. They could risk everything and not boast, they could suffer and not groan ; death, for them, had no terrors.

PHILIP SIDNEY AND HIS BROTHER ROBERT

FROM AN ENGRAVING BY LACOUR AFTER THE PICTURE AT PENSHURST

# CHAPTER XIII

## PHILIP'S BROTHERS

IT is curious that we should be taught with such pertinacity that distinguished men are prevented of boasting the existence of distinguished sons. Is it true that a wise man usually has a fool for his heir ? He very often has, but quite as often he has not. That the heir and his father do not often understand each other, do not judge an event, or even an emotion, by quite the same rules, is certain. Neither are to blame for this. But however unfortunate in the avenues of middle-class life such a catastrophe may be, it is not an unusual one.

Our own private study of history in later life not only compels to erase a considerable number of names from our catalogue of heroes, but also to cancel many *obiter dicta* our masters taught us to respect. It was a favourite maxim that distinguished talent skips a generation, just as

we are often told now that certain diseases and a disposition to insanity pass from grandsire direct to the grand-
child, the intervening parent showing no tendency to
degeneration physically, mentally, or morally. The idea is
played with in Charles Mathews's famous old farce, " My
Awful Dad " ; though it must be confessed that the parent
is no less delightful than disreputable and the son, model
of excellence though he be, is decidedly uninteresting.
But all these sweeping assertions only contain an element
of truth, certainly not a whole truth or nearly a whole
truth. There are numerous families in which generation
after generation of men and women of conspicuous merit
and value are counted. The Sidney family was emphatically one of these. Sir Henry's father was a man of note
in his day, and himself, as we know, was a statesman of
more than usual industry and ability. Philip inherited
qualities not less famous. But in the halo that covers him
we are too apt to overlook the real distinction of his
brothers, who achieved honour and dignity for themselves
by their own laudable exertions. It is perhaps a little
hard that both Robert and Thomas must suffer a cloud to
rest over their achievements, that they must stand well
in the shadow lest any ray of the full sun should be withheld from Philip.

Of neither could it be said, as has been said so often
of their brother, that he was " the nearest approach
perhaps to the ideal of the perfect knight that has ever
appeared." The eulogy was not by any means wholly
true even of him, and the constant reiteration of the phrase
has in reality done his memory some ill service. The
reality was fine enough to need no such fantastic superlatives. His character and exploits doubtless inspired his
brothers to honourable conduct, but it was the true man
whom they had seen and loved they would design to
emulate, not the half-human half-fairy creation of later
legend.

Of the two Robert held the larger place in the public view. This was natural enough, as on Philip's death he became head of the family. He was born in the November of 1563, nine years later than his elder brother and six years earlier than Thomas, whose birth occurred in March, 1569. Of their boyhood we know little, and that chiefly is negative knowledge. Robert succeeded to his brother Philip's tutor, Robert Dorset, afterwards Dean of Chester, but did not attend school at Shrewsbury, nor was he ever a student at Oxford. He was also less favoured in the way of preferment, for we find no allusion to his being made a vicar and holding a living either in Wales or anywhere else. The most interesting allusion we get as to plans for his future deals with an obscure marriage project apparently contemplated for him when he was in his eleventh year. The facts of the case are somewhat difficult to understand; briefly, they would appear to have been as follows. An idea seems to have been entertained by Sir Henry of marrying his son Philip to the daughter of the eccentric Lord Berkeley. As her father's heiress, the alliance would have been a comfortable one from Sir Henry's point of view. Some such suggestion must have been made to Lord Berkeley, though what actual shape the negotiations took is not related. The only reference we have is in a most extraordinary letter written, presumably with authority, to Lord Berkeley and signed by Nicholas Poyntz, Richard Berkeley, Thomas Throckmorton, and Giles Poyntz. It runs as follows : " Because you are over-resolutely determined to have your daughter to inherit your land, and not to give the same to any heir male of your house, which is a great pity, we think it necessary for you upon reasonable conditions to accept the offer of Mr. Philip Sidney if the same be again made. If also a further offer be made by Mr. Robert Sidney for one of your daughters, we likewise hold the same nothing necessary for you to refuse." The signature,

Richard Berkeley, suggests that one of the writers at any rate had decidedly personal views in the matter of his relative's strange resolution.  Neither of the Sidney boys became his lordship's son-in-law, and the mystery is only deepened by Sir Henry's silence, for he was wont to be eager and anxious when suggestions were launched concerning the marriages of his children.  The letter, indeed, is almost as odd as was the man to whom it was addressed, and not less candid than a communication he received from more august hands on another occasion.  After a visit from Elizabeth and her courtiers he found his beloved deer park, he lived chiefly for hunting, so despoiled that in a fit of anger he evicted the deer and turned his forest into pasture land.  On news of this violent proceeding coming to the Queen's ear she also, as was not unusual, gave way to an explosion of temper.  Her message was, however, no bit of idle impertinence.  It was a stern reprimand, an order to behave himself better in future, and it closed with a scarcely veiled threat.  " Be careful," said the plain-spoken princess, " for my Lord of Leicester desires to possess Berkeley Castle."

When Robert, following the example of Philip, went abroad to complete his studies, the already distinguished courtier was far from forgetful of the young traveller. Indeed, they held each other in the greatest affection. Robert seems to have regarded his brilliant brother as almost a second father, this being, no doubt, the reason why he did not resent the somewhat pompous advice of which he was from time to time the recipient.  True it is, as we have seen, this advice was well gilded with the kindly assurance that " there is nothing I spend so pleaseth me as that which is for you " ; and again, " For £200 a year assure yourself, if the estates of England remain, you shall not fail of it ; use it to your best profit." It was not hard for Robert to believe the assertion " yet

shall not any brother living be better loved than you of
me." He would understand, too, that in heeding Philip's
counsels he was pleasing his father, for Sir Henry thus
admonished him: "*Perge perge*, my Robin, in the filial
fear of God, and in the meanest imagination of yourself,
and to the loving direction of your most loving brother.
Imitate his virtues, exercises, and studies and actions. He
is the rare ornament of this age, the very formula that all
well-disposed young gentlemen of our Court do form also
their manners and life by. In truth—I speak it without
flattery of him or of myself—he hath the most rare virtues
that ever I found in any man. Once again I say, imitate
him." This high praise he never tired of repeating when-
soever occasion offered. Yet that he thought highly of
his other sons is evident, for in a letter to Sir Francis
Walsingham, he says: "I, having three sons: one of
excellent good proof, one of great good proof, and the
third not to be despaired of, but very well to be liked."
Thomas receives, perhaps, a moderate compliment only,
but the distinction between " excellent good " and " great
good " is less marked than that between these eulogies and
a "not to be despaired of." Thomas, at the time, was hardly
old enough to trouble his head about the wording of his
father's letters even if he read them. He might, if he
thought of the matter, reasonably console himself with
the reflection that " very well to be liked " is more than
average commendation. Sir Henry, to use a homely
phrase, regarded "his geese as swans," and he had
reason, for, like the ugly duckling in the fairy tale, they
all turned out to be really swans.

Philip's letters range from grave to gay, from politics to
pocket-money, and music, horsemanship, and fencing all
claim his attention. They have a historic value because
they show what sort of life a young man in Robert's
position was expected to pursue. Though serious matters

are seriously discussed, manly exercises and graceful
accomplishments get their full meed of attention. With
regard to music he is very serious. "Now, sweet brother,
take a delight to keep and increase your music." We are
nowhere told that Robert shared his brother's unduly sober
disposition or was ever a prey to melancholy and neuras-
thenia. It is likely that he was, for the writer adds
as a reason for his advice : "You will not believe what
a want I find of it in my melancholy times." With
regard to horsemanship the scholar is bidden read
*La Gloria del Cavallo;* by a study of this volume
he is told he will learn more in a month than others,
content only to practise the art and not study it as
well, will acquire in a year. The advice is more
practical, probably, than at first hearing it sounds. Certainly the injunction to have a care for the "bitting,
saddling, and curing of horses," is worthy of attention,
and is, I am told, a duty too often neglected in our own
day. Robert, in Philip's view, did not lose much by
evading an Oxford training. "So you can speak and
write good open Latin, not barbarously, I never require
great study in Ciceronianism, the chief abuse of Oxford,
*qui dum verba sectantur res ipsas negligunt."* Perhaps
something too much of style is taught in modern Oxford,
but it is not now open to this very direct snub.

Indeed the warning against excessive Ciceronianism is
decidedly amusing. Delivered though it is with all the
authority he could muster, the voice is not the voice of
Philip but of Languet. When Philip had been engaged
on his own studies he strove hard, and with method, to
acquire the style of Cicero. The letters, especially, of the
orator were constantly on his table. After translating a
passage into English he would try his best to retranslate
it into Latin, using the very words and phrases of the
great original. At this exercise he became too proficient
to please Languet, who warned him of the danger he

was incurring.  This warning he now passes on to his brother.

His comments on playing " at weapons " may be quoted in full, for this sport and tennis seem to have been the cricket and football of the time.

"When you play at weapons, I would have you get thick caps and braziers, and play out your play lustily, for indeed ticks and dalliance are nothing in earnest, for the time of the one and the other greatly differs ; and use as well the blow as the thrust ; it is good in itself, and besides exercises breath and strength, and will make you a strong man at the tourney and barriers.  First, in any case, practise the single sword, and then with the dagger ; let no day pass without an hour or two such exercise ; the rest study or confer diligently, and so shall you come home to my comfort and credit."  Robert was not a good penman, or so Philip thought.  On this defect in handwriting he chaffs his brother good-humouredly : " I would, by the way, your worship would learn a better hand ; you write worse than I, and I write evil enough."  Following this come the remarks on diet and complexion already referred to.  Philip's writing was not at all the evil thing he declares it to be.  The specimens at the Record Office show a clear and legible hand enough.

It will be seen that Philip found no difficulty in accepting the *rôle* of indulgent parent ; nor was opposition raised by the younger brother.  "My comfort and my credit " are curious words to have used to a boy barely nine years his junior.  Even more curious is the letter, often quoted and here again set down, in which comprehensive advice is given as to what to learn and what to avoid among the peoples Robert proposed to visit.  The letter is shrewd, but does not err on the side of charity ; on reading it the lad may well have wondered of what use and benefit foreign travel could possibly be to him.

" Even in the Kingdom of China, which is almost as far as the Antipodes from us, their good laws and customs are

to be learned ; but to know their riches and power is of
little purpose for us, since that can neither advance nor
hinder us.  But in our neighbour countries, both these
things are to be marked, as well the latter, which contain
things for themselves, as the former, which seek to know
both those, and how their riches and power may be to
us available, or otherwise.  The countries fittest for both
these are those you are going into.  France is above all
other most needful for us to mark, especially in the former
kind ; next is Spain and the Low Countries ; then Germany, which in my opinion excels all others as much in
the latter consideration, as the other doth in the former,
yet neither are void of neither ; for as Germany, methinks,
doth excel in good laws, and well administering of justice,
so are we likewise to consider in it the many princes with
whom we may have league, the places of trade, and means
to draw both soldiers and furniture thence in time of need.
So on the other side, as in France and Spain, we are
principally to mark how they stand towards us both in
power and inclination ; so are they not without good and
fitting use, even in the generality of wisdom to be known.
As in France, the courts of parliament, their subaltern
jurisdiction, and their continual keeping of paid soldiers.
In Spain, their good and grave proceedings ; their keeping
so many provinces under them, and by what manner, with
the true points of honour ; wherein since they have the
most open conceit, if they seem over curious, it is an easy
matter to cut off when a man sees the bottom.  Flanders
likewise, besides the neighbourhood with us, and the
annexed considerations thereunto, hath divers things to be
learned, especially their governing their merchants and
other trades.  Also for Italy, we know not what we have, or
can have, to do with them, but to buy their silks and wines ;
and as for the other point, except Venice, whose good
laws and customs we can hardly proportion to ourselves,
because they are quite of a contrary government ; there is
little there but tyrannous oppression, and servile yielding
to them that have little or no right over them.  And
for the men you shall have there, although indeed some be
excellently learned, yet are they all given to counterfeit
learning, as a man shall learn among them more false
grounds of things than in any place else that I know ; for
from a tapster upwards, they are all discoursers in certain

matters and qualities, as horsemanship, weapons, painting, and such are better there than in other countries ; but for other matters, as well, if not better, you shall have them in nearer places."

Despite their pedantry, curious to modern ears, Robert must have appreciated these letters as certainly as he loved the man who wrote them. He would not have said of them, as Philip himself did, "Lord, what babble I write!" Also, it would seem that he took to heart the lessons therein conveyed for, when twenty-one years old, he married Barbara Gamage, in later years the friend and patroness of Ben Jonson. This in itself is proof that she was no ordinary woman, and she won his "peculiar strain of generous applause." So gifted a lady was not likely to have married a fool or a sot, nor would she have made a friend of one, though the little man and fine poet Drummond, forgetting all decency and the laws of hospitality, called "rare Ben" both. Jonson was enthusiastic in his friendships, and his firm belief in the honesty of his comrades made him slow to detect dishonesty. But though he praised sparingly he praised lavishly and delightedly where he recognised merit, and the conversation of Barbara Gamage charmed him, or he would less often have been her guest.

Robert's wooing was no less impetuous than successful. He possessed none of Philip's caution in affairs of the heart. Like young Lochinvar, the ballad hero, he was impetuous and peremptory, and he did not allow the possibility of failure. The game he played was a daring one, and involved him in a serious danger. Barbara Gamage was very rich, which fact, added to her beauty and spirit, caused her to have many suitors. Of all these Robert would seem to have stood the least chance of obtaining the lady. A young gentleman named Herbert Crofts was generally regarded as the favoured swain. He was used, indeed, to boast himself the favoured candidate,

and in his own mind regarded the business as settled
His friends at Court were numerous and powerful, and the
Queen was not at all opposed to his claims.  The heiress
was lodged with her uncle, Sir Edward Stradley, at St.
Donatt's Castle, and he did not much relish the position
of guardian.  Elizabeth determined to see the lady for
herself, and at her command, Sir Walter Raleigh, a
kinsman of Barbara's, wrote as follows :—

"Her Majesty hath now thrice caused letters to be
written unto you that you suffer not my kinswoman to be
bought and sold without Her Majesty's privilege to the
consent and the advice of my Lord Chamberlain and
myself, her father's cousin-germayne, considering she hath
not any nearer kin nor better.  I doubt not but that all
other persuasions sett aparte, you will satisfy Her Highness, and withal do us that courtesie as to acquaint us
with her matchinge.

"Your most willing friend,

"W. RALEIGH."

Sir Edward could not find much pleasure in the
contents, or manner, of this epistle.  The bearer of the
message arrived at the Castle just two hours after
Robert and Barbara had contrived a hasty marriage.
It is quite likely they had got wind of the plot against
their happiness, and daringly forestalled it.  Raleigh and
the Queen, too, were powerless to sever the knot thus
legally tied, and could only bluster.  This they did, and
Mr. Crofts, the cocksure claimant, joined in the chorus.
Luckily for Barbara and her husband, the lady was of
age, and the Crown had no sort of jurisdiction over her.
An order was promptly issued that the lady and all her
possessions should immediately be surrendered to the
Queen's custody, to be held at her Majesty's pleasure.
There was indeed much cry but little wool.  Robert
had won his bride by his own promptitude and nerve.
Nor did he have to wait long for the Royal pardon.

Both parties to the contract were happy together for many years, till in 1621 Barbara died. Their son Robert was famous in his day, and lived a life worthy of the great traditions he inherited.

A month after his marriage with Barbara Gamage, Robert stood, by his brother, as sponsor to his sister Lady Pembroke's second son, who was called Philip. Two years after these events trouble in the Netherlands came, and Robert went with Philip to precede and await his uncle Leicester, whose title eventually became his own by a second creation. Accompanying the Earl went Thomas and other young and gay cavaliers, including the ill-starred Earl of Essex, Stella's brother. Robert, in such business as was forward, had acquitted himself with credit. No objection seems to have been raised to his appointment to the important post of deputy in charge of Rammekins Castle. Leicester's insolent incompetence was immediately apparent: Philip's rash bid for further glory was soon to be paid in full. They— and they are many—who praise him for his foolish deed, forget or ignore the fact that it hindered the cause and, to put it prosaically, was not a good example to two young men, one of whom regarded him as a very wise parent. After the fatal wound his brothers were with the sufferer whenever possible. But both Thomas and Robert were brave and useful, so they could not always be spared. Robert was present when Philip died. His grief we learn was passionate, nor could he control it in the presence of the dying man. "Love my memory, cherish my friends," said Philip gently, "their faith to me may assure you they are honest. But above all govern your will and affections by the will and word of your Creator; in me beholding the end of this world with all her vanities." No mention is made of a last message to Thomas, who may not have been present. It has been said that he was; but it may also be said that Robert was his favourite brother. He cannot have forgotten, in his subsequent career, that when Philip was asked to give a sign of his "inward joy and consolation in God," though he could not speak he "held his hand up and stretched it a little while." As the nearest relative present when the end came, it was, I like to think, Robert who placed Philip's hands across his breast in the attitude of prayer. Thomas, we are told, was also present, though no special words were spoken to him by the dying. But Thomas, it must be remembered, was never Philip's particular care, and was at this time, though gallantly fighting his country's enemies, a youngster not yet out of his teens. It is hardly probable that so youthful a witness, sincerely though he mourned, can have fully appreciated the importance of this sad event.

After Philip's death Robert was sent on a mission to Scotland, and then, returning to Holland, was appointed Governor of Flushing—a position of importance. To this duty was added the command of a body of cavalry. His career as a soldier was a notable one; he was badly wounded at Steenwyck and played a conspicuous part at the important battle near Turnhout, in Belgium. In this affair Prince Maurice showed himself a worthy successor of his father, exhibiting high talent both as a strategist and a leader of troops in action. The Count of Varax, a commander of some ability, was killed, and his men proved unequal to the task of facing the Dutch cavalry. Waning hopes were rekindled by this success, the first of a series obtained by the skill and valour of the young prince.

A few years later Robert was employed on the delicate negotiations between Elizabeth and her froward young lover, the Earl of Essex. This employment was not of a nature to be eagerly sought after. Diplomatic genius was needed if an old and angry Queen, whom he had called "as crooked in mind as in body," and the man who boasted that he could compel her into obedience to his wishes, were to be reconciled. Robert cannot have cared for a task so delicate, though it says much for his reputation that he should have been chosen. Lady Essex was Philip's widow. We can therefore the more easily picture him as an unwilling ambassador. The intrigue between Elizabeth and Essex has yet to be written; even plausible explanations at present avoid discovery. The treason of the Earl, for which he suffered, not with too much dignity—his speech is a raving collection of incongruities—was very small beer. His contract with O'Neil was honourable and fair. Opposed to a hero, he treated his enemy becomingly. What Elizabeth expected to get in the way of pecuniary profit out of Ireland is a secret that is buried with her. Parsimony, like other faults, unbalances the reason. A more parsimonious potentate than the daughter of Henry Tudor has not before, or since, degraded a throne. She had risked money in the Earl's enterprise, and because a return was not immediate she was angry with him. When the culprit was in prison she made a tragic farce more tragic by sending a bowl of broth to the sufferer. To the doctor who attended Essex she declared that, did not a regard for her honour restrain her, she would herself visit the prisoner. This date, 1601, is somewhat late for the discovery of "honour." It is impossible not to echo Lady Teazle's sentiment, "Don't you think we had better leave honour out of the question?" Joseph Surface, before he was found out, would have been a friend of hers. In this, as in other cases, she anticipated Sheridan with marked ability. Essex was killed, and the Queen mourned, not forgetting to abuse those who had expedited her orders. It is satisfactory to know that the remnants of her popularity were buried in the grave of Essex. Neither he nor she deserve much praise. The genuine popularity of Essex was increased when men remembered—and at this time men had long memories concerning the Queen's faults—that he was the victim of the caprice of a foolish and vindictive old woman.

When James, a conceited sovereign too, though with still less reason, came to the throne, he made Robert a baron.  Two years later he advanced him to the dignity of a viscount, and thirteen years later he became Earl of Leicester.  Of these later years considerable information is afforded to us.  We know that he was interested in adventure across the sea, and was a member of the Virginia, East India, and North-West Passage Companies.  In 1616, on the surrender of Flushing, he became a Knight of the Garter.  In addition to these desirable honours he achieved success as a poet, or at least as a librettist.  For many of Dowland's songs he invented the words.  He knew Ben Jonson, who describes in verse the life he lived at Penshurst.  Probably the evening of a strenuous career was pleasant ; the poet's verses are without merit and not quite truthful.  If we could get at the opinion of the " painted partridge " we should find him, in the words of the immortal Buzfuz, " a most unwilling witness."  Here are the lines Jonson wrote and critics profess to admire.  Their real interest is purely topographical and gastronomic.

> " And the tops
> Fertile of wood, Ashore and Sidney's copp's,
> To crown thy open table doth provide
> The purple pheasant, with the speckled side :
> The painted partridge lies in every field,
> And for thy mess is willing to be killed.
> And if the high-swol'n Medway fail thy dish,
> Thou hast thy ponds, that pay thee tribute fish,
> Fat aged carps that run into thy net,
> And pikes, now weary their own kind to eat,
> As loth the second draught or cast to stay,
> Officiously at first themselves betray."

There are many more verses ; from them we may conclude that the Earl's table was one that flowed with

> " All that hospitality doth know,"

and that Penshurst inspired healthy appetites and bad
poetry.

Robert attained to higher honours than Philip because
he lived longer.  Such credentials as he acquired would, it
must be allowed, have gone far to gratify the recipient
himself and please even an exacting and expectant parent.
He was a great man in his day, and filled his exalted
position with dignity.  On the death of Barbara Lord
Leicester, as Robert then was, lived quietly at Penshurst.
He was poor, being but ill-rewarded for his services to the
Crown.  By cruel experience he discovered, as his father
before him had discovered, the wisdom of the ancient
advice, " Put not your trust in princes nor in any child of
man."  He was in bad health also, being a martyr to gout
and stone.  When he had completed his sixty-third year
he caused universal amazement by marrying Sarah Blount,
widow of Sir Thomas Smythe, of Boundes Park.  This
second wedding, though less romantic than the stolen
Welsh marriage of forty years before, caused much comment.  But before the gossips had done with their chatter-
ing, a few weeks only after the ceremony, the Earl and his
new Countess were dead.  Lady Leicester survived her
husband a bare handful of days.  " She will not stay long
after my lord your father," wrote his agent Rowland White
to the new Earl.  Indeed, this second marriage was a contract between two whom Death had already stamped with
his seal.

Of Thomas, after Zutphen, we hear very little.  How he
won his knighthood is not certain.  That he attained this
honour proves his worth in the eyes of his contemporaries.
Probably he was a wise man, had flung away ambition, and
to the end of his days was content to be " very well liked."

# CHAPTER XIV

## DYER—GREVILLE—SPENSER

D R. JOHNSON, in sportive mood, declared once to an astonished circle that "one could say a great deal about a cabbage." It follows that much might be written concerning the friendships of the Elizabethan age—a wealthy subject indeed. Men in those days felt more kindly disposed towards each other than they do now, or we cloak our feelings as though in some curious way ashamed of them, whereas the Sidneys and Dyers proclaimed proudly to the world the names of the men, no less than the names of the women, whom they loved. Of those whom Philip delighted to honour Dyer and Greville hold pride of place. He writes of this close friendship in some notable verse :—

> "My two and I be met
> A blessed happy trinity,
>   As three most jointly set
> In firmest bonds of unity.
>     Join hearts and hands, so let it be ;
>     Make but one mind in bodies three.

> Welcome my two to me,
> The number best beloved ;
> Within the heart you be
> In friendship unremoved.
>     Join hearts and hands, so let it be ;
>     Make but one mind in bodies three."

His prayer is, " Grant me with those two remaining." History can show many examples of romantic friendship but none worthier notice and admiration than that existing between these three brilliant courtiers and men of letters.   To us Philip's name stands out most prominently of the three, but Dyer, as a poet, had the greater reputation at the time.   Only one of his poems is now familiar to the general reader because it is frequently found in anthologies. It must be confessed that it is not of a quality to be easily galvanised into life.   The student of the period finds it pleasing enough, but it stirs his curiosity more than his enthusiasm.   To have written a set of verses that are become a part of the nation's heritage is to have accomplished no mean thing.   A single sonnet made Blanco White immortal, yet few could name the Lord Chancellor or Prime Minister at the date it was written.   On *My Mind to me a Kingdom is*, the reputation of Edmund Dyer is firmly based.   That he had unusual merits and virtues is certain. Languet, who looked so critically at the gallants of Elizabeth's Court, and was so curt in his condemnation of the majority of them, calls him " a gem added to my treasure."   Spenser, of the *Faëry Queen*, speaks of him as " in a manner our only English poet."   Such eulogy is, of course, absurdly extravagant.   One must remember that Spenser was speaking of one greatly his superior in station, and that rank, then as now, greatly dazzled even critical eyes.   But it is interesting to read in a letter of his how gratified he was at the constant marks of appreciation and kindness shown to him by Philip and Dyer.   Their intimacy was never broken nor was it willingly that so often they dwelt apart. Of all these men Greville, Dyer, Philip, and Spenser, it may be truly said that they compared minds and cherished private virtues. It cannot be said, either, that their romantic affection for each other prevented each going his separate way at the call of duty.

Dyer was an old friend of the Sidneys, and indirectly he owed his introduction at the Court to them. Leicester, never dethroned, was often threatened. Powerful people plotted his downfall, but they schemed in vain. Unscrupulous and vicious the Earl was, but he had the merits of his defects. In graver matters than personal intrigue his wisdom is always to seek. Where his private comfort was concerned he was very shrewd. Too wise, and far too selfish to be jealous, at a moment of danger he enticed the more attractive of the younger men to accept him as their leader. So was it that under his auspices Dyer made his first bow to the Queen. The young man learnt the arts of his sponsor easily. A severe judgment passed on him would be absurd. Even so great a man as Raleigh condescended to most ignominious devices when out of favour. Elizabeth was always flattered by any performance, however extravagant, if it tended to prove the despair her displeasure could engender in the hearts of her servants. When Dyer fell into temporary disgrace he contracted a temporary consumption. " It was made the Queen believe that his sickness came because of the continuance of her displeasure towards him, so that unless she would forgive him he was not like to recover; and hereupon her Majesty hath forgiven him and sent unto him a very comfortable message." Thus a pleasant gossip of the Court tells the story. Dyer quickly recovered from his painful ailment; the smiles of the Queen were more potent than doctors in this as in other serious cases. If the illness was assumed —no doubt it was—Dyer had learnt one lesson from his patron Leicester. The Earl was more than once ill when it suited his purpose not to be well. He, indeed, as his

FULKE GREVILLE

AFTER THE PICTURE IN THE COLLECTION OF THE RT. HON. LORD WILLOUGHBY DE BROKE

royal mistress candidly said of him, could "change into all colours save white, which is innocency." The young poet's trick did no harm, however, and reads like the artifice of a modern public schoolboy who has not fully prepared his lessons. Favours bestowed on the Queen's attendants were not bestowed gratuitously. So in the New Year of 1578 we find Dyer presenting her a kirtle of lawn embroidered with flowers of gold. This would be graciously accepted and his delinquencies forgotten.

Dyer, as did most of his contemporaries, took considerable interest in the adventures of the voyagers penetrating the secrets of the New World. The £25, a considerable sum, that he risked in one of Frobisher's voyages was probably advanced through the urgency of Philip. What resulted from the explorer's efforts we have seen, and Dyer, like many another speculator before and since, lost his money.

Neither fruitless hazard nor palace ceremonies occupied the whole of his time. He busied himself seriously with literary work and helped to found a literary club of which Philip was the leading member, though Spenser also attended and contributed to the record of its transactions. Such an association as the Areopagus is familiar enough among literay men to-day. At the period of its formation it was decidedly a novelty. It says much for the value placed on learning and letters that Dyer and Sidney gave to it their time and their enthusiasm. That the "republic of letters" is no idle phrase is proved by the good fellowship of the members, who—Spenser was not nobly born—were by no means necessarily on an equality in other affairs of life. A rival institution was started by the Earl of Oxford, and the members of the two societies abused one another with hearty good will.

Members of the Areopagus set before themselves a considerable task. They were a self-constituted academy for the preservation of the English language, and they hoped to attain "a general surceasing and silence of bald rhymers." Admirable as the second object was, it did not meet with the success it deserved. We have "bald rhymers" with us still, nor is the world likely to be at any time destitute of them. "A little Pyrrhonism sits prettily enough on the philosopher," is Bouillion's dictum. It is not good, however, to arrive at right results by wrong methods. The methods of Areopagus were very wrong. Philip Sidney and Spenser, by adopting them, wrote verse of an indifferent quality. The rigid classical forms imposed were utterly unsuited to the English tongue. The hexameter cannot be handled with any dexterity by even the foremost of our poets. Kingsley has done it better than any one else, but a rigid classicist would detect flaws in *Andromeda*; this can be said for it that in attempts by other authors it would be difficult to detect the merits. Good was achieved by the society, for the language was not settled and the frequent debates must have taught the experimenters the right use of words and their proper value. The more famous members abandoned the stringent rules when writing, not for exercise, but in set earnest. This fact condemns the boasted object of the club, yet probably these men would have written less well but for the voluntary discipline to which they at one period subjected themselves. To Gabriel Harvey, poet and pedant, we owe this if nothing else, and the debt is not a small one, that he had great influence with his younger contemporaries. He used, ceaselessly, to show them how necessary it is to treat words with a becoming reverence.

Dyer had his share of travel and diplomacy, interesting to him one may suppose, but the details do not concern us greatly now. As is the case with many people of importance in their day, to a later generation he is become little more than a name. His titles to remembrance are three, that he was Philip's friend; that Lady Mary, no

mean judge, called him a "noble gentleman"; and that
he wrote one beautiful lyric.

He acted as a pall bearer at Philip's funeral. He
inherited half of Philip's library.

But of all names associated with Philip Sidney that of
Fulke Greville comes most readily to the lips. In his
biography of the Zutphen hero he boasts, touchingly, that
" he chose me for his beloved Achates." Greville had
a long and successful career, but he always remembered
that there are, for the wise who value them, treasures
greater than rubies, decorations more lustrous and splendid
than those bestowed by the favour of princes. After a
long and far from unsuccessful life, his own achievements,
creditable though they were his titles fairly won, make
no extravagant reward. The distinction that gave him a
niche in the temple was the five words of eulogy he
caused to be engraved on his tomb:—

"FRIEND $\left\{ \begin{array}{l} \text{TO}^1 \\ \text{OF} \end{array} \right\}$ SIR PHILIP SIDNEY."

There is a difficulty in writing of such men as Greville.
The bishop, the successful schoolmaster, gets the history
of his prosaic career enshrined in two portly volumes.
But only men of his own generation read them. Dr.
Keate is a name to us, a synonym for flogging, he takes
his place in the dictionary, but he has ceased to be a
personality. So it is with men like Fulke Greville: an
index is incomplete and slovenly without due reference,
yet there is very little to learn when the page indicated
has been consulted. One wishes there had been a Clarendon to write of the Westerns and Falklands of Elizabeth's
time. For in the main only a few things happen of
importance at any period. Processions have flaunted it
in all ages, but in what a minority are the leaders of those

---

¹ Both quoted.

hilarities whose names we can recall! So with a man like Fulke Greville, who knew his place, as it were, and did good work and appreciated better, it would be pleasant and profitable to know more. Dates and facts are easy enough to collect, but of the man, save in so far as he reveals himself in the pages of the book he wrote about his friend, we know nothing except by a hint or two. One might almost say of him, and think the matter ended, what Clarendon wrote of Lindsey: "He had very many friends and very few enemies, and died generally regretted." This colourless epitaph applies to many, and is as favourable a one as a reasonable man should expect. To have friends is to argue yourself a person of qualities ; to be regretted is a compliment not paid to every man.

Immortality was not despised by Greville. He wished to be remembered, and he attained his desire in five words, dying in great content and comfort at having discovered them.

A kinsman of the Sidney family, he enjoyed those advantages and inconveniences which in his day birth gave to a man. He could enter the Court, though his creditors could not : once inside they could only whistle in the courtyard. But men of Greville's and Sidney's calibre, if Greville had debts, wished to pay them, and contrived to do so.

Greville and Philip entered Shrewsbury School together ; after their schooling they both proceeded to Oxford. Here, for reasons not discoverable, they were placed in separate keeping. Sidney entered at Christ Church and his friend at Broadgates Hall, now Pembroke College, Dr. Johnson's "nest of singing birds."

During their University careers the school friendship increased. It is futile to speculate, but one may quite reasonably suppose that they were close companions in study and in sport. As such they remained during the few years Providence allowed them to be together.

Fulke Greville played the part of Philip's attendant shadow. Of his own initiative it would seem that he did very little. A man of quality, and parts, he found that preferment came his way. Perhaps he had ambition, but one fancies he was content with a competency. Accompanying Philip on various missions no very prominent part was ever allotted to him, nor for all that we know was it desired. Where Philip Sidney was, so seems to have been his rule, the second fiddle must be reserved for Fulke Greville. He would have become jealous if another hand had touched that instrument.

His value as a biographer is due to this capacity for hero worship. The merits of his hero may be exaggerated, his defects unduly condoned, but no one can doubt the sincerity of the writer who effaces himself. It is not a model biography, it is not always quite intelligible, but it proves two important things—one, that he gloried in his friendship with Philip; secondly, that on occasion he could write fine prose. Taking his friend's view of the political situation at a given time, and willingly sharing Philip's dislike of Burleigh, he writes, surely a fine sentence: "Stirring spirits sent abroad as fuel, to keep the flames far off; and the effeminate made judges of dangers which they fear and honour which they understand not." Here we have, perhaps, as fine a sentence as he wrote, but he could coin phrases when he wished, as when of Queen Elizabeth and Philip he referred to "that princely heart of hers which was a sanctuary to him." Phrase-makers are not always strictly accurate; the occasions when the Queen's heart was a sanctuary to Philip lie as yet hidden in the dust of history. Greville was, it must be recollected, a member of the Areopagus, where such writing was encouraged and, it may be, won the approval even of Gabriel Harvey himself, the man of whom we know so little but of whom so much was thought.

Greville wrote a good prose style, sometimes an eloquent

style; he was as clever as his neighbours at turning neat verses. Where he really excelled, I think, was as a critic. With all his admiration of Philip and Philip's work, he could see defects; though he did not point them out categorically he summed them up in a sentence: " His end was not writing even while he wrote." When Scott, in praise, declared that Byron " dangled his pen with the air of a man of quality," he said what Fulke Greville meant of Sidney. Philip, though a lesser poet by many leagues, did his work more conscientiously.

It was, however, emphatically not Philip's work in the world, as he conceived it, to write poetry. Ephemeral affairs, of no lasting value or interest, save that he was concerned in them, appeared to his eyes as of graver import than the deft handling of a sonnet. In politics or in poetry Greville followed him. In 1577 he was in Philip's train on the German mission already referred to. His place was subordinate, yet his virtues must have attracted attention. For it was in his ears that William of Orange breathed that eulogy of the young ambassador, still repeated with awe. When the famous letter was written to the Queen, Greville approved its contents and bore the disgrace that followed her Majesty's reading. And he had played his part, how gracefully he does not tell us, in the masque—again Shrewsbury doubtless helped designer and follower—that honoured Francis de Bourbon in 1581. At Philip's bidding the staid Fulke Greville aped it as one of " The Four Foster children of Desire." How he acquitted himself we are not told; if badly he would have told us. He was one of " the others did well " of modern dramatic criticism.

Greville, eager and anxious like many serious men of his day, held definite religious views. These he derived from Philip. His attacks on Jesuits are torrents of eloquence. At once let it be said, though, that he was no stern Puritan, and never an enemy to harmless pleasure. It was the supposed menace to liberty far more than the hatred of doctrine that stirred the hatred of Elizabethan thinkers. Rome was disliked, but it was Spain who was loathed. Indeed, this attitude is clearly defined for us in one sentence coming from Fulke Greville's pen : "Spain, Rome, and the Jesuitical faction of France." On religious as on other matters he took Philip's line with as much knowledge of the rights of the dispute as belonged to his friend, and as much ignorance. This ignorance as to the rights and wrongs in the dispute it is only possible for they who stand far off to scoff at.

Temporal advantage came his way before long. As Clerk to the Signet to the Council of Wales he acquired a position of dignity. His friendship with Bruno five years later gave him more. It was at Greville's house the great Italian met the more earnest of his English listeners, and got shrewder and worthier attention than a university afforded to him.

In Parliament at this time he cut no great figure, that is, he did not stand forth conspicuously above his fellows. But he did good work, and served on committees that had influence. After Philip's death he arrived at the dignity of a peerage, and became Chancellor of the Exchequer. From this position he was either removed, or himself retired, somewhat mysteriously. Clarendon is vague on the business, and refers to it in one sentence, deigning no definite explanation. Long before this, however, Fulke Greville had summed up the precise value of his own work for the commonweal, and announced what estimate he put on his own value—

"Friend to Philip Sidney."

He flits through the pages of history as one who loved, and was loved by, a man of surpassing merits. Meaner credentials have made men famous.

So much has been written about Spenser, and so little is

he read it almost seems unnecessary to say more than that only as Philip Sidney's friend his life, or such details of it as we can collect, comes into the scope of this book. His parentage, if worthy, was not distinguished : the exact date of his birth remains a matter of conjecture. He gained fame and poverty ; he rests in the Abbey near Chaucer. As a poet he won, and holds, the esteem, even affection, of poets. Apart from his merits as a poet, he appears to have been a worthy person. He was not a very wise, nor was he a very generous man in political affairs. Modern politicians of violent habit should study *A View of the Present State of Ireland*, wherein the views of this most ethereal of poets are set forth with a frankness that is brutal in the extreme. He saw and understood Fairyland, but concerning the miserable people of Ireland he lacked sense to see that his own verse had been his fittest motto :—

> " One loving houre
> For many yeares of sorrow can dispence."

Language fails him when he tried to describe the villainies of the Irish. Philip Sidney took care not to hide their faults, but his outspoken criticisms are nothing compared to the vituperative outburst of the greater poet. His supposed conversation between Eudoxus and Irenæus is one of the nastiest contributions to English literature ever given by a man of experience and distinction. Unluckily Spenser's poetry is not much read : most luckily the dialogue has even fewer readers. He had little reason to be grateful to the Irish in the end ; but he misunderstood them and their aims so wilfully and so haughtily the punishment meted out to him is not to be wondered at, nor is it easy to accord him more than a few grains of sympathy. It is not necessary, fortunately, for the account makes unsavoury reading, to say more on

this matter. We are only concerned with Spenser's Irish
views because he was Philip's friend, and Philip less
emphatically shared them and probably often discussed
them with him. Moreover, Spenser, even as Sidney and
Dyer, was obliged to give up much time and labour to
uncongenial tasks. Poetry did not procure a living wage
then any more than it does now, even when the verses
came from the pens of the most accomplished masters. A
story goes that Elizabeth on one occasion was so moved
by his skill that she ordered him to be paid one hundred
pounds. Cecil seems to have boggled at the price; he did
not concern himself with the affairs of the Muses. The
Queen, not given to generosity, was this once in earnest, and
learning from the poet himself, by some indifferent rhymes
of his he placed in her hand, that the reward had not been
paid, told Cecil, and that in no minced words, to liquidate
the debt at once. It would seem that the minister
promptly obeyed.

It was at the meetings of the Areopagus that Philip
and Spenser became really intimate, so far as we can guess
at this distance of time. That he contributed verses we
know, and it is fortunate that his bid for fame does not
depend upon them. They are neither better nor worse
than any efficient poetaster might have contrived who had
had the good fortune to be educated at a decent grammar
school under a competent master. "Unhappy verse," one
effusion begins, and whosoever reads the stanzas will seize
upon the opening words as an admirable comment. It is
well, however, to linger a minute over these absurdities
of a great poet, only by doing so may lesser mortals
realise how low even the great can fall. The man who
wrote " unhappy verse " wrote also—

"They were enwombed in the sacred throne of her chaste bodie,"

and this—

"And after all came Life, and lastly Death—
Death with most grim and griesly visage seen,
Yet is he nought but parting of the breath ;
Ne ought to see, but like a shade to weene ;
Unbodied, unsouled, unheard, unscene ;
But life was like a fair young lusty boy,
Such as they faine Dan Cupid to have beene ;
Full of delightful health and lively joy,
Deck't all with flowers and wings of gold fit to employ."

Here is a very different singer to him of the "unhappy
verse." Yet Philip and Spenser both suffered from the
curious influence of Gabriel Harvey. This man was an
enthusiast and a pedant. He had the greatest of all
qualities in a tutor, for he transmitted his enthusiasm to his
pupils. Loving good learning himself, he cajoled others
into loving what was worthy of admiration. His fault lay
in this, that he could not be brought to see that form is
not everything, and that alien forms cannot be right or
alive. On these alien forms he pinned his faith. Ascham,
a much greater scholar than Harvey could claim to be,
gave a very modified approval of the scheme for writing
English verse in Latin metres. He knew his classics and
his English too well to share the enthusiasm of the
would-be reformers. "Although Carmen Hexametrum
doth rather trot and hobble than smoothly in our English
tongue, yet I am sure our English tongue will receive
Carmen Iambicum as naturally as either Greek or Latin,"
was his verdict and astute prophecy. This half-hearted
patronage was not to Harvey's mind. Spenser while at
Pembroke Hall, Cambridge, studied under his guidance,
and the falling away of so great a poet as Spenser became,
once he broke his fetters, must have bewildered the worthy
tutor not a little.

The Areopagus, already mentioned, to which precious
society Spenser for a time belonged, has been described
as an assembly "where should be decided the questions
between the upholders of classical metres and those who

favoured the native rhymes. War was declared against rhyme, and language was forced into the most frightful measures ; long and short came in, and hexameters made their appearance surpassed only by the unfortunate Stanihurst. All the members of the Areopagus—Sidney, Dyer, Fulke Greville, and Spenser above all—fortunately gave up their metrical efforts, Harvey alone remaining faithful to the old hobby, with little loss to English literature, for as a poet, neither in genius, dignity, or form did he distinguish himself." In fairness it should be added of him that, however absurd his theories, he possessed the rare gift of inspiring the enthusiasm without which no great work is done.

Leaving Cambridge, Spenser, in 1576, went into Lancashire and remained there for a year. It was then that he followed Harvey's advice in a practical manner, and arriving in London found lodging at Leicester House. Here he frequently met Philip, and their friendship was warm and sincere. They must have influenced each other greatly, and mostly, if not altogether, for good. Each had a tendency to be too grave and serious, and there is little of humour to be found in the works of either. Much of the gross jesting in vogue was distasteful to them, of course. But a spice of humour goes far to keep a book alive. Life, though a serious affair enough, is less serious than they would have us suppose. The neglect both poets suffer from is largely due to want of gaiety.

In 1579 Spenser published *The Shepherd's Calendar*, and dedicated it "to the noble and vertuous Gentleman, most worthy of all titles both of learning and chevalrie, Master Philip Sidney." During his stay in London he wrote much, and passed his time in the company of men of letters. His life, however, was not at all free from care. He had enemies at Court, and the promotion he wished for was long in coming, nor was it of the kind desired when it did come. Many reasons have been urged for the

scant attention bestowed upon him by the great.  For his
own part he did not hesitate to attribute it to " malicious tongues."  Dedicating his *Colin Clout's come Home
Again* to Sir Walter Raleigh, he prays the famous
courtier " with your good countenance protest against the
malice of evil mouths which are always wide open to carpe
at and misconstrue my simple meaning."  He would hardly
have made so open and direct a statement without cause.
Frequent references to these attacks on him occur in his
poems.  But it may very well be that Burleigh did not
look kindly on the poet any more than he smiled on the
owner of Leicester House.  Apart also from his dislike of
Leicester and all who followed him, it is quite probable
that in his opinion something too much was made of the
singers of the day.  Men of affairs are apt to adopt this
view.  It is difficult to imagine Cecil caring much for
works of fancy ; he had, he considered, graver concerns
with which to occupy his mind.  He may have understood that the poet's posthumous fame would be greater
and nobler, and more in touch with the glory of his
country than his own.  But he loved his country, and had
to serve it the best way he could.  Spenser's subsequent
friendship with Essex further spoilt his chances of promotion.  He was unlucky in his patrons, though fortunate
in his friendships.

At last, in 1580, Lord Gray of Wilton, on becoming
Lord-Lieutenant of Ireland, made Spenser his private
secretary.  This promotion was due to the good offices of
Sir Henry Sidney, aroused by Philip's entreaties.

Though Philip and Spenser had met often, but met
only during a period of very few months, their liking
for each other was sincere and cordial ; on Spenser's side,
if we may judge by his written words, he felt a most warm
affection for Philip.  But there is scant reason, indeed,
for the belief, so erroneously held, that an intimate friendship existed between the two.  Philip was the last man

in the world to become the intimate of any man on the sudden. There are few indeed to whom he expressed his thoughts. His circle was a narrow one, though his interests and sympathies were generous. I think Flügel is wrong in saying so emphatically that "the English have wished to establish from the few facts known" that the two were bosom friends, or, in Tudor phrase, bedfellows. The English, to our shame be it said, do not greatly concern themselves in the matter. In supposing that we do the German critic pays us a compliment we hardly deserve now, however apposite it would have been, and more gratefully appreciated, in the days of Horace Walpole. It is plain, from this if from no other reason, that on the one side Spenser's pride and reserve, also his irritability, and on the other Philip's interest in alien matters which commanded his attention, made any real intimacy between the two an impossibility. The most we can say is that we conjecture, not without proof, a closer intimacy would have been more than agreeable to both.

That this friendship would be more sought by Spenser than by Philip is not an unreasonable supposition. If the latter needed a patron, as he did on several occasions, the better poet, being of lesser rank, certainly had still greater need of one. But there are many traces in Spenser's work of the profound regard in which he held the writer of *Arcadia*; tributes occur to the man and the man's work which prove, beyond cavil, the generous nature of Spenser's admiration. On the other hand, Philip is by no means so enthusiastic in return. Perhaps in the multitude of his avocations he found it impossible to give due attention to everything that fell from so prolific a pen. To Grosart, more than to any one else, we owe the real explanation of the relationship existing between the two men. He calls them the complement of each other, like globes of dew. "Everywhere I find Spenser missing and mourning his friend." At the same

time he comes to the conclusion that their friendship
was more formal than real. Yet Spenser must have had
personal experience of Philip's great gentleness, for he
mentions it in *The Ruins of Time*, and also to Harvey, in
a letter. From the dedication of the poem, dedicated
to the Countess of Pembroke, I quote the opening lines.
They seem to me to show that their author cherished
the certain hope of a close association with the lady's
brother in the near future, the two having, hitherto, not
been on terms of familiarity.

" Most Honourable and bountifull Ladie, there be long
sithens deepe sowed in my brest the seede of most entire
love and humble affection unto that most brave Knight,
your noble brother deceased ; which, taking roote, began
in his life somewhat to bud forth, and to shew themselves
to him, as then in the weakness of their first spring ; and
would in their riper strength (had it pleased high God till
then to draw out his daies) spired forth fruit of much
affection." A natural desire to think of the two poets
as linked together by tender ties of love and mutual
confidence has firmly established the tradition of a friendship between them that did not, in fact, exist. Philip's
praise of *The Shepherd's Calendar* is tempered by
a touch of asperity. The censure may be deserved, but,
one hopes, it would have been conveyed a little more
gently had their connection been closer : *The Shepherd's
Calendar* hath much poetrie in his Eclogues, indeed
worthy the reading, if I be not deceived. That same
framing of his style to an old rusticke language, I dare not
allow : since neither Theocritus in Greeke, Virgill in
Latin, nor Sanazara in Italian, did affect it."

To leave London was hard, but it would have been
folly for Spenser to refuse the position. Indeed, this was
the beginning of very substantial preferment, for he
quickly became Clerk of Decrees and Recognisance in the
Chancery Court of Ireland. Relinquishing this position

seven years later, he became Clerk to the Council of
Munster. Few poets prospered so well as he now and
for eighteen years. In addition to his office he received
substantial grants of land. But he seems always to have
taken a jaundiced view of life.

True, Ireland was further from London than it is to-day,
but he had the means and leisure to make frequent
journeys to the English capital. He was a man, however,
who could not be contented or satisfied. For all his ethereal
dreams he liked worldly comfort, and he liked it best
in London. He did not attempt to like or understand the
people among whom his lot was cast. The severest
measures for governing the Irish were cordially approved
of by him. Though Lord Gray's stern rule caused so
much discontent and disgust that at last Elizabeth, not
very willingly, recalled him, Spenser speaks of him with
enthusiasm. The difference between Spenser the poet
and Spenser the man is remarkable. Beautiful as were
his dreams and his verses, his life was querulous and not
at all beautiful. Some of his ideas when set down in prose
savour of cruelty.

His life, moreover, was not near so lonely as he would
have us believe. There were people of culture and distinction in the Irish capital, and some of them frequently
visited him. At his, or a, cottage near Dublin, Lodovick
Bryskett wrote *A Discourse of Civil Life* ; *containing the
Ethike Part of Moral Philosophie.* Every one was much
in earnest, one surmises, scarcely more intelligible than
Bryskett himself. The real aim, that of encouraging the
study of Moral Philosophy in English, was excellent. But
Bryskett's ideas on Plato and Aristotle are confusing. He
envied the Italians whose writers had made a union of the
two possible ; he desired to perform, with the aid of his
colleagues, a similar task for the less fortunate English.
He was, as Spenser, an admirer of Lord Gray, and the work
was dedicated to the retired Viceroy. It was ridiculous

of Spenser to grumble in his well-paid exile. He had
pleasant society and plenty of good talk, quite as good
as that afforded at meetings of the Areopagus. We have
the philosopher's own account to show that the poet
was active in the debates. Bryskett was not entirely
devoted, however, to philosophical studies; being a sensible
man he was not above succeeding Spenser, when the time
came, as Clerk to the Council of Munster.

Spenser was in Ireland when he heard of Philip's death.
His poem on the occasion is not worthy of him or his
hero. It has been suggested that he felt a grief too deep
for tears. This may be so. He must have been satisfied
himself with his copy of verses, since they were printed
and are preserved. No artist is the best judge of his own
work. Shelley did better by Keats and Tennyson, in one
phrase, by Byron. Yet Spenser knew and loved Philip
greatly. Perhaps philosophers are forbidden to show
emotion. At Kilcoltman Castle he entertained Raleigh
more than once. This was his new residence near
Doneraile.

In 1590 appeared the earlier books of *The Faëry
Queen.* This poem is diffuse, though full of extraordinary beauty. Whether it was ever finished we cannot
know. The common belief is that it was, and that the
six concluding books perished by fire. As we have it,
there is enough for satisfaction, almost for satiety. Noble
though it be it is unhuman, filled with wondrous imagery
all traces of passion are absent. Spenser was so great
a poet that to compare him with Dyer, or even Philip,
is absurd. Yet, possessed of all his wondrous powers,
he could not accomplish verses so haunting as *My
Mind to me a Kingdom is.* His mind, unfortunately
for himself, was a most turbulent kingdom, and he found
within its confines not merely "present joys," but worries
of a serious kind. A pleasant story has it that when
Lord Southampton read the manuscript he ordered his

servant to give twenty pounds to the author.  Continuing his study, he cried out with delight, "Give the man another twenty pounds."  Once again, excited by a beautiful passage, he sent down a further sum of twenty pounds.  An additional gift of a like sum marked his continued delight in the poet's masterpiece.  His appetite growing with what it fed upon, he became cautious. Putting the script aside, he gave a final order to his man : "Turn that fellow out of the house, for if I read further I shall be ruined."

Certainly Spenser had not to wait for his applause : it came to him as immediately as to a great actor.  He was regarded by all, in the phrase of Nash, quoted by Disraeli, as "Heavenly Spenser."  And Disraeli concurs : " I have often thought that among the numerous critics of Spenser the truest was that of his keen and witty contemporary ; for this town wit has stamped all our poet's excellencies by one felicitous word."  Meanwhile Heaven was not particularly kind to him.  As an "undertaker," that is one who had acquired a forfeited estate, and was expected to produce order out of chaos, his daily life was not free from anxiety.  His temper towards the Irish did not ease his task.  More intimate troubles than differences with his Irish tenants were his also.  When in Lancashire he had loved a Rosalind who did not return his passion.  As is the manner of poets, he never tired of expressing his adoration in verse.  He wishes to die, nay, thinks death is the only solace left to him.  His poem,his *Faëry Queen*, became irksome to him.  He declares that he cannot finish the writing of it.  He did, it would seem, finish the poem, though we have it not.  The lady he married, and composed for her a poem, the *Epithalamium*, of great beauty.  One cannot help thinking that Spenser was a difficult and even unpleasant man to deal with.  Not successful in the exact manner he wishes, yet eloquent enough to win a coy mistress, he grumbles.  It is impossible not to think that he was his own executioner. Tragedy and misfortune came to him : a careful study of events at the time goes far to justify a belief that he was not blameless in hurrying the catastrophe. When, in 1595, he crossed to England, he had with him the second three books of *The Faëry Queen* and his abominable production, *A View of the Present State of Ireland*. This pamphlet, if not exactly his death-warrant, explains his ruin. Sorry for his own woes, he was not in the least sympathetic to other people in their troubles. Una, fairies, and dragons he could sympathise with, they were his children ; but there is not a direct note of decent human passion in the whole body of his work. Consequently its fame is more traditional than real.

The following year, 1596, he became friend to the Earl of Essex. Visiting the Earl's house in the Strand, where is now Essex Street, he met many men, even Shakespeare, and looked to improve his fortunes. He should have dined on the petal of a lily and quenched his thirst with a dewdrop. There is really little to admire in Spenser as a man. Diplomacy, if he desired advancement, was not one of his gifts. King James, the most learned fool in Europe, was furious at the allusions to his mother under the pseudonym Dunessa. He breathed threatenings and slaughter, and demanded instant reparation. The poet seems to have forgotten that the Scotch King was next heir to the throne of the two kingdoms.

When he returned to Ireland he was made Sheriff of Cork. This was, it is conjectured, in 1597. The year following an insurrection—and little wonder if Spenser reflected the views of his official leaders—broke out. He was now affluent, famous, and probably discontented. Burleigh's death decidedly was an advantage to him. But this advantage he was not allowed to cull. Though poets themselves, the insurgents could not tolerate the presence of Spenser among them. He reigned in the

EDMUND SPENSER

AFTER A PICTURE BY T. UWINS IN THE COLLECTION OF THE RT. HON.
THE EARL OF KINNOUL

castle of the Desmonds, he had written savagely of them and their aspirations. Like Erskine, he might have complained that "there was too much Goddamn butter and Ireland." A very terrible reward was the fruit of his labours. Pent-up anger found a loophole; the outspoken and unsympathetic lord of the castle had to fly with his wife and children. Some assert that not all the children were saved. He reached London to find death in a tavern, and Ben Jonson asserts that he died "for lack of bread." This is an exaggeration; certain moneys were at his command. But his affairs were in disorder, his spirit and his nerve were broken. He abused a people with unpardonable virulence; the people heard the insult and swamped him in the wave raised against oppressors. The violence of the mob must be condemned, yet it can also be understood. Sympathy with Spenser is not unalloyed. The rebels had their argument and it is a powerful one; there is merit in their plea if not in their actions.

# CHAPTER XV

## THREE FAMOUS CONTEMPORARIES—LEICESTER, DU MORNAY, AND LANGUET

Leicester's character—His brilliance—Quickly a favourite—His crimes—Amy Robsart—Dreams of marriage with Elizabeth—His hatred of Simier—A curious incident—Secret marriage—Failures in Holland—Recalled and restored to favour—His death, probably by poison—Du Mornay—His serious character—Narrow religious views—At St. Bartholomew massacre—Diplomat and author—at Ivry—Hubert Languet—Birth—Early repute—Gravity of character—Nature of his letters—Lack of humour—Devotion to Philip—His influence—His schemes—His courage—Melancthon—Hatred of greed—Lived humbly—Friendship with the Sidney family—Tutors Robert—His death

SIDNEY'S sonnets rank next to Shakespeare's in merit and the mystery that surrounds them. But I cannot help thinking that the poems are clear and intelligible, and the really mysterious utterance of Philip's was that above all things he prided himself on being a Dudley. It is difficult to discover what possible cause of pride there could be in the relationship. A certain delight in ostentation, but not for his own glory, Philip showed, almost boyishly, more than once. This trait, greatly refined, is the sole link that would seem to bind him to his uncle's house. His mother did not share her brother's love of frippery and trappings. Not one other bond of union connected the two men than this love of pageantry and show, in one case a selfish desire for personal glorification, in the other, however foolish, an earnest determination to exact homage and admiration for the sake of the Queen and cause he served.  There is scarcely a word to be said in favour of the man whom, there is proof, Elizabeth sincerely loved and mourned, over whose death she wept, and the austere young knight who called him uncle.

Brilliantly clever in advancing his own interests Leicester certainly was.  Not many men would have looked, or hoped, for more than peaceful seclusion and a modest competence who were cursed with such an immediate ancestry as he. His grandfather was the infamous John Dudley, " cater- pillar of the Commonwealth," whose extortions as a tax- gatherer made his name loathed throughout England. His dishonesty and his harshness brought him to the scaffold, and no one mourned his death, unless it were the politic and avaricious king who profited by his exactions but dare not allow them to continue.  The Tudors only cared for those who were directly useful to the royal House.  Leicester's father, clever, vain, inordi- nately ambitious, obtained a dukedom, but not improperly was executed, having attempted to place his daughter-in- law, Lady Jane Grey, on the throne—a notable case of vaulting ambition o'erleaping itself—and he caused the deaths of those worthy to live.  Here was not a solid foundation on which to build a career, yet Leicester was always in favour and grasping the honours and rewards due to his betters.

Early success came to him chiefly because of his hand- some appearance.  No one disputed his claim to be accounted the handsomest man in Europe.  Elizabeth would have none but well-favoured people about her ; the humblest of her pages was to be something more than competent in his duties.  He must be pleasing to look upon.  So Leicester had the great advantage of attracting the eye of his royal mistress by the striking

qualities of his form and figure; and, despite his failures,
even crimes, he managed to keep captive her admiration
till his death.   In his picture his face is long, with a high
and somewhat broad forehead, arched eyebrows, not thick
but dark, humorous but shifty eyes, full lips half hidden
by a heavy, carefully tended moustache, a short, two-
peaked beard, and a nose large, hooked, and almost
Hebraic.   It is a handsome face, undeniably, not at all
an attractive one.  Contemporaries did not dispute the taste
that acclaimed his beauty; even Sussex, who on his death-
bed bade men beware of "the black gipsy," could not
decry the looks of his enemy.   He seems to have retained
his splendid appearance to the end of his life.   In complexion he was, for an Englishman, extremely dark.
Hence he earned the title "gipsy."   His disposition was
dark as his appearance.

From the very first he became a favourite with the
Queen, and the hold he obtained over her never weakened
save in the rare and short intervals of royal anger.   Whatever his crimes, his follies, or his blunders, they were
quickly condoned, and, if not forgotten, completely
forgiven.   So rapid was his rise to power that there was
early talk of his looking to become the Queen's consort.
Elizabeth's attitude towards him was scarcely that of a
monarch to a subject, however illustrious.   Her infatuation seems to have been real and not feigned.   Probably
he was the only man for whom she had a warmer affection
than mere friendship.

Gossip is never the whole truth and not often even half the
truth.   Certainly the gossip of Elizabeth's Court was rife,
and, it may be said, rather more than usually malevolent,
whenever the names of the haughty Princess and her
boastful, swaggering courtier were spoken.  Nevers, the
French Ambassador, more than hints at caresses warmer
than are usual between friends; he hints at kisses and
much else of a highly reprehensible and undignified nature.

Nor is he the only one who has left us piquant comments on the nature of their comradeship. But however much Leicester may have counted on success, it is not probable that the Queen seriously contemplated a union. Leicester's reputation was a very bad one. He stopped at nothing to gain his ends where women were concerned. " His lordship hath a special fortune, that when he desireth any woman's favour, whatsoever person standeth in the way hath the luck to die quickly," grimly comments one of his critics.

That Leicester was an adept in the little known mystery of poisons is not to be disputed. He may not have been guilty as often as was rumoured, but cases of murder can be brought home to him. The belief that he poisoned Lord Sheffield was not ill-founded. The death of Lady Sheffield by poisoning is rather damning evidence, if not really conclusive, against him ; for he had married her on the death of her husband. Other tragic deaths of both men and women have been nearly brought home to him, if not quite. At the time people with common accord attributed them to his plots and evil designs, a curious circumstance being that in each case the man stood in his path or his lust for the woman had been sated.

These accusations of poisoning, well founded as is probable, were the more readily believed because at this time poisons were not infrequently resorted to by those who wished to make away with their enemies as quietly as possible. It has been said of Leicester that even Italy could not show a subtler adept in the poisoner's art than he. A craft understood by few, it was a doubly dangerous device in skilful hands, for the risk of detection was slight indeed. Men possibly exaggerated the dangers they ran, an unseen enemy always invoking a panic terror greater than the fear a visible danger can command. When Ben Jonson reset his comedy, *Every Man in his Humour*, placing the scene at home and altering the

Italian names and manners for English ones, he did not alter his allusion to the custom of poisoning. The jealous Kitely is still made to exclaim—

> "Now, God forbid.  O me !  Now I remember
> My wife drank to me last, and changed the cup ;
> And bade me wear this cursed suit to-day."

Elizabeth was blamed, on several occasions, we read, because she did not murder Mary of Scotland in this quiet and convenient way.   Her reason for not doing so is probably this, that she desired by a more public execution to strike immediate terror into the hearts of England's enemies and Mary's friends.   That she made a show of sorrowful anger when the deed was done does not affect this supposition. Elizabeth knew how to blow hot and cold ; and if the execution of the Queen of Scots was justified, as many then thought and some still think, beheading was decidedly a dramatic and impressive punishment.   For several years Elizabeth herself was in danger from the poisoner and lived in constant fear of doctored dish and fatal goblet.   But the would-be murderer did not confine his efforts to tampering with meat and drink.   In 1598 the Queen's saddle was alleged to have been infected, and two men were hanged for the crime.   A fire was made at Smithfield of many dresses, some furniture, and a girdle, though for whom they had been prepared I cannot discover.   The chair of the Earl of Essex was found, in Gifford's words, "rubbed with some deleterious mixture."   The horror inspired by these devilish and underhand methods prompted by revenge or jealousy can be readily understood.   Among the various reasons, put forward by Languet and others, to deter men of the north travelling in Italy, it is curious not to find any reference to the Venetian and Milanese way of destroying an enemy.   Even Genoa, a home of the Jesuits and the Inquisition, therefore to be avoided like the plague, was not more dangerous than London. Yet when Philip was in Genoa Languet conjured up many a menace, and trembled for the safety of his friend.

The exact truth as to Amy Robsart, Leicester's beautiful and unfortunate first wife, will perhaps never be known. The Earl stood his trial, in a manner, before a coroner's jury, but very little was elicited. The verdict arrived at was that she fell downstairs; how she came to fall was not disclosed by the evidence, and no blame was attached to anybody. Professing to urge the jury to discover the truth, it is not unlikely that the Earl had taken the necessary steps to ensure a comfortable acquittal before the inquest began. Elizabeth, despite her admiration, to call it by no stronger term, must have been perfectly aware of both gossip and fact. Had no other considerations caused her to refrain from marriage with the Earl, and there were many reasons that weighed with her, Cecil's opposition being not the least, she wisely decided that while he remained merely a lover and a subject he might be managed, but would become dangerous were he to obtain the exalted rank towards which his ambition goaded him. She, indeed, at first encouraged a scheme whereby he was to wed Mary Queen of Scots. Later, on the uncompromising rejoinder of that high-spirited sovereign that she could never so far demean herself and dishonour her rank, Elizabeth gracefully withdrew her suggestion.

Leicester, flying at higher game, was indolent in the matter, and did not express the slightest desire to claim the beautiful Scotch queen for his bride. He went so far as to urge on the Duke of Norfolk to take his place as suitor. Unfortunately for himself, the Duke played a somewhat double game, and not skilfully. Professing to fall in with the views of Elizabeth, who objected to any such match, he was all the while corresponding on the suggested arrangement. The letters fell into Leicester's hands, and with unspeakable meanness, he showed them to the

Queen. By this act of treachery the Earl advanced one more step in favour, while the unlucky Duke was sent to the Tower to reflect on the practical advantages accruing from honesty to those not nimble enough to tread warily more devious paths. Leicester's subsequent incivility towards his victim is only what that victim might have expected.

He never relinquisned his deep design to become consort—it is hinted that he dreamed even of sharing the throne. In 1578 there was, as we have seen, much talk of the proposed Anjou marriage. The Duke sent over one Simier, a man skilled in courtly arts, to herald his own visit and prepare the ground. Neither the marriage project nor the ambassador of the Prince pleased the haughty nobleman. His displeasure was shared by most, but whereas Philip's horror at the alliance was patriotic, as was general, Leicester's was entirely personal and selfish. Losing no time, he invented a story which he whispered to the Queen. Simier had become a great favourite, and his popularity was gall and wormwood. People now living can be found, in the rural districts of Sussex, Devonshire, and elsewhere, who believe firmly in the existence of witches. Very few decades have passed since great and wise judges, clad in the awesome splendour of scarlet and ermine, spoke the death sentence over unfortunate folk whom a jury had declared to be in league with the powers of evil. In the sixteenth century the belief was universal. Bearing this in mind, Leicester's story was not so naïve as it would seem to the educated of our own day. He declared that Simier's influence was due absolutely to his knowledge of magic.

Elizabeth does not seem to have taken this information seriously. She thought, not unreasonably, we may conjecture, that any skill in magic arts noticeable at the Court of England was exhibited by herself. Even had Simier been guilty of witchcraft, no great harm could have

PHILIP DU MORNAY
FROM AN ENGRAVING BY L. GAULTIER

happened to him in England; he was Anjou's subject.
Accusations of witchcraft proving futile, a further attempt
to discredit the envoy was tried. True, there is no direct
evidence implicating Leicester, yet I think he must have
arranged the performance : he was the only person who
could reasonably be expected to profit should the attempt
prove successful. Simier and the Queen enjoying a voyage
on the Thames in one of the royal barges, a gun went off,
unmistakably aimed at one or other of them. By great
good fortune neither was hit, though an inoffensive barge-
man was wounded. Elizabeth roundly declared that she
herself was not the object aimed at. She declared, with
the regal pride that became her so well on this and other
difficult occasions, that she would believe of her subjects
" nothing parents would not believe of their own children."
On the gallows the maladroit sportsman was pardoned,
his story was accepted that the fowling-piece went off by
accident. The incident is a curious one. The intended
victim, Simier, did not lose the Queen's favour ; attempts
to shatter her Majesty's courage were useless. Fear, till
Death, a more powerful sovereign than herself, threatened
her, she did not know.

Simier had a shrewd notion of his enemy's plots and
plans, and took a most pertinent revenge. It came to his
ears, little escaped them, that Leicester had secretly
married the Countess of Essex. Promptly, not it may
be conceded wrongly, considering the affronts offered to
himself, and that he was Anjou's emissary whose interests
he was bound loyally to serve, he enlightened Elizabeth
on this rather, to her, insulting performance of the flamboyant Earl. That glittering nobleman found it convenient to retire from Court life for a season.

Punishments to Leicester were little more than the
sham indignities meted out to children who are bidden
stand in the corner. Very soon he acquired his old footing
at Court, and knew himself restored to power and favour.

The story of his magnificent hospitalities is too well known to repeat.

Some six years after the Simier episodes the Prince of Orange was shot at and killed by a fanatic. Several previous attempts on his life had been made. Balthasar Gerard claimed the glory, or dishonour, of having slain the wisest and bravest prince in Europe. Rumour said that Parma or the Jesuits had inspired the murder. I cannot find sufficient evidence to implicate either. The Jesuits at this time had become adepts in the *rôle* of scapegoat : Parma, incomparably the greatest general in Europe, was chivalrous and far from cruel. He was not an Alva, and he was not the man to destroy in an underhand manner his ablest opponent in the great game of war.

The murder of this mighty prince shocked but did not surprise. Not for the first time had an attack been made on his life. Reasons are easy to discover why he of all men had bitterer enemies than often fall to the lot even of rulers. His extreme toleration in matters of religion offended all parties. Catholics abused him because he protected the Protestants, who showed their gratitude by expressing disgust at his leniency towards the followers of an older faith. But though never safe from the assassin's knife, the publication of the Ban, as it was called, written by King Philip at the instigation of Cardinal Granville, was in very truth his death-warrant. Titles and honours were offered to whoso should be the murderer. Penalties were threatened against those who should speak to him or provide him with meat, drink, and raiment. William's answer to this insolent document was lengthy, conclusive, and really eloquent. Its very vehemence, while the further enraging his enemies, filled many of his supporters with uneasiness. Some of the more important cautiously drifted into security. Meanwhile the sovereignty of the United States was pressed upon him. This he consistently refused to accept. Self-advancement was no part of William's creed. Often he lacked necessaries ; at his death he was possessed only of a hundred guilders. He decided that Anjou was the man to choose, and the Valois prince came to Holland and abandoned his philanderings at the English Court. The choice was a curious one, but dictated by necessity. Among other reasons it was flattering to Elizabeth. Yet it is a strange partnership to consider, that between the man who "every time he put off his hat won a subject from the King of Spain, and one who disgusted brusque Henry of Navarre into the outspoken opinion, *Il me tromperai bien, s'il ne trompe tous ceux qui se féront en luy.*" Navarre judged shrewdly. That Leicester was glad to see the last of the Duke is easily believed. It is not unlikely also, that, judging by his subsequent aspirations expressed at no distant date, he was already considering his own chances of being offered the post the Prince declined to take. Anjou, as was to be expected, behaved abominably and disgusted every one. William none the less stuck doggedly to his choice. To offend Elizabeth would have been dangerous to the welfare of the cause, and she had told him bluntly "not to torment a prince of such quality and merit." Then a terrible event happened, and a St. Bartholomew was sought to be repeated in Antwerp, with the object, that must have been known to Anjou, of killing William. With cries of "Anjou, the mass, kill, kill !" soldiers rushed through the streets massacring all whom they met, and storming the houses of the citizens. Here they were unsuccessful, and the sturdy burghers successfully defended themselves with admirable courage. Anjou's misdeeds made it wiser for him to quit the scenes of his extravagancies, crimes, and follies.

But even when Holland was rid of the Valois fool, the life of her leader was no safer than before. One Añastros made a determined effort to slay the Prince as he was leaving the dining-room. The assassin was clearly mad and gloried in his crime.  William was severely wounded and all thought he was dying.  He himself felt that his last hour had come.  Even in his agony he peremptorily forbade his assailant to be tortured—a fine touch of generosity in such an age, a glowing proof of the tolerant and well-balanced judgment that so distinguished him. Unfortunately this command was forgotten on a still sadder occasion.  For the Prince recovered, though his wife died from shock, only to receive in his body the bullets of Balthasar.  This man, posing as Protestant and destitute, actually bought his murderous weapon with the money William had, in pity, given to him.  Death was instantaneous.  The tortures the villain suffered are too horrible to relate in detail.  Europe was seething with horror, exultation, and excitement.  Leicester's chance to wipe out the memory of his own errors by some glorious deed had come.  But his vanity and incompetence spoilt the opportunity Fate had thrown into his hands.  Here is approached the most discreditable chapter in a discreditable career.

In their despair the Hollanders turned to the English Queen for aid and counsel.  She refused, very graciously, their offer to make her their sovereign.  Affairs went from bad to worse.  St. Aldegonde seceded.  City after city fell into Spanish hands.  Parma was able and not cruel ; he won recruits.  The sun seemed set for ever on the Protestant cause.  A commission crossed to England to interview Elizabeth, to entreat her.  But she resolutely declined the honour it urged her to accept.  Help, and substantial help, she offered, and her proposal was accepted. On certain terms, not ungenerous to her own interests as was usual with her, she supplied men and means for the furtherance of the campaign.  Unhappily she placed Leicester, "whose public life was contemptible, whose private life was stained by the darkest suspicions," at the head of the troops with the resounding title of Governor-

General. The immediate result of this choice was lamentable. On landing in the provinces, the Earl conducted
himself with arrogance, amazing even in one so lost to
all sense of decency and duty. Banquets and displays
followed in quick succession ; at these he made a fine
figure. His splendour dazzled the simple-living Dutchmen. Boasts that he was of royal blood and should, of
right, stand higher than he did were often on his lips.
And amid all this junketting his soldiers were forgotten,
starving, and in rags.

He aimed at becoming Captain and Admiral-General of
the United Provinces, and for a brief while his ambition
was realised. Almost absolute power for a moment seemed
within his grasp. He treated with contempt the arguments
of sober men who opposed his rise to this unprecedented
power. Crime never deterred his schemes, and when
de Hemert lost Grave that unfortunate man was executed.
Indignation throughout Holland was intense. An easy
victory at Dœsborg did nothing to restore him to favour ;
Zutphen was a blunder, and Sidney was slain. Elizabeth
herself was furious with her absurd and cruel representative. That a subject of hers should dare to accept a
sovereignty she herself had refused cut her pride to the
quick. By the August of 1587 every one had had more than
enough of the glittering impostor, that "blaze of straw,"
as he was contemptuously labelled. Governors whom he
appointed proved treacherous, towns fell into Spanish
hands, hatred of the English became scarcely less acute
than loathing for the Spaniards. Yet Leicester persisted
in his madly arrogant career.

But his time was not quite come, and more stupid
actions were to put a seal on his incapacity. By his
dilatoriness, or a constitutional inability to see events in
their right proportions, he allowed Sluys to fall. This
town was of the utmost importance, yet he neglected to
supply the citizens with provisions, and one of the strongest

of his outposts passed of necessity into Spanish hands. The capture of Sluys, following as it did hard on the refusal of the Dutch to export rye for the English market, raised the agitation against Leicester to fever heat. He seems to have been unaware of the enormity of his failures, nor could he perceive the magnitude of his laziness and absurdity. To him, evidently, all events tended to his own glory and power. Nor did he regard any other concern of any importance at any period of his life. Yet is it curious to find that in the midst of these reverses he was actually flattering himself that the crown he aimed at was within his grasp. With superb impertinence he wrote a letter suggesting that the sovereignty of the Netherlands should be conferred upon his unworthy self. This audacious suggestion was received with contempt. But the audacity of the proposal is equalled by its folly. It was not at all likely that level-headed men would accept such a malevolent popinjay as successor to the noble William whose death they lamented. Even the momentary juxtaposition of the two names seems an insult to the memory of the hero done to death. Prince Maurice and Barneveld aroused the adventurer's jealousy. It is said he had designs, carefully prepared, to seize both and imprison them. This design he had neither the wit nor pluck to put into execution. Some nobles of Utrecht suffered from his infantile endeavours to play the tyrant. How a man playing for great stakes could have handled his cards so badly was a mystery in his own day and remains an enigma still.

His schemes failed, and at last, none too soon, he was recalled. The Queen, after an outburst of temper, this time more than justified, forgave him and restored him to favour. Her infatuation for him is amazing; but he seems to have exercised an influence over her that no other man could accomplish. He actually took his seat at the council convoked to consider his own shortcomings. What tremendous power he possessed is easily gathered from the fate meted out to his accuser, Lord Buckhurst. This intrepid and outspoken nobleman was kept a close prisoner in his own house—that truly was a concession—for some months. In 1588 the dreadful days of the Armada came. The terror of the threatened invasion hung like a cloud over the kingdom. Drake, and such as he, perhaps certain of ultimate victory, could play bowls quietly on Plymouth Hoe; for the ordinary citizen the signs of the times were disquieting and anxious. The Queen, as usual with her at a crisis, proved her courage, never doubted, and the good sense that could distinguish her at times. But, to the horror of every one, she put the incompetent Leicester in command at Tilbury. With the consummate impudence that characterised him, he accepted the responsibility. Very fortunately he was not called upon to display either his courage or his skill. He did, however, contrive to display a childish jealousy of Hunsdon—no great commander, but brave and honest—and to make himself ridiculous.

The Armada was beaten—indeed destroyed—and Leicester was afforded no single chance of making himself dangerously ridiculous.

Not many months after Howard of Effingham's victory the Earl died. That he wished to poison his wife is declared by competent historians; that she poisoned him is probable and often asserted. For England, at any rate, it must have been good to know that the man was beyond the power of doing injury. Elizabeth alone was overwhelmed with grief; yet even she remembered at this bitter moment that her favourite owed her money. She took immediate care that all debts due to her were paid from his estate. A very dangerous and a very wicked man was dead. It will always be a mystery how a man of Sidney's temperament, of his austerity, of his honesty, of his genius, could set down in writing the extraordinary confession that most of all he prided himself on being a Dudley.

The circle of Sidney's intimates was a small one. He did not live long enough, and was out of favour too decidedly and for too long a period, to make many close friendships. Probably he was not the man to have made them even had the chance been given him. Reserved and somewhat haughty, his was not a nature to win popularity, nor does he seem to have desired or courted the favour of the many. Such friendships as he had were close and tender, but they were rare. Perhaps the man he revered most was Hubert Languet, whose reputation was European, whose virtue was a byword.

Languet, a Burgundian, was born at Vitreaux in 1518. His reputation for learning was early acquired, for when less than thirty he became Professor of Civil Law at the University of Padua, then a most famous centre of learning. Theology seems to have attracted him from the first, and after two years' practice of his professorial duties he relinquished them to follow Melancthon, whose doctrines he accepted.

From Padua he went to Wittenberg and remained there till his master died in 1560. Melancthon appears to have thought of Languet much as Languet in after years thought of Philip Sidney. We are told that he had, even as we are told Philip had, a soft and melodious voice. It is said that he was also of a fine and delicate nature. These qualities he may easily have inherited from his ancestors, people of distinction at Vitreaux.

How a boy so gently raised as Languet was could have cared for Melancthon is a problem no one now can decide. We must take facts as they are. Melancthon came from Britten in the Rhenish Palatine. His father was called the "locksmith of Heidelberg." His qualifications to expound theology are obvious. Men of note on both sides could flaunt credentials of no greater value. It is recorded of him, however, that he studied assiduously. He made himself a proficient in law, in medicine, and in theology. By what authorities he was passed as proficient in any one of these studies is not recorded. This at least may be said for him, that Erasmus had a high opinion of his learning, and said so. "Immortal God, what promise is there in this young man, this boy! His attainments in both literatures are equally valuable. What ingenuity and acumen, what purity of language, what beauty of expression, what a memory for the most unfamiliar things, what a wide extant of reading!" To quote this encomium is fair, but one must not forget who was the author of the panegyric. Erasmus was always too much a "Mr. Facing-both-ways" to inspire real confidence. Both sides in the controversy quote him, but the party that quotes him most often is the one he had not courage to join. Melancthon would have had those who disagreed with him, supposing they were peasants, hunted down. Luther was more humane. One would have had them destroyed, the other wanted to spare all he could. Yet a German writer of repute declares that Languet must have been "captivated by the gentleness of this son of the 'locksmith of Heidelberg.'" Languet was captivated by Melancthon, who must have possessed personal charm. But it is idle to pretend that an undue portion of human feeling was a chief characteristic. He was a masterful man, and, like most masterful men of the time, did not care how cruel his methods were if he could get his own way. The greatest enemies of Kings and Popes are very often those who would like to be Kings or Popes themselves. German peasants did not willingly submit to the authority of this man with the melodious voice, so he was willing to slaughter them by the thousand. Languet became broader-minded as the shadows of old age crept round him. An unhappy strife arose between Lutherans and other Reformers with regard to details to be observed at the administration of the Lord's Supper. An unhappier cause of quarrel could hardly have arisen, since they who averred that they knew the proper method were attacking the sanctuaries of both parties. The aggressive power was Spain—a power they both professed to hate.

To one used to the idea of the gay and debonnair Frenchman, this staid man, austerely virtuous, destitute of humour, is a curious figure. That he meant well, despite his bigotry, dared a good deal, and would have braved more had he been called upon, is clear from the conduct of his life and the trend of his writings. Languet's fault is that he was too virtuous and too anxious. He saw no merit in an opponent, and communicated to Philip much of that bigotry which soils the knight's otherwise beautiful character. Men in the sixteenth century were, it would seem, utterly incapable of taking a balanced view of theological controversy. The man who agreed with the speaker was hugged, the man who opposed him anathematised. It is not very difficult to understand the state of things. Religious persecution exists now, in England, and with less excuse. Philip's sombre temper appealed greatly to Languet, and quickly he assumed the office of mentor; from this he was never dismissed. The hero of Zutphen died too soon after his master to cast about for a new leader. It is the custom in most books that I have read to glorify this friendship in extravagant terms. I cannot think that it brought to Philip much happiness. He was devoted to his master, but he was a boy, though an unduly sober one. Languet, surprising in a Frenchman, seems to have been dull as well as learned. His letters, from which I have made extracts, make one marvel at Philip's complacency in answering any of them. They are ponderous, dull, and observe that sort of piety akin to what may be supposed to be the correspondence of a successful speculator.

Languet knew Sidney's reputation, had a just estimate of the boy's ability. He seems to have thought that Philip was in duty bound to sacrifice everything, including the

HUBERT LANGUET

promise of a great career, for the Protestant cause. It is
very difficult to get into the minds of these people ; not
easy to understand how such men as Languet could influence a Sidney, or how either could honestly behave in the
way that too often they did. Charity was, one fancies, a
word not tabulated in their dictionaries. Languet's letters
have become famous, and they who have not read them
are pleased to praise them highly. They are at once
bitter, stupid, querulous, and long-winded. If Philip is
at Court, he is accused of wasting his time ; if he is not in
attendance he is told he ought to be. When Philip does
not write—and what boy of his age ever wrote a letter
willingly ?—he is remonstrated with, much after the manner
of Mr. Plowden admonishing a juvenile offender.

It is odd that Sidney put up with these letters ; their
gush and piety are sickening enough to-day. But we
have it on record that he received the letters gladly, and
noted their contents with care. Languet must have had
personal qualities that he could not communicate to the
written page. Difficult, indeed, is it to picture a high-
spirited boy receiving his lugubrious and sermonising
epistles with even a show of patience. He had " papist "
and "atheist " on the brain, and apparently an indulgence
in any wholesome frivolity was bound to make a man one
or the other. This, most unfortunately, Philip seems to
have accepted as gospel truth. Always preternaturally
old, Languet's letters were not calculated to make him
younger. Languet was a learned man, even a wise man in
some respects : he saw the meaning of events clearly, but
his letters to Philip make only sorrowful reading. His
attacks on Philip's supposed idleness are morbidly ridiculous. What could a sensitive boy make of such a
sentence as this : " My noble Sidney, you must avoid that
persistent siren, Sloth "? Sloth was a siren who sang to
Philip in vain. He might, indeed, have thought more and
written less with advantage. He was, too, willing to take

his principles, arguments, and prejudices from such men as Languet. This facility of absorption has not tended to improve his reputation.

Languet came of a good stock ; his learning was beyond dispute ; at times he was wise, almost always he was honest. His greatest fault, to modern eyes, is his portentous lack of humour. Apparently he was debarred, by some curious physical defect, from observing the lighter side of any question. Not improbably his honesty conduced to his stolidity. " I hope," he writes to Philip in the April of 1574, "if you have not done what you promised me, about correcting your pronunciation, that you will do it now. I think it is most essential and yet perfectly easy." This was not a too cheerful letter for a boy to receive, but there is one written five years later, which frees Sidney from blame in any fault he may have committed : " Now I will treat you frankly, as I am accustomed to do, for I am sure our friendship has reached a mark at which neither of us can be offended at any freedom of the other." The freedom was mostly shown by Languet. The friendship was not without value. On the records it is not easy to account Languet a great man ; it is quite easy, and incontrovertible, to account Sidney a rather foolish one. They were both for all that was right, as they conceived ; but, like certain intemperate orators and others of our own day, they hurt their reputations and did harm to their cause. Preaching freedom piously, they were intolerant in fact. Over and over again it has been shown, by experience and theory, that people of this sort are not a valuable asset to any community. Languet had one gleam of common sense. He writes to Philip in the March of 1580 : "For our men do more harm to those who pay them than to their enemies." The conclusion of the letter in which this phrase occurs is Jesuitical, in Languet's meaning of the term, to the extreme.

It is the fashion of historians to extol Languet. Reasons

for so curious a eulogy are not given. He cared for Sidney for four reasons. The boy was astoundingly clever, good-looking as people accounted looks, well born—an important asset—and very earnest. Languet was earnest and creditably born, but he was not more honest than Philip, nor was he more able. He was a pedagogue, and sometimes an annoying one.

Yet his letters have a vogue. They have been translated into various languages. One cannot help thinking that better letters have gone unpublished. Languet's morals were beyond reproach. Indeed, his immaculate virtue tends to make the reader angry. His sense of humour was not developed ; his outlook on life and the trend of events was a narrow one. His Catholic opponents were not generous, but they knew how to strike ; the Huguenot was querulous and always allowed " I dare not " to be handmaiden to " I would." He was a conceited old man and a morbid one. His letters to Sidney were enough to damp the ardour of any recipient. There are no great works extant to his credit ; there are some hundred pages that tell against him. He meant well, and achieved a fame that most certainly he never deserved. I cannot find, and I have tried, among Elizabethans another example of one who gained so great honour on such slight grounds, and of one who was an intellectual snob and fanatic yet was able to persuade people he was of vast importance. Languet was very wise and very stupid. He was a man who made wisdom rather irritating. He was, in a word, a prig. His letters prove it. Philip's character would not have been hurt by an occasional indulgence in the more harmless frivolities of his time, in junkettings suited to his youth. Nor would his health have suffered. No small part of his premature solemnity was due to Languet's teaching and admonition. What the exact charm of his companionship was is difficult to discover. He was no hypocrite, but at the same time

was certainly not intended, either by himself or Providence, to play the *rôle* of martyr.   His frequent employment on diplomatic missions on behalf of the Protestant
princes of Germany doubtless taught him some of the
wiles of the serpent.   As a shrewd writer says of him,
" He promoted the cause not so much by forward devotion
and zeal as by the management and the arts of diplomacy."
That he was convinced of the rightness of his cause is
beyond dispute ; so also it is beyond dispute that he did
not severely labour, if at all, on its behalf.   When not
actually employed he lived comfortably in Frankfort, and
to him came many men of importance.   In them he
instilled a zeal more active, though I think not more
sincere, than his own.   His travels were extensive, he
had many difficult negotiations to conduct ; but his life
was only once in danger, for he always could protect
himself in the folds of an ambassador's robe.   While
speaking his own convictions he was also only echoing
those of some reigning potentate, whose mouthpiece he
was.   However important at the time his labours may
have been—and important they certainly were considered
by his contemporaries—they make dull enough reading
to-day.

   For good or ill Christendom is divided roughly, so far as
Europe is concerned, into two schools of religious thought
—the Catholic and the non-Catholic.   Petty intrigues
of petty princes, of sometimes unduly arrogant bishops
and dour ministers of infant creeds, are not profitable or
even interesting reading.   The map of Europe does not
look like anything these clever, eager people expected to
make it.   Neither party to the religious controversy has
converted its opponent.   The New Learning and the Old
Wisdom are not yet reconciled.   But Languet was no
coward, and probably if martyrdom had been his lot
he would have accepted his fate bravely.   The most
that can be urged is that he was not anxious for heroic

honours, and preferred the shop of his friend Wechel to
the fiercer glories of the stake.   This is not surprising, and
he cannot be reasonably blamed.   But the ultimate fatuity
of many of the disputes in which he acted as spokesman
or director, the barren controversies of the schoolmen in
which he took part, are neither romantic nor profitable.
Consequently we find the life of a man who was of importance in his day .no very exhilarating reading.   Yet he
could speak out boldly when the occasion was thrust upon
him.   A King of France was made to learn this, and
Languet's life was in danger during the Bartholomew massacres as the result of his courage.   In
escaping uninjured he contrived to save the life of
Wechel, the Frankfort bookseller, with whom he made
his home.

The house of Christian Wechel was in some cases the
dwelling-place, and in all cases the club, of refugees from
France.   Christian so far back as 1530 had established
himself, with reputation, at Frankfort.   Convinced Protestant though he was, he allowed his son Andrew to
settle in Paris, doubtless hoping by this arrangement to
increase the business connections of the firm.   The
bigotry or foolishness of the authorities there had seriously
hampered Andrew's movements and plans.   The massacres of St. Bartholomew did not improve his chances of
success, and he was glad enough to escape the fury of the
mob and hurry to Frankfort.   Here, in safety, he was able
to continue and improve the trade Christian had initiated,
and his own learning and scholarship attracted many
fugitives of distinction to the city, for in his parlour could
always be heard good talk, whether of a theological trend
or more usefully employed in animated controversy as to
the rival merits of the writers of antiquity.   Philip, of
course, knew of the erudite bookseller, and visited him
directly he arrived at the Rhenish city.   Perhaps they
travelled there together, since both fled from the same

place, the same persecution.  It was at Wechel's house
that Languet and Philip met for the first time.

Languet had, a few years before his meeting with
Philip, met that other Philip, Philip du Mornay, with
whose virtues and wisdom Europe was familiar ; and the
friendsi ip between the old scholar and the young Frenchman lasted till death parted them.  Philip Sidney accompanied Languet to Vienna, and it was when they separated
in the autumn of 1573 that the curious interchange of
letters began.  As has been shown, the younger man's
visit to Venice did not please Languet, and caused him
anxiety.  This feeling of unrest is curious, for he expected
Philip to do great things for Christianity, and the Protestant cause in particular.  Opportunities to study the
disposition of his pupil had been frequent for many
months.  Venetian gaieties were not likely to absorb the
attention of so sober-minded a youth.  This he must have
known, yet never ceased from fretting until he knew his
*protégé* was safe on his homeward journey and the wicked
city of the Adriatic would see him no more.  Venice,
in reality, was at that time the best school in Europe
for a budding politician.  Christianity in Europe was, with
rare exceptions, scarcely more than a label men attached
to their sleeves.  Even its most sacred truths were dis-
honoured and defiled by the rancour and quarrels of
contending factions.  While Christians abused and slew
each other the relentlessly powerful Turk was strengthening his position and extending his territories.  Venice
first, and all Italy afterwards, seemed inevitably destined to
destruction by the Mohammedan flood.  In the Council
Chamber Philip could hear wise and timely words, and
learn from the way the danger was met more of policy
and statesmanship than even Languet could teach him.
But the sage was fearful and jealous.  He hated the young
man to be away from him, imagined perils that were
vague, temptations that for Philip had neither danger nor

charm.   A lonely man, despite the fame and the consideration he enjoyed, in the midst of his strenuous labours
his heart yearned after and feared for his boyish friend.
He does not seem to have approved of Philip's ambition
unless exercised under his own direction.   He forgot that
many playing important parts in the European drama
were young, and had won their spurs when even younger
than his beloved English disciple.

Towards the end of his life he bcame more tolerant,
and endeavoured to influence his contemporaries, though
his efforts were in vain.   His wise attitude in the troublesome dispute concerning the Lord's Supper, a quarrel
that divided Lutherans and Calvinists into bitterly hostile
parties, did not commend itself to the majority of Germans.
These dangerous dissensions that in a moment of grave
peril threatened such disaster to the Reformed faith made
him weary of life.   Bitterly he writes: "What should I
fear from the machinations of priests, when I see that my
life is of no use to any one, that Death only can release me
from all the suffering I have endured!   What can be
worse for a man than to look upon the crime that has been
committed, for ten or twelve years now, in our miserable
France and in the Netherlands!   I did not fear the hatred
of the priests!   For life and death are in the hands of God,
and they could do nothing against me without His
sanction."

Feeling that he himself was superior to priestly persuasion and keen enough to outwit clerical designs, he
could not feel perfectly happy about Philip.   By a process
of reasoning that seems somewhat foolish now, he persuaded himself that Italy was not a country in which the
lad should linger.   The anxiety he displayed reveals a
want of faith in the stability, one might write obstinacy, of
the young man's temperament.   Of all men Philip least
needed such solemn admonition as is contained in a letter
he wrote to his pupil as follows: " Nothing is more

dangerous to a noble mind than the insidious way in
which a man's strength, ability, and mind are gradually
degraded into slaves ; for this wretched servitude is the
aim and object of the intrigues to which, in Italy, you now
expose yourself.   Is it not better for you, with your talents,
fitter for you when your future is considered, that you
should piously declare with your lips and treasure, in your
heart, your faith, that you should defend the good cause
of the oppressed against unjust powers " ("injustice and
power " is the exact translation,) "and nerve yourself to
sacrifice your life for your country?   These lessons [things]
you can learn better in Germany than in Italy ; and this is
why I keep on urging you to return here."   Religion, at
the time this letter was written, did not appeal to Italian
brains as providing a subject of agreeable controversy.   In
the peninsula men accepted announced truths very
calmly and did not dispute their credentials or the authority
of those who propounded them.   A Genoese or Venetian
gallant would have refused to wear a ready-made suit of
doublet and hose : a ready-made religion saved him a
good deal of trouble.   His concern was, as the poet of
*Galuppi, Baldassaro* reminds us, with

"Balls and masks begun at midnight, ending ever at mid-day.
When they made up fresh adventures for the morrow."

Languet had not the slightest cause for anxiety.   He
invented, so far as Philip is concerned, his own troubles,
and his uneasiness speaks well for his affection but hardly
convinces us that he was thoroughly acquainted with Philip's
immobile habit of mind when contemplating Churches and
creeds.   Justice compels us to realise that had Philip been
other than he was alarm would have been natural.   Italy,
ever since the "Knightly days of the Earl of Surrey and the
fair Geraldine," had chiefly attracted young men of noble
and illustrious families who travelled in search of culture

and knowledge.   That " The Unfortunate Traveller " of
Nash's fancy never was in Italy at all is as certain as
anything can be ; the legend, however, was in the air long
years before that ingenious author gave to it the dignity
of print.   Many of these youthful voyagers did fall victims
to the allurements of the Catholic Church, we are told,
Genoa especially being a dangerous and ungodly home of
the Jesuits.   But Genoa was in close league with Spain,
and a voyage in Spain was more likely than a sojourn in
Italy, at this time, to destroy the immature faith of boyish
Protestants.   Even the son of the great Prince of Orange
remained at Philip's Court willingly, a loyal Catholic and
Spaniard by choice.   Men scarcely less distinguished than
Languet frowned severely on this habit of foreign travel
south of the Alps and Pyrenees.   As the political situation
in Europe then was, a political reason for this opposition
would not, even now, read unreasonably.   The squabbling
Protestant sects, forgetful almost always of the truth that
unity is strength, did universally regard with alarm and
horror these excursions, and contrived in their disapproval
to discover a common platform.   Roger Ascham was not
less lachrymose than Languet.   He loved, he tells us, the
Italian language almost as well as he loved the older
classics.   The land of its birth he regarded with an
almost ludicrous suspicion.   His advice is very direct and
outspoken : " If you must go there, then you must go with
the wisest teaching of the wisest men (apart from the
Holy Scriptures) ; and you must beware of the enchant-
ments of Circe, from which nothing can save you but
godly means."   He warns his reader to avoid the dissolute
books to be found in the Italian shops, and says they are
even more pernicious than "all that has been printed " in
the Jesuit colleges of Louvain.   Absurd as this warmth of
abuse may sound to most modern ears, it passed for good
and well-weighed sense not only with fellow-scholars like
Languet but also with such men as Sackville and

Walsingham, who were statesmen first and theologians afterwards. And it must always be borne in mind that, lamentably narrow as such an outlook is, men honestly believed that eternal damnation was the inevitable fate of those whose religious beliefs differed from their own. Such an attitude is not, of course, now universal. But it is still held by some otherwise quite sane and not unkindly people. From observation of these we may get a faint notion of the bitterness that animated men of opposing creeds in the second half of the sixteenth century. As yet that simple and useful creed, " Trust in God and keep your powder dry," beloved of Nelson, had not been invented or thought of.

A horror of money seems to have been a characteristic of the Burgundian wiseacre. He knew, it could not have been concealed from him, that the Sidney's were poor, and his friend often at a loss for ready cash. Men, in most ways good and honourable, had become somewhat unscrupulous in their pursuit of wealth. The lax habits, in this matter, of his contemporaries made Languet nervous for the conduct of his pupil. He writes very seriously on this matter several times ; two extracts will suffice : " But if your desire of fame and glory makes your present activity irksome to you, place before you the example of the old Chandoses and Talbots ; you will obtain greater honour and glory by following their steps than if you could obtain all the wealth which the Spaniards have brought over from their new world, on the strength of which they have insulted all the nations of Europe, and so disgusted them with their insolence, that they now feel, and perhaps will soon feel, still more that they have erred in their reckoning." But greed of gold was not only a Spanish and Papist vice, as the writer very well knew. It was indeed a universal vice, a craze for the precious metal possessed men like a disease. The rich freight of the Spanish galleons stirred men to adventure and robbery.

It was not only love of liberty and Christian zeal for reformed Churches that inspired the men of Northern Europe. Languet knew this, his own hands and inclinations were very clean, and he writes again: "If what you say about Frobisher is true, you have stumbled on that gift of nature which is of all the most fatal and baneful to mankind, yet which men so madly covet, as it, more than anything else in the world, stirs them to incur every kind of risk. I fear that England, crazed by the love of gold, will just empty herself into these islands that Frobisher has been finding." Later, in the same letter, he adopts a tone of eloquence and high morality most edifying, for the lesson was dictated by both heart and brain. They, of our own day, who measure success by the size of their bank balances, giving, too, consideration to the bearers of full purses, would not find in a Languet an agreeable or comfortable companion. This wisdom none called in question, he did not mince words, and he remained poor in his rooms over the shop of the Frankfort bookseller, when he might have been wealthy and richly housed. It is noteworthy to remember in judging him, that familiar with the palaces of princes, he was content to live in lodgings. And there was particular reason for his anxiety. The possession of great wealth could in no way enhance Philip's great reputation. Quite conceivably riches thirsted for and acquired, might have, as they had in so many cases, notably in Elizabeth herself, an ugly trick of besmirching a noble character. Philip's desire for them was natural enough. Want of money, he knew, had ruined his father's peace of mind. He himself was rather given to extravagance, was generous to a fault, and had a too exalted idea of his rank, overestimating the total expenditure looked for in one circumstanced as he was. Languet writes: "Do I, therefore, think that you should reject these treasures that God has thrown in your way? Anything but that. Nay; I thoroughly admire the high

spirit, the perseverance, and even the good fortune of
Frobisher.  He deserves great rewards.  But I am thinking of you, for you seem to rejoice in the circumstance as
if it was the best thing possible for your country, especially
as I noticed in you last spring a certain longing to undertake this kind of enterprise ; and if Frobisher's foolish
hope of finding a north-west passage had power then to
fascinate you, what will not these golden mountains do, or
rather these islands all of gold, as I daresay they shape
themselves day and night in your mind ?   Beware, I
do beseech you, and never let 'the cursed hunger after
gold,' whereof the poet speaks, creep over that spirit of
yours, into which nothing has hitherto been admitted save
the love of goodness and the desire of earning the goodwill of all men.   If these golden islands are fixing themselves too deeply in your thoughts, turn them out before
they possess you, and keep yourself safe till you can serve
your friends or your country in a better way."

Languet had another member of the Sidney family
under his care, for in 1580, after a visit to England
and the formation there of many hearty friendships, with
Lady Sidney, Sir Henry, Fulke Greville, and the poet
Dyer, whose friendship he likened to a gem added to his
treasures, Robert Sidney was bade look to him as mentor.
The boy does not seem to have shared all Philip's remarkable qualities, though it is difficult not to believe that he
was somewhat more human.  He married Barbara Gamage,
who, as a friend of Ben Jonson's, must have been dowered
with more than common wit.  Robert was Philip's heir.
His career was honourable and is elsewhere discussed.
The Earl of Leicester's wealth fell to him, and he was
created a baron, a viscount, and finally Earl of Leicester.
These distinctions, however gratifying to the recipient, are
not indicative of his superior conduct in epoch-making
events.   The picture of him,.standing arm in arm with
Philip, is curious.  Neither are conspicuously prepossessing,

and they are very much alike ; but Philip looks sullen, and
Robert looks sly ; both have thin legs and hands, and
large feet ; Robert's hair waves one way, Sidney's the
other.   For portraiture of this kind it could scarcely have
been necessary for either to sit.   But, indeed, most of the
portraits of this age seem to have been fashioned in one
and the same mould.   Languet was delighted with the
picture Philip sent him from Venice, but this was painted
by Veronese, and Languet said of it, " It looks to me so
beautiful and true a likeness of you that I feel there is
nothing in the world I prize so much ; I think, though,
that the artist has made you look too sad and thoughtful ;
I should have liked it better if your face had had a merrier
look when you sat for the painting."   What this picture
was like we shall never know.   We must be as content as
we can with the efforts of Zucchero and others worse than
he.

Robert and Languet seem to have been friendly ; there
is not, however, any sign that the Huguenot scholar
regarded his charge as more than an amiable young man
of high birth, whom it was pleasant to teach, but who was
in no sense a companion, especially when the discussion
was of great matters.

Languet's end was not happy.   For him the future had
no terrors, but he was unhappy at the condition of the
affairs he had to leave.   Those he cared for seemed to be
players in a losing game.   Even Philip du Plessy du
Mornay could not cheer him.   A kind of cowardice seems
to have chilled him.   Yet perhaps it was less cowardice
than despair.   Believing in God and the Reformed Faith, he
saw the banner of the army waver ; he was glad to leave
the world, a curious example of the faith that put its trust
in Him who defends the right.   He had been a good friend
to Philip and a wise one, but he was too sombre ; in his
anxieties for the causes he espoused and the friends he
loved, he rendered needlessly unhappy, destroying some of

the good that may fairly be attributed to his learning, piety, and statecraft.

In some ways du Mornay was the most famous of Philip's friends. Oddly enough they bore the same Christian name, and they had the same ideals and mutual theories as to the necessity for self-effacement. Both were modest in all that concerned themselves, both were of high rank and distinguished lineage. There is nothing astonishing in the friendship that sprang up between the two men, or perhaps we should say the two youths approaching manhood. The French Philip was, however, some years older than his English namesake. But he was very young when he and Sidney met, and he was a long way from being middle aged when Philip died. It can hardly be contended that Philip du Mornay was always a successful ambassador. His efforts in England in 1577 to raise enthusiasm for Henry of Navarre and the French Protestant cause were not fortunate. "I am delighted to hear that you have become intimate with du Plessy," writes Languet. It must have been pleasant for him to know that the two young men whose future seemed so brilliant had met, liked, and saw much of each other. Of the two, Philip was probably the old man's favourite, but of Mornay he speaks always in terms of great eulogy and affection. The natures of the two companions were alike. Both were prematurely serious, both eminently sober and religious in their habits, both were imbued with a hatred of the Papacy and Spain. On du Mornay no more than on Philip was a sense of humour conspicuously bestowed, and he would seem to have had something less than the Englishman's success as a diplomatist. It must, however, be always remembered that as regards his English missions, at any rate, he was confronted with a sovereign whose plan was to promise much and perform little. His manners were, from every account, perfect ; his wisdom caused admiration ; his generosity and kindness of heart inspired affection ; his learning prompted warm admiration.

The narrowness of view that distinguished his ideas on religious questions is not at all astonishing. The horrors of St. Bartholomew when he was either waking or sleeping passed before his eyes. A tragedy so frightful was not easily forgiven or forgotten. He was in Paris during the massacre, and had resided there some time previously. Like Philip Sidney, indeed like older and wiser, because more experienced, men than either, he did not see the storm brewing. An illusion of universal peace and amity between rival factions lulled him, as it had others, into a belief that the cruel days of massacre and persecution were over. With others equally credulous he had a rude awakening, and was, himself, a fugitive and witness of the horrors perpetrated. Whether he and Philip Sidney met in Paris is not quite certain. Probably they did, but had no chance of becoming intimate. The real beginning of their friendship dates from the day the Frenchman presented, in London, to his English namesake Languet's letter of introduction. This friendship was the most valuable asset du Mornay derived from his embassy. Certainly the Protestant cause got scant help from England's Protestant Queen. During the next year, 1578, Philip du Mornay returned to England, this time with a wife and a baby. The closeness of the friendship between the two men is evidenced by the fact that Sidney stood godfather to the little girl.

Du Mornay did not confine himself to ineffectual diplomacy. Earnest and eloquent, the products of his pen attracted attention. Among other things he wrote *A Work concerning the Trueness of the Christian Religion.* This Philip Sidney thought much of and partially translated. He had no time to finish the work, but handed over the *De Veritata Christiana*, such was the original title, to a competent translator. When finished, the English version was, amazing though the fact appears, dedicated, by Philip's express command, to the exemplary

Earl of Leicester. What pleasure the Earl of Leicester took in a reading of the volume is not recorded. Leicester escaped one epidemic of his era, he was not theologically mad.

The tragedy of Zutphen completed, du Mornay was still active, reasonable, and heroic ; his conduct at Ivry, four years after Sidney's death, has found its chroniclers, and not undeservedly.

# CHAPTER XVI

## SIR FRANCIS WALSINGHAM

His upright character—Ambassador in Paris—Badly served—His
shrewdness overestimated—Secretary of State—Advises Philip
—Interest in Frobisher's voyages—Negotiates French alliance
—Marries his daughter to Philip—Her character and conduct
—Mary Queen of Scots—Visits James—Fooled by Gray—
Early death.

IN strange contrast to Leicester was another man
who exercised great influence over Philip. But any
attempt to do justice to the career of Sir Francis
Walsingham would be to exceed my object and the
necessary limitations set me. His career was a long one,
and he was held in great regard by his contemporaries.
For us he is chiefly interesting as Philip's friend and the
friend of Philip's father, and as standing, eventually, almost
in the position of a second father to Sir Henry Sidney's
son. That he was a man of virtue and honour cannot be
disputed ; that he was endowed with conspicuous foresight
and ability we are told by those who have presumably
fitted themselves to speak with authority. The latter half
of this glowing estimate is at least open to doubt. So far
as we can judge he would seem to have been easily deceived
on more than one occasion : his honesty as a man somewhat spoiled his career as a statesman. His value was of
a twofold quality, he obeyed orders and he did not ask
for rewards. Such qualifications were inestimable in the

eyes of a mean and imperious Sovereign, but from the
possession of them, when bare of initiative or respectable
cunning, we cannot expect to see a statesman of the first
rank evolved.   We look in vain for any permanent contribution on Walsingham's part to the building up of his
country's history, and his very personality is scarcely more
real to us than that conjured up in our imaginations by
the frequent repetition of a particular name in documents
and despatches.   When the great Victorian poet told us
so much of *People of Importance in their Day*, he might
well have found a corner for Sir Francis in his gallery.   Of
importance in his day he was, but in our day he carries
little more distinction with him than many another who
obeyed orders faithfully three hundred years ago.   In his
letters there is a curious timidity and irresolution displayed—not timidity or irresolution of a frightened man
anxious about his individual conduct in anything that
concerns himself, but the nervous wariness of the second-
rate statesman who too often lets " I dare not wait upon
I would."   Such, as it seems to me, is his character, that
of a man compelling respect but in no way calling for
excessive admiration.

Walsingham's first meeting with Philip was in Paris, on
the eve of St. Bartholomew.   Yet the Ambassador, so
well served by his spies as Hallam asserts, was ridiculously
ignorant of the conspiracy, and no one was more surprised
than he when the massacre occurred.   Either his spies or
his intelligence were decidedly to seek on this lamentable occasion.   And he did not see that the Huguenots
themselves were much to blame for the crimes that agitated
Paris, and of which they were the principal victims.
Macaulay, staunch defender of Huguenot and Protestant,
admits that "beyond all doubt the proceedings of the
Huguenots, from the conspiracy of Amboise to the battle
of Montcontour, had given much more trouble to the French
monarchy than the Catholics had ever given to the English

monarchy since the Reformation, and that, too, with much
less excuse." The wisdom of Mr. Secretary Walsingham
did not enable him to grasp a truth that stared him daily
in the face. Yet to his care Philip was confided when the
boy first visited Paris.

Both Walsingham and Cecil were, indeed, very badly
served by their agents at this time. Had Cecil been at
all aware of the trouble to come it is unlikely that he
would have despatched a special embassy to Paris, there
to take conspicuous part in the rejoicings and congratulations attending the royal wedding. And we may be quite
certain that he would have prevented so young a boy as
Philip taking so great a risk as a resident in the French
capital necessarily incurred. The deeds of the St. Bartholomew eve aroused scarcely less horror by the Thames
than in the city on the Seine. A hideous example was
suddenly presented of the monstrous cruelties partisans of
rival creeds were capable of exercising. So astounding
a performance must have needed careful preparation, and
it is foolish to suggest that the first of English statesmen
was served by men of even moderate capacity and fidelity,
since he only learnt the terrible news when it became
common property.

There is this excuse for Cecil, that he was in London ;
there can be little for Walsingham, who was in Paris, in a
great position too, as Elizabeth's ambassador. Reading
by the light of later knowledge it seems incredible that
he should have had no inkling of what was to be attempted.
He had, however, no premonition, and his reputation for
foresight and vigilance would seem to rest on a very
infirm foundation. His character as a man it were impertinent to criticise. It is above indiscreet praise or
unmannerly blame. In all things that he understood he
advised shrewdly and kindly. Scrupulously honest himself he had the misfortune—in a statesman it is nothing
less—to believe in the honesty of others. Believe no man

till you have tested his qualities, is the pessimistic lesson
history seems to preach ; Walsingham was too blind or
too honourable to accept such a doctrine. To labour the
point is useless. Judged by a reasonable standard he was
wanting, a shrewder head than his was needed. In other
affairs, outside the scope of this book, he showed no very
unusual talents. The fiction, beloved of historians, that
he was a man of genius and perspicacity is a fairy tale.
The efficient spies by whom he was served are part of the
illusion, and inspired Mr. Hallam to speak pontifically,
which he was fond of doing when least well advised. He
makes some amends when he says : " Walsingham himself,
sagacious as he was, fell into the snares of that den of
treachery, giving credit to the young King's assurances
almost on the very eve of St. Bartholomew."

This sagacity, here alluded to, is not apparent in much
that Walsingham did now or at any other time when an
ability to read the warning signs of future events would
have been useful. His rise to eminence was due much
more to honesty than to talent. Dozens of men, many of
genius, surrounded the Queen at Greenwich. The meanest
of these was abler than the ambassador. But, for the
most part, these courtiers played their cards primarily
with a view to their own advantage, emolument, and preferment. Cecil knew this, no man better, and it was to
his and the Queen's advantage to utilise the services of a
man who obeyed without much questioning and who
sought for no personal advantage. On the whole, for
such clever intriguers a better servant could not have been
found. Such routine work as his various offices made
necessary he did, no doubt, admirably. When not called
upon to initiate a policy—he seldom was—his knowledge
of the " rule of thumb" made him invaluable. The in-
dustrious and honest clerk to a swindling firm could not
be more useful than he was. His honest belief in the
integrity of his employers gave them an appearance of

probity they did not deserve, and has built for him the
reputation of a profundity which he never possessed.

There is a saying, extremely popular in Lancashire, and
not unknown elsewhere, that "a ricketty gate hangs a
long time." Walsingham's failure to anticipate the massacre of St. Bartholomew did not work to his dis-
advantage, as it should have done. After seeing Philip
safely away from the scene of slaughter and confusion
he returned to England. He was made a Secretary of
State. But the honour was not the idle one familiar to
us to-day. It did not mean that having proved himself
a failure he had earned a fuller title and permanent
obscurity. For some years to come he was employed
in matters of vital importance to his Sovereign and his
country. Meanwhile, in the midst of the turmoil at
Paris, he had found time to consider the virtues and
accomplishments, no less than the safety, of Philip.
Deeply stirred by the, as he conceived it, duplicity of
the Catholic Church, entirely forgetful of the edifying
squabbles which enlivened existence for supporters of
the Reformed Churches, he became convinced that Philip
had become a Catholic. All Languet's eloquence was
needed to disabuse the sagacious statesman who has
won Hallam's regard. As we know, the Roman Church
could not have displayed its arts more hopelessly than
in an effort to persuade this turgid and sincere Protestant,
who thought that Rome was a synonym for hell and
that the Pope was the devil. So great was Walsingham's
fear, that Philip, on Languet's advice, made a point of
meeting certain ministers of unimpeachable austerity.
It was a real anxiety that agitated Walsingham, caused
by a sincere love for the boy. That Philip would be
eventually his son-in-law, was a scheme that had not
entered the elder man's head. But it is difficult to
discover wherein the sagacity of a man is proved who
could think a massacre, attended by every sort of

horror, would prove a powerful enough argument to
cause a clever and learned youth to forsake the faith
of his father and accept that odiously flaunted by a
gang of assassins. And it must be remembered that
Philip was well out of danger before this nervous
anxiety was exhibited : hence there is little or no excuse
for so absurd a supposition : and our belief in the
astuteness of an excellent gentleman receives another
rude shock.

When immediately under the gaze of Cecil, Lord
Burleigh, he seems to have done useful work. Relieved
from the necessity of taking the initiative, he could obey
orders with alacrity and skill. To Philip he was a very
good and assiduous friend : also a sensible one. The
affection he showed to the boy was cordially returned.
Next only to Languet and his father, Philip seems to have
looked to Walsingham with confidence, and to have
obeyed such injunctions as the older man thought fit to
put forward from time to time in the arrangement of his
purely personal conduct and affairs. In such a *rôle*, no
doubt, Sir Francis appeared to advantage ; and the
absence, often protracted, of Sir Henry, made such a
director as he was of real advantage, even when it did
not seem necessary to accept his counsel. At least
Philip could talk to him freely, and probably availed
himself of the privilege gratefully and frequently. In
minor, but not unimportant matters, his precepts would be
practical and worthy serious consideration. It came
about, therefore, that Walsingham, many years before
Philip's marriage, stood much in the relation of a father
to his future son-in-law. When Philip was sent once
more abroad, he wrote to the Secretary of State with
commendable regularity and in considerable detail. At
the conclusion of the embassy to Germany it was
Walsingham who had the gratification of first announcing the success achieved to his old friend, Sir Henry

Sidney ; he did so somewhat quaintly in the following words :—

" I am to impart unto you the return of the young gentleman, Mr. Sidney your son, whose message, very sufficiently performed, and the relating thereof, is no less gratefully received and well liked of her Majesty, than the honourable opinion he hath left behind with all the princes with whom he had to negotiate hath left a most sweet savour and grateful remembrance of his name in those parts. The gentleman hath given no small arguments of great hope, the fruits whereof I doubt not but your lordship shall reap, as the benefit of the good parts that are in him, and whereof he hath given some taste in this voyage, is to redound to more than your lordship and himself. There hath not been any gentleman, I am sure, these many years, that hath gone through so honourable a charge with as great commendations as he ; in consideration whereof I could not but communicate this part of my joy with your lordship, being no less refreshing unto me in these my troublesome businesses than the soil is to the chafed stag."

In Elizabeth's day men wrote to each other picturesque and flamboyant letters. A certain unstudied eloquence seemed to animate everybody who put his thoughts on paper. Apart from this, then universal, characteristic, the words are sincerely meant, and Walsingham's unwearied attentions to Philip prove the truth of his assertion that the young man's success was hardly less refreshing to himself than it must be to the father of such a prodigy.

When Frobisher contemplated his famous voyage, in 1575, Philip was, we know, an eager listener to the adventurer's stories. He was easily persuaded that a North-west passage to the Indies was likely to be discovered by any one sufficiently hardy to face the accompanying dangers, and not unwilling to share them. For this attitude of mind his few years and the encouragement sailor-men received from his uncle Warwick are responsible. But it is a little disconcerting to find that Sir Francis also had his dreams of illimitable wealth, and was willing to risk a substantial sum, poor though he was, in the vain hope of thus securing a large fortune. His example must have removed effectually any scruples that Philip may have entertained. As, however, the Spaniards were to be the principal sufferers through the success of the expedition, and no one seems to have doubted of a triumphal issue, it cannot be supposed that he was troubled with many twinges of a conscience never very sensitive where Catholics and Spaniards were concerned. It may be, and it is not a merely fanciful suggestion, that Walsingham was stirred to regard the speculation favourably by Philip's enthusiasm. Some colour is lent to this suggestion by the fact that each adventured a similar sum. Be this as it may, pupil and guardian were involved in the sum of £25 a piece in Frobisher's expedition, the amount, as money was then reckoned, was considerable, and both of them could not easily afford to lose half a guinea each of the fifty they jointly subscribed.

In spite of his repeated failures, Walsingham had as much credit with his contemporaries as has been accorded to him by subsequent historians. An understanding of his career is necessary to us only so far as it touches upon that of Philip. Having already shown strange ineptitude on a terribly important occasion in the year 1582, we find him once more at Paris engaged on a mission at once serious and delicate. A petulant letter, already quoted, proves how cordially he loathed his task, and how thoroughly incompetent he was to bring it to a satisfactory issue. His orders were to bring about an alliance with France against Spain, which object being fulfilled the Queen might look favourably on the Duke of Anjou's suit. For four months the unlucky ambassador struggled and schemed in the French capital, and, when he at length returned to England, he had neither enhanced his own reputation nor advanced matters by so far as an ell. This failure does not seem to have annoyed his employers or to have lowered him in their estimation. Following hard upon his useless endeavours, Anjou came to England to woo the Queen in person. The Duke was not more favoured by fortune than the secretary ; the dual alliance against Spain was never formally signed.

Walsingham endeavoured to the very best of his ability to help his *protégé*, and by the year 1583 appears to have had a most worthy cause for his solicitude. Till that date he was animated by admiration, in which all shared, and a steady affection for the young man who had acquired for himself a fame already European, which then meant little less than world-wide. In this year something more than his love of Philip and devotion to his old friend Sir Henry stirred him to further exertion. Not unlike Polonius in many ways, he was akin to him in that he had a fair daughter. This daughter he proposed, to himself, that Philip should marry. With this project in his mind he arranged, as beneficially as he could, for the welfare of his daughter's chosen husband, and by no means frowned on Philip's unpleasantly impetuous desire to become rich at the expense of unoffensive adherents to the old faith. It cannot be alleged with any justice that he plotted to bring about a union that was undoubtedly extremely pleasing to him. Wealth, as told in sovereigns, the young people could not expect, for their elders had none to give them. Yet though many a rich young bachelor was to be had for the asking, he preferred Philip for his unique merits, and could reckon with agreeable confidence on a career for him of prosperity and added renown.

Satisfactory as the alliance was to both families, there appears but little of romance in the history how Frances

Walsingham was "wooed married and a'." Philip's failure
as a lover, when he dreamed of Penelope Devereux and
never attempted the realisation of his visions, may have
made him chary of enacting the *rôle* of the devout lover.
At the very time, too, when preparations were being made
for his marriage he was busy about the verses not inspired
by his bride. He was fond of her, there can be no
question, and as men have discovered before and since
1585, a happy enough marriage can be contrived between
parties who have mutual respect and a common desire to
help each other. Some years before the wedding, when
Frances was barely fourteen, he had written to Walsingham : " The country affords no other stuff for letters, but
humble salutations, which humbly and heartily I send to
yourself, my good lady, and my exceeding like to be good
friend." Who the "good friend" was is not revealed, but it is
not at all unlikely that the writer referred to the secretary's
daughter. Mr. Fox-Bourne says it is "reasonable to
assume" as much. Though no definite plans were made
till nearly two years later, this conjecture of the historian's
is probably fair comment. Dissolved from such an interpretation the phrase is rather meaningless, for there is
no one else, with such knowledge as we have, to whom
it can be made to refer. Allusions there are, not a few, to
the ardent ladies who were more than willing to become
Philip's wife. Their names have not come down to us,
and maybe only existed in the imagination of Sir Henry
Sidney. He was anxious enough for the proposed marriage.
" I most willingly agree, and protest I joy in the alliance
with all my heart," he writes. He cannot resist, however,
declaring that " far greater and far richer marriages " were
not beyond Philip's reach. He more than suggests that,
had he chosen to do so, he could have brought about
a contract that would have eased him appreciably from
the burden of his debts and restored him to favour at
Court. His sentences are almost incoherent, and with

much labour I cannot discover exactly what he means. Mr. Fox Bourne hopes "that Sir Henry never had any serious thought of selling his son." A suggestion such as this cannot, I think, be entertained. At the same time the old saying " Do not marry for money, but marry where money is," must have sounded wholesome doctrine in the ears of a father deeply in debt, who saw little chance of once more becoming solvent. If it were true, as reported, that candidates for Philip's favours " ventured as far as modesty would permit to signify their affections unto him," and that their arts were seen by everyone save, presumably, the man for whom they were displayed, the guardian of the Welsh borders was only human in his boast ; and it would not deceive Walsingham. The fact is that Philip was too strong for either, and their excessive adulation led logically to their implicit obedience. So it does not astonish us to find that Sir Henry, forgetting the great fortune that his son might have wedded, can prattle of "the joyful love and great liking between our most dear and sweet children, whom God bless. . . . Commend me most heartily to my good lady cousin and sister, your wife, and bless and buss our sweet daughter." Sir Francis was not given to these hysterical outbursts. But, once Philip had decided for himself, the opinions of the two elder men, had they been unfavourable, would have received no more than a courteous hearing. They would not have influenced the intending bridegroom. This both men knew, one important bit of knowledge Sir Francis probably kept to himself.

The marriage, as we have said, does not reveal Philip to us as an ardent lover. Miss Frances Walsingham would seem to have been as prosaic as her future husband. Very young though she was she, like Philip, had found opportunity to become the heroine of a romance, and her father was not by any means ignorant of the same. Whether Sir Henry or his son suspected anything is not known ; their writings do not suggest in any way that they were cognisant of the young woman's secret. This secret was sufficiently serious to make it abundantly clear why Walsingham was more than eager to see the precocious Frances married. The whole affair is a great mystery, but it is clear that Frances and an unlucky gentleman in the Marshalsea Prison either were already man and wife or proposed to become so at the earliest opportunity. The prisoner's name was John Wickerson, and concerning him I can find nothing of importance. It is not too much to suppose that he was a gentleman, or he could not have had hope of becoming, even in fancy, son-in-law to a man in Walsingham's position. Only a man of some social distinction could have had an opportunity of speaking to her. His captivity in the Marshalsea suggests that he was extravagant, also that his friends were not in a position to relieve his pecuniary necessities. More detailed and accurate knowledge would be welcome : but that Walsingham regarded the affair very seriously is certain. His comment, scrawled on the back of the captive's petition for release, is extant and may be seen. "Desires to be enlarged after his long imprisonment, and that I would not any longer continue my dislike of his contract with Mistress Frances." Mistress Frances was decidedly precocious. When she married Philip she was a child not far advanced in her teens. Moreover, this petition raises an interesting question, Was she free to marry Philip ? I confess to being unable to decide the point. From Wickerson's own words it would be easy to argue that the girl was already married. This, probably, was not so, but it is extremely difficult to understand this part of the petition, that for two years he had languished in confinement because of his "rash contract of matrimony with Mistress Frances, which to relinquish would be a perpetual scruple and worm in conscience and hazard of body and soul." He then proceeds to comment on " his perilous state," and suggests that they should be allowed to perform "their said contract in the holy state of matrimony." Wickerson when he left the Marshalsea was convinced that he had better be wise and seek some other lady on whom to bestow his favours. We do not hear of him again, we do not know that he ever got free of the Marshalsea. We do know, on irrefutable evidence, that the lady was easily consoled. Indeed, it is difficult, had not Philip cared for her it would be useless to advance any argument in her favour. Not long after Philip's death she married the Earl of Essex, and later, when her father was dead and the Earl had been murdered with an appearance of legality on the scaffold, she calmly married the Earl of Clanricarde. It is impossible either to like or respect a woman who could be so insensible to grief and so disloyal to a memory. That she could choose a second husband, her first being Philip Sidney, is contemptible ; to have decided on a third is disgusting. She does not seem to have worried herself over the fate of Wickerson.

Walsingham had a domestic triumph. His failure in an affair of State was soon to follow. In this absurd farce Philip played a very important part. He was as easily hoodwinked as his father-in-law.

For eighteen years the ill-treated Queen of the Scots had been kept in various prisons. Her complicity in the murder of her cousin—if it was a murder, which is probable, but it has never been proved—and other alleged eccentricities on her part in no way exculpate Elizabeth. The conduct of the English Sovereign throughout the whole miserable episode is unsupported by a single sentence of constitutional law, and is most feebly supported by a reference to plots that did not exist, or were of scant importance if there was any truth in the words of the informers. King James, the timid and very foolish person he afterwards proved himself to be in

England, was showing himself to be weak minded and
ridiculous.   That a halo of romance should environ a
Stuart is indeed difficult to understand.   No royal house
shows a history so completely contemptible.   Every promise
was consistently broken by its members, every pledge was
ignored, and, in a desire to show that each held his
position by a divine authority, tricks were resorted to
that it is disconcerting to attribute to the direct interven-
tion and advice of the "something not ourselves that
makes for righteousness."   There is no episode, save
Flodden Field and the reign of Charles II., that sheds the
slightest lustre on the house of Stuart.   James, however,
was crafty, as many cowards and lunatics are.   Walsingham, with respectable qualifications, was no match for him.
And he found a rather complicated problem awaiting his
solution in Edinburgh.   His failures in Paris made him
peculiarly competent to deal with it.   The problem
Walsingham was called upon to settle was not difficult if
he could have influenced the contending parties.   That he
was unequal to the task should have been clear to the
London authorities.   Apparently it was not, or they
assumed ignorance.   He had been told that rival factions
in Scotland were playing at shuttlecock with Scotland's
King.   This was true, and even James himself, an adept,
can scarcely ever have appeared so absurd.   Having leant
to Arran and Lennox, he left them suddenly and declared
for Gowrie.   Getting weary of his new masters, he
announced that his affections were all on the side of his
original captors.   The rival parties called a halt and stood
glaring at each other.   During the truce Walsingham, considerably perturbed we may suppose, clothed in not a rag
of authority, arrived.   Mary, the real Queen of Scotland,
was in England, a prisoner.   James in desperation, disliking
advice, and not willing to relinquish a throne, decided
to become a Catholic.   On this portentous decision a
storm arose.   The King thought that he might expect

help from a considerable party in England ; it is said that
his mother assured him of this help.  The English minister
was properly horrified, and patched up a truce between the
monarch and Arran ; and having done precisely nothing,
probably looked for the rewards and honours that so often
decorate the foreheads of the inept—sometimes of the
criminally dangerous, which is worse.

Meanwhile Philip turned his attention to Scotland,
and he discovered a danger in the troubles there as yet
unsuspected.  He felt certain that Spain, his old enemy,
was the instigator of all these troubles north of the
Tweed.  Not a shred of evidence can be produced to support
his view.  With such a theory buzzing in his bonnet evidence
would be, for him, merely an unnecessary inconvenience.
He fell into an ingeniously contrived trap as the result of his
precipitancy.  An exceedingly clever and charming man,
handsome beyond belief, came to London and sought him
out.  The visitor was no other than the Master of Gray,
and his mission was of a nature to appeal to Philip.  An
alliance, so the amiable traveller announced, was sought
to be accomplished between Elizabeth and James.  By the
terms of this the two monarchs were to swear eternal
friendship and Mary was to be left languishing in prison.
James was mean enough to allow his mother to suffer
far worse trials than imprisonment.  The arrangement was
decidedly to the advantage of the Queen.  Gray did not
hide himself in London, and Philip delightedly believed
the truth of the story.  Unfortunately for "all high
hopes" Gray was an unmitigated scamp.  He had cheated
every man with whom he had worked, and it is odd that
no suggestion of his treachery had reached London, for
both Gowrie and Arran had reason to complain of his
double dealing.  What were his exact motives in coming
to London it is not easy to discover.  That, whatever they
were, he most completely deceived Philip and others, is
on the record.  He posed as a violent Protestant ; he was

a very unworthy Catholic. This assumption of piety made him at once beloved and trusted; no one for a moment suspected his duplicity. Gray left London much regretted by his dupes. On his return he wrote letters to Philip full of eloquence and affection. Nay, to whomsoever he wrote he inserted messages of overwhelming regard: "Pray him do according to the postscript in my letter; for in that stands my weal, and otherwise my overthrow." The intention of the postscript is lost, but it was probably an adroit design to fool Philip to the top of his bent. And Walsingham must have been fooled too, for in the offer of a pension to James he was advised by Philip. The idea was to persuade James, always greedy and without dignity, to accept a yearly income on condition that he would pay no heed to Spanish intrigues. The King showed his disgust at the inadequacy of the insult proposed by refusing, haughtily, to pocket it. So Gray passes from sight again, after his meteoric career, and we have no distinct information as to why he visited London. His residence in our capital does not add to Walsingham's laurels, and Philip, when he learnt all, must have felt foolish. Not long after this episode Philip went to the Netherlands. Walsingham's life was also practically finished. He was only fifty-four when he died. Impossible though it is to appraise his merits so highly as do many commentators, for his failures seem more frequent than his successes, it is easy and fitting to give him honour. He was very honest, very loyal, very unselfish, and to attain such praise is to be distinguished. He was not remarkably astute, and served better than he commanded.

# CHAPTER XVII

## PENELOPE DEVEREUX AND THE SONNETS

Penelope Devereux—Philip's *Astrophel and Stella*—Its source of inspiration—A boy and girl attachment—Approval of Essex—His death—Penelope tires of dull wooing—Marries Lord Rich—Later becomes mistress of Blount—Then marries him—Curious story—The sonnets—Their meaning, merit, and history considered

IT is sometimes said that Philip was of grave and even taciturn temper. His own declaration that he never was a boy is pathetic and probably true. His early employment on affairs usually assigned to older men would strengthen and confirm his natural habit of mind. Glorying in pageantry, as he confesses, a taste fostered in his school days, the world was for him from the first a fight and not a masquerade. His self-control gave way once or twice, his sense of justice was not always equally balanced; but though he died at thirty-two, it was Nestor men mourned rather than the singer and courtier. As one of his panegyrists says : " So general the lamentations at his funerals, that a face thereat might be sooner found without eyes, than eyes without tears. It was accounted a sin for any Gentleman of Quality, for many months after, to appear at Court or City in any light or gaudy apparel ; and though a private subject, such solemnities were performed at his interment for the quality and multitude of mourners, that few Princes in

Christendom have exceeded, if any equalled, the sad
magnificence thereof." And another says :—

> "*Huncque precor licest nostris celebrare camaenis*
> *Cujus in exequiis Anglia tota gemit.*"

Another poet celebrates his virtues thus :—

> "England, Netherlands, the Heaven and the Arts,
> The souldiers and the World have made six parts
> Of the noble Sidney."

His death was sincerely grieved by friend and foe
throughout Europe, which had hardly been the case if
his reputation rested on a set of verses unknown even
to the vast majority of his countrymen. Yet these verses
are the most poignant document of himself that he has left
to posterity, and are a curious contrast to the Languet
letters. *Astrophel and Stella* is poetry of a high order,
nearly always pitched in a fine key, though often indiscreet. Not less extraordinary than this passionate outburst of a greatly reserved man is the cause that inspired
him, his love for Penelope Devereux, a daughter of the
Earl of Essex. And a further fact is something more
than curious, that the sonnets were indited to her after she
had become Lady Rich. But what is more amazing still
is that such a woman could have inspired such a man.
That the homage of Philip was far from displeasing to
Penelope cannot be doubted. The more frivolous and
heartless she was the more her vanity would be flattered
by the attentions of such a man. It is impossible to suppose
that her heart was stirred by his addresses, and had
her earlier life been happier than it was, there is no scrap
of evidence to prove that she would at any time have been
willing to comply with her father's dying wishes. Whatever were the charms of Penelope Devereux, and some she
must have had, she was not of a meek or yielding disposi-

tion. The domestic virtues were not taught her by Lady Essex, or their growth encouraged by her surroundings. One hesitates to say of such greatly placed ladies, though Dr. Johnson said it of one in scarcely less exalted a position : " The woman's a whore, and there's an end on't." Even worse than incontinence has been charged against the mother. Penelope has not been suspected of murder, but she refused to acknowledge her bridegroom at the altar, and, as soon as she could, left him and went off to live with Charles Blount, whose wife and Countess she at last became in fact, but whose claim to be so considered was allowed by every one, including the Queen, during the intervening years before her pretension could be legally established.

They first met at Chartley, when Philip was in attendance on the Earl of Leicester and the Queen, during a royal progress through the Midlands. Philip was then twenty years old, and " Stella," to give her the name by which the poet celebrated her beauty, was only twelve. Their youth would, however, be no inseparable barrier to their union in that age of early marriages. Probably, except perhaps between the young people themselves, there was no talk of an alliance. The Earl of Essex was in Ireland, serving a thankless woman, who was availing herself of the hospitality afforded by his beautiful seat in Warwickshire. Leicester was very busy flattering and deceiving the Queen and making love to Lady Essex. It is unlikely that a boy and girl attachment, if such began at Chartley, would attract the notice of older and more august personages. Be this as it may, when the Earl a year later returned from Ireland he quickly took a fancy to Philip and rapidly grew to love him and show for him the tenderest affection and admiration. He dreamed, it is certain, of a marriage, and doubtless solaced his disappointments and tempered thoughts of his Sovereign's ingratitude, by contemplating the happiness of the two for whom he cherished affection so deep and sincere. That he regarded the affair as settled is, I think, certain, since from this time he always spoke of Philip as his adopted son. On his appointment as Earl Marshal of Ireland, a post long promised to him, he took Philip with him. The position he had accepted was a difficult one, and a thankless one for a sad man tired and heart-broken in his prime. Probably, keeping the tragic secret to himself, he knew there was truth in the rumour that Leicester did not grudge him this splendidly sounding but barren preferment. Leicester was said by some to have advocated it, and gossip has this much support, that, soon after her lord's death, the Countess was secretly married to the unscrupulous and brilliant advocate of the noble man whom she had first professed to honour and obey. Very soon after the Earl Marshal's arrival in Dublin he was taken violently ill. What medical skill could do was done, but unavailingly. Before Philip, on a visit to Sir Henry, could return to the capital the Earl was dead. His last hours were worthy of the active years that preceded them. Lamenting that men would not turn more to religion and less to politics, he spoke of the frailness of women and trusted that God would help his daughters "lest they should learn of the vile world." In uttering these words it is not too much to suppose that his thoughts were turned to the ingratitude of the Queen, the lively conduct of his wife, and the future felicity of Penelope. His message to Philip I have already quoted, "If God move their hearts, I wish that he might match with my daughter. I call him son—he so wise, virtuous, and godly. If he go on in the course he hath begun he will be as famous and worthy a gentleman as ever England bred."

Essex died, there is no doubt, comforted by the reflection that, at no distant date after his demise, the two would be joined in wedlock. The dying Earl, perhaps in a mood of tacit forgiveness, did not mention his wife in his last hours. There is no proof forthcoming that he died of poison administered by an hireling of Leicester's; there is no suggestion that Essex suspected poison. We may set against these facts in Leicester's favour two points that tell against him. He had been involved in scandal before, and with clearer reason. How Amy Robsart died none know to this day; a great number readily and confidently became, though not at the moment, assured he was the voluntary executioner of Essex. If all the crimes attributed to him were true, his own death, and the scandal surrounding it, in which rumours of poison played a chief part, was a fitting if tardy punishment. The story, though not in the least an improbable one, is not sufficiently corroborated. One curious comment may be made on it, that within two years of her husband's death Lady Essex married Leicester; and there is little doubt but that then they were merely formally ratifying a contract made in secret some months earlier.

Penelope would seem to have inherited her mother's qualities. There is little in her conduct at this, or any later period of her career, to remind the student of her relation to her illustrious father either in character or action. She was the child of her mother; her life story shows that. This makes it the more curious that she, of all women, should have excited the passion of so austere a lover, who was never austere when he hymned her praises.

Whatever may have been the young girl's feelings, none the less, and despite the value Philip must have felt in the approval of Essex, he proved at first a very laggard in love. He conceived, perhaps rightly, that the events of the day called for his continuous remark and even interference. A young woman of Penelope's spirit was not likely to think the Protestant cause in Europe so important a matter as the assiduous attentions a lover owes to his lady. These attentions the lover forgot or neglected to pay. It is quite possible that he wished to serve his country, and by his distinction in her service prove himself worthy both of England and his mistress. A young woman in love may not appreciate this platonic species of devotion. It is quite certain that the Lady Penelope had small taste to receive passion so decorously robed. Philip has been unfairly abused for being dilatory. The blame is not wholly deserved. This Penelope was averse to the spinning and undoing of webs while her lover tarried. She discovered that four years spent in such an occupation were tiresome and profitless. She stayed an appreciable time with Lady Sydney's sister, Lady Huntingdon, with what benefit is not discoverable.

There were, too, other reasons than Philip's dilatoriness against the match. Sir Henry Sidney hated Essex almost as fervently as he detested Ormonde. "For that their malice," he exclaims in a letter, "I take God to record I could brook nothing of them both." It may well be doubted, none the less, whether he would have advanced active opposition to the union. His finances were not in a position to permit aggressive displeasure. His wife was bitterly lamenting that her debts prevented "my going on in any course of honourable living"; and Philip was scarcely solvent, even being worried about a bootmaker's bill. Leicester probably was not deeply interested in promoting the scheme. He and Lady Mary were never warmly friendly, and if the woman was the less cordial of the two she certainly cannot be blamed. Leicester's secret marriage to Penelope's mother may have caused him to regard the scheme without enthusiasm. One inclines to think, however, that the real cause was the gallant's tardy wooing and the lady's not unnatural pique. He expressed his love too late, and then it was for Lady Rich, no longer Penelope Devereux, his passion, too long smouldering, burst into flame.

The "proper gentleman" whom Penelope married was

the son and heir of the late Lord Chancellor, and was Rich
in name, estates, and money, rich in everything but virtue.
The marriage was ardently sought by Earl Huntingdon,
the Queen's approval anxiously craved. The Earl can
have had but poor abilities as a judge of character, though
he understood the value of money, and his eagerness in
the matter seems almost indecent. But Penelope and her
sister were both, as it were, his charges ; he was probably
really conscientious and desirous of doing his best for
them. He is not the only man who has thought of happiness as shackled to titles and estates. Elizabeth, who the
previous year had asked to " be put in mind of these young
ladies," graciously gave her consent, and Penelope became
Lady Rich. Her consent is hardly likely to have been
asked, nor, if she really cared for Philip, would she have
been likely to withhold it even had her friends condescended to the formality of seeking her approval. Many
years after the ceremony, her second husband, the Earl of
Devonshire, makes some very grave charges. They are
levelled at Penelope's worldly friends, and assert, with
emphasis, that she was forced into the marriage against
her will by those who should have protected her. A
further charge is made ; no one denies that Rich was
unscrupulous and brutal and unpleasant, that he robbed
her of her dowry, and turned her adrift to live on an
allowance. It must be remembered, however, that this
is in a statement made to King James, who was quite
easily deluded. Also it has to be remembered that Sir
Charles Blount kept her as his mistress, that she bore him
children while filling that position. She became Countess
of Devonshire, her protector had become an Earl, which fact
is creditable to Blount, so soon as Lord Rich divorced her.
When he did she had been married to Rich for twenty
years and more. The pious and wise James would not
recognise her as the Countess of Devonshire ; he could not
deny her right to the title. Two years after her marriage
the unhappy lady died.

There is a curious story concerning the divorce of Penelope and Lord Rich. It is asserted that from the first she was badly treated by her husband, that for twelve years she had been left practically a widow, that she was continually urged to confess her fault with a "nameless stranger." The "nameless stranger" is her counsel in this matter, and he is pleading, quite properly, for his mistress. She was the mother of his children, and the divorce obtained, he promptly married her.

This story, even as the sonnets, is curious, and may be written around. It cannot be told (there are no data) intelligently or intelligibly. James was hardly the man to act as *censor morum* with even a shadow of authority, yet one cannot help wishing that Philip's love had centred on a lady concerning whose career there was less mystery and less need for an apology. There seems a reason for rejoicing that—

> "Thou art my Wit and thou my Virtue art,"

is not correct in fact ; Philip gathered wit and virtue from other branches. That he meant what he wrote is, I think, certain.

> "'Fool,' said my Muse to me, 'look in thy heart and write.'"

Shelley wrote of Philip thus :—

> "Sidney as he fought
> And as he fell, and as he lived and loved,
> Sublimely mild, a spirit without spot."

Shelley was an enthusiast and not capable of weighing evidence coldly. Was there a "spot" is the question critics and biographers debate over with warmth and ingenuity. The consensus of opinion is that Shelley's verdict would be upheld on appeal. The pity is that so many famous pens should have wasted ink on a barren

speculation.  For my own part, I am not anxious to avoid
the direct meaning of the sonnets.  The atmosphere in
which Philip was reared tended to a laxity reprehensible
enough to-day : whatever his fault in the case of Lady
Rich, it was virtue compared to the conduct of his
superiors.  He loved once, and with his usual outspoken
honesty confessed his emotions.  As he has never been
convicted of a lie, I prefer to believe that when he wrote
he meant what he said.  Some assert the sonnet sequence
is a beautiful effort of the imagination.  It is a record of
hard fact illuminated and made lovely by touches of
imagination.  This view is, one surmises, more true than
any plausible excuse or effort to explain away the real
meaning of the verses.

> "For to be wise and love exceeds man's might,"

says Shakespeare, our supreme authority ; other poets and
philosophers have played with the same truth.  Philip
was a man ; he was only a little wiser than other men
called upon to face a similar trial.

For this view there should be quoted his own defence,
put into one of his sonnets, written in extenuation of the
folly of which a friend had reproved him.

> "Alas ! have I not pain enough, my friend,
> Upon whose breast a fiercer gripe doth tier
> Than did on him who first stole down the fire,
> While Love on me doth all his quiver spend ;
> But with your Rubarb words ye must contend
> To grieve me worse, in saying that Desire
> Doth plunge my well-formed soul even in the mire
> Of sinful thoughts, which do in ruin end ?
> If that be sin which doth the manners frame,
> Well stayed with truth in word and faith of deed,
> Ready of wit and fearing naught but shame ;
> If that be sin which in fixed hearts doth breed
> A loathing of all loose unchastity,
> Then love is sin, and let me sinful be."

These fine lines, full of sincerity, emphatic and wistful, prove beyond reasonable doubt how seriously Philip regarded his passion for Lady Rich. That his affection was returned is less certain, but two sonnets seem to suggest that it was. We could hardly expect even such slight response as indicated, since it was the lady herself who prevented the romance from becoming something more than indiscreet. Whatever her faults may have been, and they seem to have been considerable, it is clear that she had a nice care of Sidney's honour, and restrained him at the one period of his career when there was danger of his lapse from the high code of morality he had set up for himself and truly lived by. Commentators have done him scant justice in endeavouring to explain away an episode that needs no explanation.

"I cannot brag of word, much less of deed,"

he says; and again it seems well to believe him, for on his death-bed he refers to passages in his life which, unless they were a sick man's ravings, can have no meaning save that they refer to this unfortunate infatuation. He was not the man to shirk a truth even if it told against him, and they who apologise for him scarcely do him the honour they intend. Greater men than he have temporarily fallen a victim to desires too strong to smack of wisdom.

"*La feuille tombe à terre, ainsi tombe la beauté*,"

Even the noblest of men has his moments of weakness.

Sidney heralded Shakespeare in two ways: he wrote sonnets, and in writing them produced a mystery. "Who was Mr. W. H.?" is a question that will continue, probably, to agitate critics for all time. If not for all time, at least until that far-off day when the merits of the poems themselves will engage critical pens more earnestly than the discussions as to occasions, or occasion, on which the verses were written. A poet is driven to write by his own emotions, but those emotions are his private trouble or solace according as they made for his personal happiness or sorrow. Their real value lies in this, that to those suffering or rejoicing they are a willing assistance to the dumb. The " mute, inglorious Milton " is everywhere, and the real poets speak for him when he needs their help. The immediate cause of the inspiration that fired the lines is not the business of the man who lights his own bit of tinder at the flame. Sidney and Shakespeare have been victims to this intrusive criticism for so lengthy a period, it is not easy to write about either without touching a matter one would willingly have ignored. Most of Sidney's critics remind us of certain noisy people who, having firmly established a negation, make a comfortable living by abusing the precise inconvenience they have begun by assuring us does not exist.

A great many worthy pens have been employed to prove to us that Sidney's affections for Lady Rich were of a specially innocuous quality. Possibly they were; but this is not very obvious, as it is undisputed that she inspired them. Had " Astrophel and Stella " been a collection of elegant society verse, a hundred fair inspirers might, without scandal, have tricked him into a ballade. Unfortunately Philip was a great poet. He was, too, in the habit of saying what he meant, and taking the consequences. I cannot find any reason to suggest that he was not most deeply and seriously in earnest when he wrote some of the noblest love poetry in the language. What these poems say, I think, admits of no interpretation save one. If this suggestion is correct, their writer cannot deserve blame, unless a man is only to be admired if he is a saint, or is devoid of all passion and feeling. In considering this question, a question I have shunned, it has seemed to me that his unswerving truthfulness, his deep feeling, and his utter lack of humour, must be remembered. And, finally, the atmosphere of the Court, the constant habits of all the great personages therein assembled, to which no one ever thought of objecting, must be recognised. His liaison with Lady Rich was perhaps an indiscretion, certainly nothing more, in the eyes of Philip's contemporaries. That blame attached to it may have occurred to him, it never occurred to them. He himself had the cleanest record of any man in England, a record that few men, inspired by the higher standards proclaimed to-day, could show. His best friend and the truest guardian of his memory and virtue is he who recognises, not evades or denies, the origin of these poems.

So much, I think, must be said, and without hesitation. So much, I suggest, must be repeated, often if necessary.

*Astrophel and Stella* was a collection of private metrical documents, shown to friends who understood his feelings, but not by him given to the world. To men not his intimates he seemed chiefly swayed by the laudable ambitions that animate the statesman and the soldier. These people would guess that he wrote fugitive verse in his spare moments. It was the fashion for men of breeding and position to dally with the muses. A certain dexterity in rhyming was expected of those who claimed to be considered in society and at Court. The Queen herself wrote, and expected those about her to evolve a distych on occasion. But that Philip's poetry was better than such effusions none but those of his own circle could know or even suppose. When not reflecting on the real tragedy of his life his performances are no better and no worse than the efforts of his humbler contemporaries. A " thin diet of dainty words " is not the banquet set before us in his great sonnet sequence. That Languet knew the truth seems almost certain, if we interpret some of his letters correctly. " Whatever may come of it, I pray that it may be for your happiness." Earlier in the same letter the old man says, "What you say about marrying, in fun, I do not take seriously. But don't rely too much on your fixity of purpose. People wiser than you have been caught in that net. What I most care about is that you should be *safely* caught in it." The italics are mine. Then he adds that "Fate has most to do in affairs of this kind, so you must not fancy that you can bind and direct the matter so as to ensure success, and to give you, in every respect, all you desire." These curious words were written before Penelope became Lady Rich. More curious still are some words of Philip's own writing : "As regards yourself, of whom I am so unworthy, I have already told you long ago what I thought, if only briefly, yet as well as I was able to at that time." In the words of Marlowe :—

> "It lies not in our power to love or hate,
> For love in us is overcome by fate."

The Huguenot, speaking in prose, was clearly of the same creed as the author of the couplet. As the years advanced Philip found himself more and more devoted to the lady by whom, when she was yet a very young girl, he had been attracted. It was this passion that made him a poet. For, as he confessed, he became a poet one half against his will. He felt too deeply to proclaim his emotions from the house tops.

Controversy is still active as to the order in which the sonnets should be arranged, and rival editors have rival theories. For the purposes of this book the disputes are academic and unimportant. Their meaning, in whatever order they are placed, seems clear, and it is not now our business to consider of them as literature. They are to be regarded merely as shorthand notes giving us a clue to the truth in the most disputed episode in Philip's short life. They throw a searchlight on his own humour and the conduct of the woman he sincerely loved. Though they were not published till some years after his death, but read merely by a select few within this circle, their surpassing merits were rightly apprised. It is quite possible that Lord Rich knew of them, even if he had not read them. That, despite their naïve sincerity, he took no steps towards obtaining a divorce is strong evidence, apart from the internal evidence provided by the poems themselves, that if Philip was unwisely impetuous through "love and desire of loving converse that steals the wits even of the wise," the lady had a strict care for the proprieties in this affair at any rate.

We do not know whether Philip arranged the order of the sonnets himself ; nor, as has been ingeniously suggested, can we feel assured that he deliberately disarranged them the better to conceal their real meaning. Not improbably they were not at first fixed in any precise sequence. Philip's friends knew their meaning and could hardly be expected to anticipate the controversy that was to arise over them in succeeding generations. Poets and persons of a glowing fancy many of his friends and presumable editors were. But their imaginations did not rise to the heights of believing that the truthful Philip did not mean precisely what he said. This attitude has only been adopted by critics of a later generation, who seem to shudder somewhat at the outspoken nature of their hero ; this very outspokenness being his finest quality. The series of sonnets has been divided by Mrs. Mary Ward into three sections, and she suggests them very cleverly. The first deals with the stirring of the poet's love, his desire to praise his mistress and his determination to lay any glory his deeds have brought him at her feet. The theory is tenable and interesting. But the poet rounds on himself " by outbursts of moral sensitiveness eminently characteristic." In the second section she places the poems that seem to show that Stella relents. Crudely put, this means that Lady Rich relents.

"Gone is the winter of my misery,
My spring appears : O see what here doth grow,
For Stella hath, with words where faith doth shine,
Of her high heart given me the monarchy."

The first line may have suggested Shakespeare's lines :—

"Now is the winter of our discontent
Made glorious summer by this sun of York."

In the third section the inevitable separation is dwelt upon, and this separation comes about not by Philip's wish but the lady's insistence.[1]   "See what it is to love," the critic suggests as the inevitable last words of the sequence.   Personally, I wish she had done more than preface a tiny selection, contained in a volume of extracts culled from many gardens ; for I believe she has, better than any, understood the real drift of *Astrophel and Stella.*

"The short yet eventful life of Sidney," says a German critic, "only half belongs to English literature." These are wise words.   It belongs to every age and every country where are found men passionate, honest, gentle, and brave.

---

[1] "Forced by Stella's laws of duty to depart."   A line not to be overlooked, this.

# CHAPTER XVIII

## MARY SIDNEY—THE "ARCADIA" AND "THE DEFENCE OF POESY"

Horace Walpole as critic—His estimate of *Arcadia* and its author —A laboured novel—Its style—Its place in literature—Philip's own view of its merits—His reason for writing it—His method of composition—The story—Milton and the prayer—*Arcadia*, though very long, remains unfinished—*The Defence of Poesy*— A noble treatise—Date of composition—A literary quarrel— What is a poet ?—Philip's definition—Analysis of the treatise and comments thereon—Its wisdom, wit, and logic

THE inspirer of *Arcadia* had nothing in common with the lady of the Sonnets. Mary Sidney, Countess of Pembroke, was Philip's favourite sister and his most intimate friend. Remarkable even in an age of famous women, she seems to have had scholarship enough to share his studies, stood loyally by him in the hours of trial and danger, and at all times was for him a tender and understanding friend. Her position as Lady Pembroke was a great one, but she did not seek to shine in the empty revels of the Court. Undeniably beautiful, she did not care to rival the splendours of other women not less fair. Her chief delight was to live quietly at Wilton, and there entertain fittingly the poets and men of talent whom Philip brought with him. Her piety, wit, and charm caused her to be loved and esteemed during

SIR PHILIP SIDNEY
AFTER A MINIATURE

her life, and she was mourned sincerely and for long when
at last Death called her.

She was born at Ticknell, near Bewdley, in 1561, and,
more fortunate than her sisters Margaret and Ambrosia,
lived to pass her sixtieth birthday. Of her earliest years
there is little or nothing known. That she grew up at
Penshurst carefully tended and admirably taught are
about the only certain facts that come down to us till
she reached her fourteenth year. By this time she was,
according to the notions of the age, a grown woman.
Elizabeth, willing to do a cheap favour to a family which
her parsimony pressed so cruelly, regarded the young lady
with marked approval. An opportunity occurred for her
to signify her gracious pleasure and pose in the triple *rôle*
of Queen, Samaritan, and Christian. Ambrosia Sidney
died at the age of fifteen, to the intense grief of her
parents. When the Queen heard the news she expressed
and wrote to the sorrowing father a letter it is not
possible to read without a smile. The opening sentiments
are unimpeachable, and the style is regal and condescend-
ing as became so illustrious a comforter. The concluding
passage makes one think that the condescension and
suggestion—a suggestion that was a courteously veiled
command—therein was prompted quite as much by her
own convenience as a desire to soothe the hearts of the
afflicted parents.

" GOOD SIDNEY,—Although we are well assured that,
with wisdom and great experience of worldly chances and
necessities, nothing can happen unto you so heavy but that
you can and will bear them as they ought to be rightly
taken, yet, forasmuch as we conceive the grief you yet feel
thereby, as in such cases natural parents are accustomed,
we would not have you ignorant, to ease your sorrow as
much as may be, how we take part of your grief upon us.
God hath left unto you the comfort of one daughter of
very good hope, whom if you shall think good to remove

from those parts of unpleasant air unto better in these
parts, and will send her unto us before Easter, or when
you shall think good, assure yourself that we will have a
special care of her, not doubting but, as you are well
persuaded of our favour towards yourself, so will we make
further demonstration thereof in her."

"Good Sidney" must have read his Sovereign's epistle
with a chastened feeling of gratitude. He knew its author
too well to be fooled by the seeming graciousness of the
supposed favour to be conferred on a member of his
family. In the eyes of strangers the letter seems worthy
of a great princess. But he could read between the stately
lines and cannot have gathered much consolation from his
study of them. Even at this date he was much impoverished and his chief debtor was Elizabeth, who never
intended to pay him and never did. All that the rotund
phrases really meant was this, that a rich queen would
henceforth provide board and lodging for a child of
fourteen. Moreover, his compliance with the command,
for such it was, meant a considerable expenditure on robes
and jewels and pocket-money, lest his daughter should
appear shabbily among her companions at the Court.

Wonder is, here and there, expressed that the Queen,
vain of her beauty and no longer young, should summon
into her presence so lovely a girl as Mary Sidney. I
do not think the reason is very far to seek. She was
full of confidence in the power of her own charms.
Ambassadors and courtiers, albeit for their own ends,
never ceased to dilate on them. She, nothing loth,
believed in them herself. She was satisfied that no woman
in the world could surpass her or even equal her. And
she was strong in the knowledge, too, that her position
gave her an unassailable power over all who presumed
to pose as her rivals. For them there was short shrift.
Indeed, Elizabeth, despite notable defections that aroused
her anger, seems to have been incapable of understanding

that such beauty as the gods had given to her was, at
best, the beauty that fades most quickly, the beauty, that
is, of youth and colour.  Magnificent and awe-inspiring
she was to the end of her life : but these are not the
perfections, if the poets may be credited, for which a lover
sighs.  One may admire in a Queen the qualities one
would resent in a mistress.  This extreme vanity led her
to the conclusion that her wondrous graces needed a fine
setting.  The attendants on Venus, she appears to have
argued with herself, were distinctly comely ; so, she, the
Tudor Venus, disliked to see around her either men or
women who were not beyond the criticism of the most
critical.  Her flatterers, we may be sure, found it easy
to persuade her that the beauty visible in others was but
a reflection from the glory emanating from the royal
presence.  At least she was kind to Mary, who was far
from unhappy at Court, and Philip's duties there gave
brother and sister many opportunities of seeing one
another and of strengthening the warm friendship that
had begun at Penshurst.

Some four years after her arrival at Court, years apparently uneventful save that the girl learnt many lessons
that strengthened her virtue while they gave her a
sufficiency of worldly wisdom, she became a bride.  Her
wooing could not have been romantic, her suitor was
hardly the knight to stir the poetic fancy of so young
a maid.  Sir Henry, Cecil, and Pembroke made of the
alliance a business contract.  Mary raised no objection
to her future lord, she saw that he could make her happy,
and she had for him a sincere respect.  This respect
ripened into love, and for both was a very real contentment
and sunny happiness.  The bridegroom had indeed
sterling qualities both of heart and head.  A great nobleman, he avoided the cabals of the Court and desired
no honours more conspicuous than those he possessed.
To him the smile or the frown of Queen, or Queen's

favourite, had no importance. At Wilton and at Baynard's Castle he was king; in both his wife reigned as
a much-loved queen.

Elizabeth regarded the marriage with complacency,
indeed she almost approved. Lord Pembroke was eager
for the match, and probably did not inquire in what
quarter the Queen's whims were directed. He was not,
he never had been, a lover of hers, so in going his own
course he did no injury to her vanity. His aloofness
endeared him to the harassed Sidneys as a valuable ally.
He was too greatly placed to be easily injured, too loyal
not to stand by his wife's family when distress or danger
compassed any of its members.

Wilton, though less beautiful than Penshurst, was a fair
demesne enough, and might have satisfied the desires
of a lady far more covetous of grandeur than ever was
Mary Sidney. The following description in *Arcadia* gives
us a pleasant idea of the home over which the young bride
was to rule :—

" The house itself was built of fair and strong stone, not
affecting so much any extraordinary kind of fineness
as an honourable representing of a fair stateliness." This
eulogy might be applied equally truly to the owner of
Wilton. The passage continues thus : " The lights, doors,
and stairs rather directed to the use of the guests than
to the eye of the artificer, and yet, as one chiefly heeded,
so the other not neglected ; each place handsome without
curiosity, and homely without loathsomeness ; not so
dainty as not to be trod on, nor yet slubbered up with
good fellowship ; all more lasting than beautiful, but that
the consideration of the exceeding lastingness made the
eye believe that it was exceedingly beautiful ; the servants
not so many in number as cleanly in apparel and service-
able in behaviour, testifying even in their countenances that
their master took as well care to be served as of them to
be served."

In this place, quaintly described as "homely without
loathsomeness," Philip found a frequent refuge when he
desired a retreat. His first visit was in the July of
1577. On the New Year's Day following the Countess
sent a fine present to the Queen, a doublet of lawn most
richly embroidered and lined with yellow taffeta. It is
not said that she received a gift in return. Her own was
politic, for it reminded the Queen of what she owed to the
family of the giver: also it was, there can be no doubt,
a token of sincere personal gratitude. When a child was
born Elizabeth signified her interest by consenting to
become godmother, and was represented at the christening
ceremony by Lady Warwick. This act of condescension is
the more noteworthy in that the Earl of Leicester, then in
dire disgrace, stood godfather. A greater tribute to the
real charm of the Countess, and to Philip too, who was
also in disgrace, could hardly have been paid. Perhaps
Spenser did not strain the poet's proverbial licence when
he hymned her so enthusiastically :—

> "In whose brave mind, as in a golden coffer,
>     All heavenly gifts and riches lockèd are ;
> More rich than pearls of Ind or gold of Ophir,
>     And in her sex more wonderful and rare."

Bad as the rhymes are, the homage is magnificent.

Philip remained at Wilton for many months, and *Arcadia*
was invented and written there. It is not unlikely that
the dedication is only a half-truth, and that he was, in
fact, not more than part author, though he says, " Here
now have you, most dear and most worthy to be most dear
lady, this idle work of mine." And he alludes to the
inspiration he culled from her in a striking passage :—

" You desired me to do it, and your desire to my heart
is an absolute commandment. Now it is done only for
you, only to you. If you keep it to yourself, or to such
friends who will weigh error in the balance of goodwill,

I hope for the father's sake it will be pardoned, perchance made much of, though in itself it have deformities. For, indeed, for severer eyes it is not, being but a trifle, and that triflingly handled. Your dear self can best witness the manner, being done in loose sheets of paper, *most of it in your presence*, the rest by sheets sent unto you as fast as they were done. In sum, a young head—not so well stayed as I would it were, and shall be when God will—having many, many fancies begotten in it, if it had not been in some way delivered, would have grown a monster; and more sorry might I be that they came in than that they got out."

*Arcadia* is the most substantial of " trifles." The author's pen must have travelled with miraculous rapidity. The tale, incomplete as it is, by its mere length might well represent the labour of years. That Philip carried a note-book about with him and recorded therein his fancies, even when they occurred to him on the hunting-field, hardly explains to us how so much was accomplished in so short a time. In the dedication quoted, lies the clue to the mystery. Lady Pembroke not only saw her brother write, she wrote herself, and wrote not a few pages of this book. Their joint authorship, if it can be proved, and I think the introduction goes far to prove it, would account for the rambling and often incoherent medley with which the reader is confronted. Sir William Alexander attempted to draw together the scattered strings of the argument, and edited an edition of the work. Philip himself did not think highly of the result of his own efforts. He saw, better than most of his critics, how many and how great the faults were. Its composition having proved " the most delightful of mid-May amusements," he evinced no desire that the result should be given to the world.

On his death-bed he expressed a wish that it should be burned. His sister, and we may be grateful to her, decided to disobey him. She could argue, fairly enough, that the

story was no longer his but hers.    He had given his share
in it to her, and she saw in the entangled tale, rightly, that
there was    much    worth    preserving.    She, therefore, set
herself the task of fitting together the loose parts, and
smoothing the rough places.    Whatever passages may be
assigned to her pen before Philip's death, the whole volume
when it faced the world owed a good deal of its merit to
her sisterly labours.    A proof of her loyalty and modesty
is found in the fact that she claimed no share in the merit
of the production.    Had any praise been offered to her she
would have answered that she knew what Philip had intended, and had done no more than finish the book in
accordance with his express design, a design of which she
alone had the key.    We are expressly told of what her
task consisted, " repairing a ruinous house, the mending of
some old part occasioneth the making of some new, so
here her honourable labour began in correcting the faults,
and ended in supplying the defects."    The Countess had a
great qualification for her task, apart from her minute
knowledge of Philip's intentions, apart from a recollection
of the assistance she had given him, assistance he so
clearly acknowledges, during the progress of their joint
task.    She was not new to the duties of a collaborator.
Philip anticipated the labours of certain ponderous poets
who thought they could improve on the Psalms of David
by twisting them into rhymed stanzas in which the poetry
was sacrificed to a grim and forbidding piety.    Addison
has shown that the trick may be well done, others have
emphasised the    difficulty    of    their    self-imposed    task.
Rhymed versions of the Psalms are usually atrocious.    A
favourite effort, still sung north of the Tweed, mutilates
the sublime canticle " The Lord is my Shepherd."    Yet
this version is full of merit compared to other versions
offered to us as metrical arrangements of the Psalmist's
words.    There is no excuse for these absurdities, for we
have before us the superb and moving English of our

Bible and the Book of Common Prayer. Philip, therefore, can ask for pardon with some reason, since he did not live to read their stupendous and solemn prose. It cannot be suggested, however, that his efforts were even moderately successful. The only point we need notice is that his sister was part author in his attempt to do the impossible.

On her brother's death she seems to have abandoned all active literary pursuits, save only the editing of Philip's writings. Her passion for letters, however, was as keen as ever; men of letters found in her their most cordial and admiring ally and friend. Shakespeare received much kindness at her hands, and it would be interesting to know that he discussed with her this rhymed version of the songs of David. *Arcadia*, at least, was familiar to him, and he is said to have borrowed from its pages. The instances generally quoted of the kindly theft do not stir me to any solid conviction, any more than does the oft-repeated assertion that Richardson had read and loved the romance because he gave to one of his insipid heroines the name of Pamela.

Philip left all his jewels to his sister, and she was more beautiful than they. For though she must remain for us a great name, rather than a great reality, great men loved her, and their praise of her is rich and abiding testimony of her worth.

We possess a picture of this estimable woman. Little concerning her may be learnt from it. The hands are nearly as wooden as the lace that breaks in stiff waves from her wrists. Her dress is "without form and void," her neck is completely hidden by a portentous tucker or ruffle. Her wig, or hair, whichever it is, is pushed so far back that her face seems to be starting out from it, and reminds the spectator of a rabbit peering through the bars of its cage. This face is the Sidney face, or, it would be better to say, taken from a model similar to the one used

when other Sidneys were painted.   The prim mouth, the
staring, bead-like eyes, the faint arched eyebrows, the large,
if oval, chin confront us again.   But there is nothing of
character in the picture.   It is merely one of Zucchero's
opportunities lost.

It is a fashion to sneer at Horace Walpole, at his
architectural eccentricities, his truly though unintention-
ally funny, *Castle of Otranto*, his habit of gossip—gossip
which was on the whole good-natured and always admirably amusing, and to regard him as a selfish and not very
important person.   Dr. Johnson, who could hardly be
expected to look with favour on a man carrying the name
of Walpole, might indeed have alluded to Sir Robert's
dillettante son contemptuously.   He was by no means
harsh in estimating the merits of the Strawberry Hill
magnate.   True, " he always took care to put Sir Robert
Walpole in the wrong, and to say everything he could
against the electorate of Hanover."   Writing of parliamentary reports, which it is difficult to believe were by
any one accepted as accurate, or so truthful a man would
not have chuckled over his confessed unscrupulous doings,
was not that noble dictator's mission in life.   He is found
declaring his belief that Horace, or Horry, as he was
called familiarly, collected many curious things and wrote
about them with taste.   Horace Walpole was one of the
first to see the beauty of Gray's *Odes*, and printed two of
them at his private press.   When they were attacked he
was one of their most zealous champions, and, which is
worth considering, he was not blind to their defects.   In
his letters, notably one to Lord Lytleton, he mentions the
blemishes and has anticipated the comments of later critics.
What he says concerning the *odes*, either in praise or
blame, is good sense and reason.   About the worst thing
that can be said of him is that he was unjust to Garrick as
an actor ;  he certainly admired " little Davy " as a man and
was glad of him as a neighbour.   He stuck to his guns, too.

He would not budge from his theories or opinions, and he supported them by arguments cleverly marshalled and wittily expressed. From his villa—"castle," he calls it— on the Thames he did not give laws to the world, nor in all the nine big volumes of his inimitable letters is there the slightest suggestion that he proposed to be considered as more than a shrewd and kindly man of the world, who could tell a good story better than most, and had a vast number of good stories to dole out when opportunity offered. But his correspondence shows one thing very clearly; he did not seek to give the law to others, but he claimed the right to frame for himself the regulations as to taste and manners that were to guide his own conduct. So, and this is what concerns us, he was very outspoken on the subject of Sir Philip Sidney, writing to Hume a letter which is less of a defence than a covert attack. Before considering Philip's work in some detail, I think it well to quote from this letter freely. Walpole had every right to speak, and it is interesting to observe how definitely he ranges himself in the ranks of those who, in the face of an opposition that included names not less great than the historian's, would not acknowledge the marvellous abilities of the author of the *Arcadia*. Whether we agree with Walpole or not, there is one defect in his argument. He does not see that, quite apart from all questions of literary merit, it was the traditional character of Philip which so deeply impressed not merely his contemporaries but his successors, and cheated men into the belief that the stream flowing from such a fountain must be a golden one.

"I must premise, sir, that what I am going to say is not directly to defend what you criticise; it is rather an explanation which I owe to such criticisms, and to apologise for not correcting my work in consequence of your remarks; but unhappily for me, the greater part of your notes regard passages in pages already printed off for the future edition. I will touch them in order.

" I perceive by what you and others have said to me, sir,
that the freedom I have taken with Sir Philip Sidney is
what gives most offence ; yet I think if my words are duly
weighed, it will be found that my words are too strong
rather than my argument weak. I say, *when we at this
distance of time inquire what prodigious merits excited such
admiration.* What admiration ? Why, that all the learned
of Europe praised him, all the poets of England lamented
his death, the republic of Poland thought of him for their
King. I allow Sir Philip great valour, and, from some of
his performances, good sense ; but, dear sir, compare his
talents with the admiration they occasioned, and that in
no unlettered, no unpolished age, and can we at this distance help wondering at the vastness of his character ?
Allowing as much sense as his warmest admirers can
demand for him, surely this country has produced many
men of far greater abilities who have by no means met
with a proportionate share of applause. It were a vain
parade to name them. Take Lord Bacon alone, who I
believe of all our writers, except Newton, is most known
to foreigners, and to whom Sir Philip was a puny child in
genius—how far was he from attaining an equal degree of
fame and honour ? To say the truth, I attribute the great
admiration of Sir Philip Sidney to his having so much
merit and learning for a man of rank :—

*" Rarus enim ferme sensus communis in illa Fortunâ."*

Indeed, sir, if your good sense and philosophy did not
raise you above being blinded, I should suspect that you
had conceived still more undeserved esteem from the same
surprise for another author, who is the only one that, by
being compared with Sir Philip Sidney, could make me
think the latter a very great man. I have already shown
in a note to illustrate my argument, and to excuse myself
to some gentleman who thought I had not paid attention

enough to Sir Philip's *Defence of Poesy ;* but whether one or two particular tracts are a little better or not than I have represented his general writings, it does not affect the scope of my reasoning, the whole truth of which is, as I said, that he was not a great man in proportion to his fame."

Walpole states his case ably, no reader of this letter can deny, and the reader must remember it is a private letter, not an essay composed for publication, which no less a man than Hume thought worthy of preservation. He therefore respected the writer's views, Hume not being at all the sort of person to be led by fashion, or likely to consider the son of an Earl necessarily a being superior to the son of a bricklayer. Who was in the right, Walpole or the eulogists, it is not for me to decide. My readers must form their own conclusions.

*Arcadia* as conceived by Philip Sidney, is a region no one would willingly visit. Its morals are original, even startling ; but its inhabitants are terribly given to long and affected speeches. They do not talk, they always lecture. The serious habit of the man who never was young is reflected in this laboured novel. To quote one passage is sufficient : " Animated therewith she sat down by Pamela, and taking the purse, and with affected curiosity looking upon the work : 'Fully happy is he,' said she, 'at least if he knew his own happiness, to whom a purse in this manner, and by this hand wrought, is dedicated. In faith he shall have cause to account it, not as a purse for treasure, but as a treasure itself, worthy to be pursed up in the purse of his own heart.' 'And think you so indeed ?' said Pamela, half smiling ; 'I promise you I wrought it out to make some tedious hours believe that I thought not of them ; for else I valued it but even as a very purse.'" Here we have, taken at random, an absolutely typical example of Philip's methods. Conceding that the cheat-ing of the hours is a pretty conceit, common patience

ɔoggles at the clumsy play made with the word "purse."
Nearly every page of *Arcadia* is studded with these ill-
cut gems. Honesty compels one to add that there is
scarcely a page without its beauty. I am not clever
enough to twist Philip's faults into virtues. What he did
was to adventure and explore, just as Frobisher and others
ventured and explored. The mariners were not always
successful—or not often completely successful. The
pioneer accepts occasional failure as natural and inevitable. Philip was the pioneer of the novel in English ; he
succeeded well enough to encourage others ; herein he
deserves merit and applause. To say that his own effort
is interesting for its own sake is to talk unwisely. One
critic says : " When in the Elizabethan age the literature
of tradition gave way to the literature of invention, a
decisive step in advance was made ; but the novel still
retained all the essential features of its poetic ancestry."
This would be accurate enough if we read, "the novel
began with all the essential features of its poetic
ancestry."

The nearest approach to a novelist before Sidney was
the poet Chaucer. Abundance of tales circulated, but they
were told in verse, then ground into prose, and from the
prose put back into metrical shape. Moreover, before
*Arcadia* the stories told were not original but traditional,
when they did not migrate from Italy or Navarre. Philip
stole, unwittingly or wittingly, as Shakespeare stole, the
best that came to his hand. Whatever would mend or
help his story he appropriated and wove into his text.
But in the main outline his text, good or bad, was his own.
Probably it was not too long for the lazy hours of those
at Wilton, nor, in his retreat from the Court, with its dis-
tracting hourly episodes, did the writer feel compelled to
proceed by other than leisurely stages. Ostensibly he
began the work to please his sister, then, becoming wedded
to his self-imposed task, he continued weaving plot within

plot and fantasy within fantasy, being unwilling to lay the
task aside, not seeing clearly when or how he should gather
the threads together and make an end.   Philip with his
usual, though not invariable, common-sense did not over-
estimate the value of his performance.   In his dedication
he writes : " I could well find it in my heart to cast out in
some desert of forgetfulness this child which I am loth to
father."   So Chinese a method of dealing with his offspring
would very likely have commended itself to him.   For this
very frank statement was not an affectation ; he was given
to speaking the truth about himself no less than in his
expressions of opinion concerning others.   When Beau
Brummell was introduced to a local magnate he made a
favourable impression, and for a curious reason.   The
Beau, as was his wont, had been showing a collection of
his drawings to a knot of fair admirers.   The pompous
gentleman, graciously accepting the courteous conduct of
Brummel at the moment of presentation, believing the
dandy to be merely an artist, said how gratified he was
to find the young fellow knew his place.   Philip did not
regard letters and their exemplars at all in the light this
squire regarded painters.   But he did not take his own
efforts in this branch of human endeavour too seriously.
He had other schemes of usefulness before his eyes that he
considered more important.   So, after the sentence quoted,
he continues : " But you desired me to do it, and your
desire to my heart is an absolute commandment.   Now it
is done only to you, only for you.   If you keep it to yourself, or to such friends as will lay error in the balance of
goodwill, I hope for the father's sake it will be pardoned,
perchance made much of, though in itself it has deformities.   For, indeed, for severer eyes it is not, being a trifle,
and that triflingly handled."

Here we have a most explicit statement.   The influence
the romance was destined to have never crossed his mind,
its sole purpose was to amuse the leisure hours of his sister

and her friends. Whatever its faults are, we may rejoice that she and they thought more worthily of it than did the author. A contemporary criticism is seldom of such permanent value, else should we be admiring and reading many volumes whose writers are scarcely known to most of us even by name. Into their oblivion their works and their critics have followed them.

How "trifling" was the handling we know from the knowledge we have of the way in which the book was put together. When ideas occurred to him, and they came in battalions, he used to jot them down in a pocket-book which he always carried about with him. Any loose sheet of paper, too, that lay near was requisitioned both at Wilton and in London. What he wrote in the capital was despatched at once to his sister, and what he wrote at Wilton was done immediately under her eyes, and often actually at her suggestion. A book so compiled, literally a scrapbook, was bound to fail as an artistic whole, despite the many and great virtues to be found therein. A fixed plan of composition, it is claimed by his contemporary critics, was formed in Philip's mind, and a direct moral purpose gave strength to his inspiration. It is difficult to picture Philip doing any sort of work for mere pleasure. "His aim," says Greville, "was not in writing it, either authorship itself, nor to use the treasures of his mind to serve a school, but that both his understanding and the strength of his imagination might aid his heart, and help himself and others to be good and noble, not only in words and thoughts, but also in their lives and deeds." Hence it is presumed that the aim of the composition was not entertainment, but morality, which end was to be obtained by a description of an ideal kingdom. Any such theory is at once condemned by the facts as we know them. Only one argument can be advanced in support of this contention—not much of an argument, though Flügel thinks it is sound—" that this being the chief aim of the book explains why the shepherds and shepherdesses in Sidney's *Arcadia* play so small a part, while the chief characters in the plots are assigned to people of the highest class—princes and princesses."

As the writing progressed, the original motive, if it ever existed, is lost sight of and forgotten. There is a continual want of directness and simplicity, two qualities the author very well knew how to employ, that are to be expected in a direct treatise. Though the style is often brilliant, the faults are so far from being hidden that they are lit up and made clearer. Freshness and vitality are wanting. The absence of any moral design is noteworthy, the personages—animated labels for the most part—are entirely unreal, and, therefore, non-moral. They have neither human faults nor human virtues. While this long-drawn and complicated fantasy does not deserve the sledge-hammer condemnation of the severe and austere Milton, its claims to possess ethical merits are as absurd as the harsh old Puritan's abuse. " Vain and amatorious " the romance may be, but it makes neither for good nor evil. It was written at odd moments to give pleasure to the author and his sister.

This modest ambition was more than accomplished. It is surely ridiculous to allege, as one critic does, that because " it could easily be turned to moral account," contemporary readers found the book useful. The same critic goes on : " The ladies of the upper classes required something to entertain them, to arrest their fancies with vivid scenes and complicated plots with their final *dénouement*, without leading them into devious paths like the ordinary romances, and this *Arcadia* accomplished admirably." I would put the same truth differently. Morality, save for a few, was not a matter of much importance in the reign of Elizabeth ; men and women were not squeamish in their methods of speech. Morals are of no importance in *Arcadia*, the marionettes who

enact the stories are exceedingly outspoken, the entangle-
ments make amusing puzzles, and the ladies of the upper
classes who had plenty of time on their hands sought
relief from boredom by unravelling them. Unconsciously
they absorbed, without knowing it, the beauties that
illumine so many pages of this ill-knit, and, at times,
almost unintelligible romance. Flügel is in the right when
he says, "If the *Arcadia* has now been saved from the
fate of oblivion, the form, and contents, of the *Defence of
Poesie*, completed about that time, held within itself,
through its style and matter, a certainty of everlasting
fame."

The truth of this bold utterance must be clear to any
one who studies *The Apology*. It is on this essay that
Philip's claim to be considered a master of English prose
triumphantly rests. *Arcadia* amused its author and his
his sister ; it unexpectedly gave pleasure to others at the
time. Only a scholar now cares to wade through its many
pages to search for the treasures that lie submerged
therein. For these we should be grateful, but the best
we can say for the book as a whole is that it is less dead
than *Euphues*.

The first part of Philip's book tells a story straight-
forwardly, and the story is pleasant. Two princes
are friends, both brave, chivalrous, and renowned for
martial achievements. One is Musidorus of Macedon, the
other Pyrocles of Thessaly. They voyage together, as
Philip and Greville were proposing to voyage when Drake
left them in the lurch at Plymouth. A great storm arises
and their vessel founders. The companions, though saved,
are separated. To the kings of the rival countries where
they find asylum their merits become apparent. A war
breaking out, the armies meet to wage battle. At the
head of one is Musidoras, and Pyrocles commands the other.
The battle rages long, and the two generals meet in single
combat. With more good fortune than befell Sohrab and

Rustam, recognition occurs before a blow is struck. Two such friends cannot wage deadly combat against each other. The accommodating armies agree decidedly with the views of their generals. Peace is readily declared. This happy conclusion releases the friends from their respective engagements. Renewing their interrupted journey, they set out together for Arcadia. Their adventures here are the main thesis of the many hundred pages that compose the elaborate and fantastic romance. In a few short paragraphs it is impossible to give the details. Our ideas of Arcadia are very rudely shaken. It is not the happy pastoral country we might naturally expect. Apart from the dragons and other beasts of prey, themselves dangerous and unwelcome society, there is not much pleasure to be had in conversing with the natives. To say truth, the shepherds and shepherdesses seem very little removed from the Irish peasants Philip and Spenser libelled cruelly, though of course there was an unsympathetic truth in much they said concerning the impoverished and ill-used islanders. The inhabitants of Arcadia stand a good deal in need of that " sweet subjection" Philip advocated as wholesome for the wretched people outside the pale. Mr. Lee says, " The call of realism was in Sidney's ears, the call of honesty, and his peasants divested themselves of ideal features for the ugly contours of fact." But it is odd that he should call his book " Arcadia," that he should choose a gross country to people it, when, if he wished to be realistic, he might have been pleasantly so, and taken some smiling English county for his ideal country, the dwellers in English villages for his models. The conduct of the adventurers is quite in keeping with romance. They disguise themselves on arrival at the house or hut of Dametas for no very obvious purpose. Musidorus becomes a shepherd, the better to woo the Princess Pamela, his friend puts on a woman's robe and dubs himself Zelmane. For an incredible

number of pages these strange devices fulfil their purpose.
When they arrive at the territory of King Basilius a strange
story, and intricate, of love begins.    The tale is not too
interesting nor too refined.    Musidorus, of course, loves
Pamela, and she him, despite his shepherd's garb.    Her
sister, equally beautiful, is to fall to Pyrocles.    This eccentric royal family are living in huts in a wood because
Basilius is jealous of his wife, for what reason is not clear,
nor does it matter, since Gynecia, his queen, is most virtuous as well as most beautiful.    The arrangements of the
regal dwelling are curious.    Basilius, his consort, and his
younger daughter live together in one hut; in another,
some distance removed, Pamela resides.    A most direful
family are commissioned to look after her.    They are
peasants of unsavoury aspect and conversation.    The
husband is not quite so impossible as his wife ; both are
angels compared to Mopsa, the daughter.    Shakespeare
may have had Mopsa in his mind when he drew Audrey.
Audrey as he depicts her, however, is only crude and a
little uncomfortably free of speech.    Mopsa is as ugly in
her manners as is the name she carries.    The lovers are
very successful, and as they were great princes there is no
reason why they should have to masquerade.    This mas-
querading has unpleasant consequences.    The refined
Musidorus, " of so goodly a shape and well pleasing
favour," had to pretend an affection for Mopsa.    Pyrocles
had to suffer worse penalties for seeking hospitality in a
false habit.    Both king and queen fell in love with him.
Basilius, angry with his wife, was quite willing to find
consolation.    Gynecia, not on good terms with her husband, was willing to be consoled.    The Amazon robes
Pyrocles wore had not deceived her.    He was no woman,
she knew.    Over this thin ice Philip skates dexterously.
The love of an elderly lady, virtuous and beautiful, of
course, in love with a young man, was not a problem
undiscussed at Greenwich and Hampton Court.    This

introduced confusion of sex is a favourite device of the
Elizabethan dramatists ; it is popular on the modern
stage, especially at Christmas. At this season we learn
that Robinson Crusoe was really a clever and accomplished lady who sang pathetic ballads or patriotic ditties,
and that her mother was a comic old man in petticoats.
The tangle is not a delightful one ; probably Philip found
himself in the midst of the maze before he realised where
he was. That he did not concern himself greatly about
the impropriety of a situation even a daring modern
novelist might be expected to shy at, is clear from the
touch of genuine piety he puts into his mixture to leaven
the lump. Pamela's prayer is nobly conceived and nobly
worded. Milton, who made the devil a saint, anticipating
Goethe and Sir Herbert Tree, wrote in horror: "Who would
have imagined so little fear in him of the true all-seeing
deity, so little reverence of the Holy Ghost, whose office it
is to dictate and present our Christian prayers, so little care
of truth in his last words, or honour to himself or to his
friends, or sense of his afflictions, or that sad hour which
was upon him, as immediately before his death to pop
into that hand of that grave bishop who attended him, as
a special relique of his saintly exercises, a prayer stolen
word for word from the mouth of a heathen woman pray-
ing to a heathen god ; and that in no serious book, but
in the vain amatorious poem of Sir Philip Sidney's
*Arcadia.*"

Milton was even more deficient in humour than Sidney :
he was as confirmed a bigot, and he was much less
gracious in his private life. This outburst of his over
Pamela's prayer is the impertinence of ignorance. The
man he here anathematises is Charles I. ; the bishop,
a far nobler man than Milton, is Juxon. Dr. Johnson,
with his accustomed wisdom, settled the matter once and
for all, when he said, " The use of it by adaptation was
innocent ; and they who could so noisily censure it, with

a little extension of their malice could contrive what they wanted to accuse." That Charles did use this prayer is doubtful; that he had used it is less doubtful; that he gave it to Juxon, slightly altered, is almost beyond controversy. It was among the papers he handed to the bishop on the scaffold. Theological bigotry is painful to contemplate in Philip's day, in Milton's it passes all bounds of reason. Only a few men, of no particular ability, belonging to self-advertising societies, would prolong it in our own. The prayer is as follows:—

"O All-seeing Light and Eternal Life of all things, to whom nothing is either so great that it may resist, or so small that it is contemned; look upon my misery with Thine eye of mercy, and let Thine infinite power vouchsafe to limit out some proportion of deliverance unto me, as to Thee shall seem most convenient." The phrase "quite convenient unto Thee" is, in spite of Milton, still heard in prayers delivered from ultra-reformed pulpits. The prayer nobly concludes: "Let calamity be the exercise but not the overthrow of my virtue; let their power prevail, but prevail not to destruction. Let my greatness be their prey; let my pain be the sweetness of their revenge; let them, if it seem good unto Thee, vex me with more and more punishment; but, O Lord, let never their wickedness have such a hand but that I may carry a pure mind in a pure body." The husband of three wives objected to all this almost as violently as three wives, each in their turn, saw reason to object to him. But Milton came along after Philip was gone, so the curmudgeon criticism and Chadband disapproval never disturbed him. He was in a hero's grave before they were voiced.

*Arcadia* though long enough, was never quite completed. The story was published after Philip's death. Those who are interested in its shadowy, and at times, ridiculous personages, can read the happy ending, and

feel no compunction in bidding Mopsa as elegant a
farewell as she would understand. For its time, in its
place, even for the influence it had, the book is a
great achievement. It is not a work to interest other
than scholars; but the modern novel could have not
been written if *Arcadia*, the Arcadia of Sidney, had
not been discovered. The panegyrics that followed the
publication of the book are some intimation that its
earliest readers realised the immense, though uninten-
tioned, influence it was destined to sway over all who
as modern writers present us, to-day, with a novel.

A much more serious effort on Philip's part was his
Art of Poetry. Herein he very seriously sat down to
declare the faith that was in him, and give his reasons
for that faith. He was not unsuccessful. Of its kind it
is the best treatise we have in English. Even to the
most modern of us it is right in essentials. One episode
too, if episode is the right word, has a correct and
absolute value. This relates to horsemanship, and touches
on the character of a man who is worth considering.
For he and his qualities gave Philip an opportunity,
gladly seized, of throwing a flashlight on to the society
of his time. Enthusiasm impelled Philip, gratitude for
the enthusiasm stirs us.

A considerable amount of ink seems to have been
spilt in controversy as to when Philip wrote *An Apologie
for Poetry*. Professor Arber is, I think, right in choosing
the date of publication as 1580. But the first paragraph
in his admirable reprint is somewhat loosely worded.
The professor's reference to Spenser's *Shepherd's Calendar* is helpful, the assertion that the Apology was
written "subsequent to 1579" is not. Philip may have
composed it years before he gave it to the world,
though it is not at all likely that he did. But mere
assertion is dangerous, and we have no evidence to
prove he had not been at work on it for twenty years.

So precocious a boy might have well begun serious
work before he went to Shrewsbury. I do not think
the allusions to Gosson's two rather foolish books are
at all conclusive in approximating the date. The first
was called *The School of Abuse*, which appeared in April,
1579, and the second, *An Apologie of the Schoole of
Abuse*, which electrified readers the following November.
I cannot see that either of these publications affect
*An Apologie for Poetry*. Still, great effects from little
causes spring ; and modern doctors trace intractable
diseases to the bite of a mosquito. What the quarrel
was, or between whom, will never be understood. There
was a quarrel, and, doubtless, both sides played their
parts with consummate dignity. The becoming attitude
for us of a later age is to ignore there was any dispute
at all. "The point at issue between Gosson and Sidney
seems to have been, whether uncleanness, falsity, and
effeminacy were separable or inseparable from poetry.
The *Apologie* is four times the length of those portions of Gosson's tracts that dealt with the abuses of
poetry."

We may be excused for thinking that it is a wise attitude
to understand the subject on which we argue, furthermore
whether we discuss realities or shadows. I confess, with
shame if necessary, that after three years' close study and
the reading of everything bearing on the subject, I do not
know what the controversy was about. Gosson apparently
did not find virtue on the stage ; he became a parson,
therefore, but did not die a bishop. I do not understand
what Spenser, referring to the *Schoole of Abuse*, means
when he says in a letter to Harvey, "and dedicating it to
Maister Sidney, was for his labour scorned ; if at least it
be in the goodnesse of that nature to scorn." Dr. Arber
talks of a "vindication," a vindication of what ? It is
difficult enough to get at the rights and wrongs of a serious
quarrel between men who have lived and are gone before

us : a quarrel such as this, whatever it was, does not concern us, because it is abyssmally unintelligible. Even Arber sees this, " It will be better," he sagely says, after having care-founded our worries, " to rise from the temporal controversy to the general principles comprised in the present work ; merely noting that the ultimate point at issue between Sidney and Gosson seems to have been, whether uncleanness, falsity, and effeminacy were separable or inseparable from poetry." Gosson seems to have thought himself a humourist, and designed an attack on " the poets, pipers, actors, and baffoons and other such pernicious parasites of the State." The high reputation Philip enjoyed, and his known fondness for the arts, may have prompted the foolish man to round off his jest by an impertinent dedication. If he meant his scurrilous treatise to be taken seriously his choice of a sponsor is bewildering and amazing. Philip, we learn, censured the coxcomb so far as his good nature permitted ; but it is hard to realise that the Apologie was specially designed for the refutation of a fool.

The little book is, however, far more of a eulogy than a defence ; it is a declaration of faith, and silly aspersions on that faith are quickly brushed aside before the main arguments are developed. The fire and enthusiasm of the language are remarkable, and come from the heart of one who declared and believed poetry to be " the divinest thing on earth." He made no rigid collection of rules collated from Horace and Aristotle, though he knew well the works of both, for the writing of poetry. In testing the poetry of his contemporaries he makes it evident that he considers chiefly of its spirit and truth, he praises or condemns according as the verses under discussion possess or lack these qualities. His knowledge of their necessity as ingredients in what is of any value at all makes him rejoice even over the roughest wrought folk-song. He says, " Certainly I must confesse mine own barbarousnesse ;

I never heard the old song of Percy and Douglas that I
founde not my heart moved more than with a trumpet;
and yet it is sung but by some blind Crowder, with no
rougher voice than rude stile."

He insists that a real poet cannot lie, since his sphere
is necessarily the eternal truth of things, of the heart of
man and of man's loftiest ideals. The poetic gift, he
warns us, "must not be dragged by the eares." Human
skill, he asserts, has nothing to do with the creation of
poetry, "it is a divine gift."

" There is no art delivered unto mankind that hath not
the works of nature for his principall object, without which
they could not exist . . . So doth the Astronomer look
upon the stars . . . the morall—Philosopher standeth upon
the naturall virtues, vices, or passions of man : and follow
Nature saith he therein, and though shalt not erre. The
Lawier saith, what men have determined. The Historian,
what men have done." The theme is developed with
plenty of adroit humour, the Astronomer may fall into
a ditch while locating a star, he tells us, the inquiring
Philosopher may be blind in himself, and the Mathematician,
though able " to draw forth a straight line," is quite liable
to walk in crooked ways. The "end of all earthly
learning, being virtuous action, those skils that most serve
to bring forth that, have the most title to be Princes over
all the rest : wherein if we can shew, the Poet is worthy to
have it before any other competitors."

If this Gosson is of no more importance, Philip is of
much. Whatever the merits of this illegible controversy,
Philip here gives us of his best. And that best is not only
best for his own age, but for ours and for all ages. It is
as valuable a contribution to the world's knowledge as has
been vouchsafed to us ; in this it is easy to agree with Dr.
Arber, "there is much exposition of that which will remain
for all time."

"What is a poet?" was Philip's pertinent text. Rhyme

and metre had nothing to do with a man's claim to the title. His definition would have included, and rightly, Walt Whitman, for he avers, " One may be a poet without versing and a versifier without poetry." How true this is some of us have better opportunities, or worse, than he had of knowing. " Verse being but an ornament and no cause to Poetry," is another axiom no modern reviewer will controvert. Poetry is " that fayning notable images of vertues, vices, or what else with that delightfull teaching which must be the right describing note to know a poet by." Some modern poets would shrink from so rigorous a standard : Philip himself had no reason to shirk it. Weighed in, after his successive victories, he on his own mounts was an undisputed winner. Whether it is a correct definition of poetry none knows or ever shall know. From Horace onwards men have tried to define the indefinable. Philip's definition is as good as any we have. But whether good or bad his effort is interesting because it is the earliest systematic attempt that we know of, in English, to approach so serious a problem. If we do not gain a complete and satisfactory answer we, at least, get within the magic circle wherein the answer lurks. In this solemn matter Philip is not lazy, nor does he " dangle his pen with the air of a man of quality," as Byron did to the admiration of Scott and the sorrow of those less than Sir Walter in everything save their regret. Philip wrote his treatise in deadly earnest, and put into it his best literary work. The little book proves him, when on his mettle, the completest literary artist of his day—unless we except Spenser. The creator of *Colin Clout* and the *Faëry Queen* made his confession to Harvey in an epistle prefacing *The Shepherd's Calendar*. Spenser's adulation of Harvey detracts from the value of his remarks, and does not encourage us to think highly of his critical judgment. In his postscript is this amazing sentence : " Now I trust, Mr. Harvey, that upon sight of your special friends and fellow poet's doings, or els for envie of so many unworthy Quidams, which catch at the garland which to you alone is dewe, you will be persuaded to pluck out of the hateful darknesse those so many excellent English poems of yours which lie hid, and bring them forth to eternal light." Philip most certainly did not think that Harvey was alone worthy of " the garland." The list of poets he gives us as being worthy of fame is a very short and very discriminating one, consisting of four names only.

Philip, as a recognised poet, and still more as a man of importance in other ways, did not escape the attentions of minor bards. He must have grown weary of the dedications and laudatory verses addressed to him. Many of the writers must have come under his scorn as " Poetapes, not poets."

The treatise is admirably arranged, and is full of scholarship, even of humour, and logic. Though he begins by a reference to his unfitness for the task of defending "that my unelected vocation" he loses no time in asserting that poetry is the noblest work of man. The "making" of poetry is the finest example of man's desire to create. God and the poet are the only true creators. The poet is, too, the one person who cannot lie, "he never affirms and therefore never lyeth." " For who," he quaintly says, "thinks that Esope lyed in the tales of his beasts: for who thinks that Esope writ it for actually true, were well worthy to have his name chronicled among the beastes hee writeth of." He begins his argument by invoking the aid of all men of culture, of all thinkers. He reminds us that Poetry always has been, and always must be the " first nurse " whose milk enables men eventually to " feed afterwards of tougher knowledge." This striking contention he supports with a graceful show of scholarship. Herodotus, who certainly was imaginative if he was not credulous, and many another famous writer, are claimed as poets. Plato did not really banish poets from his Republic, he expelled only the "Poet-apes." All that is best in the great prose writers, he avows, is due to the bard ; the passion, the imagination are inspired by the singer. Then he reminds his reader that the great nations of antiquity respected and revered their poets beyond soldier or statesman : to them belonged of right the chiefest honours. " Now, that Verse farre exceedeth Prose in the knitting up of the memory, the reason is manifest. The words (besides their delight which hath a great affinitie to memory), being so set, as one word cannot be lost, but the whole work fails," is another of his arguments. Further, he proudly boasts : " I list not to defend Poesie, with the help of her underling Historio-graphy." This verdict is perhaps hard on the historian, but what the writer seeks to show is that the poet is no man's debtor, that his verses do not depend on the labour of others : " Hee citeth not authorities of other Histories, but even for his entry, calleth the sweete Muses to inspire into him a good invention : in troth no labouring to tell you what is or is not, but what should or should not be." Disciples of the " Art for Art's sake " school are roughly handled. Sidney contends that poetry must " teach and delight." So it has for him a most definite and sacred purpose. Merely to delight is not enough, the aim of the true poet is to be also a schoolmaster to the world. There are three classes of poets he tells us : " They that imitate the inconceivable excellencies of God " form one division. In the next we find those who deal with moral and natural philosophy, history, and astronomy. The third and rarer class, to whom he gives precedence, are "right poets which most properly do imitate to teach and delight ; and to imitate, borrow nothing of what is, hath been, or shall be ; but range only, reined with learned dis-cretion, into the divine consideration of what may be and should be." Exalted, indeed, is the mission of the poet as Philip conceived it.

The third group he holds in the highest honour, probably, for the reason that they are the only perfect creators, the others being, in a sense, moulders of material already to hand. After again assuring us that a poem need not rhyme, he would not have loved our modern phrase "prose poet," though he anticipates it; he tells why verse is commendable. "The senate of poets have chosen verse as their fittest raiment," he says, and explains the reason. Speech he holds the greatest of human blessings, next to reason, therefore he concludes logically enough that, as verse "most doth polish that blessing of speech," it is a fitter and worthier medium than prose. Proceeding with his argument, he reminds us that learning's chief end is "to lead and draw us to as high a perfection as our degenerate souls, made worse by their clay lodgings, can be capable of." Now poetry alone can fulfil so tremendous a task. Very ingeniously, for the most part very convincingly, he unfolds his argument. Character can be formed by wise teachers, and the wisest teachers, he would have us believe, are poets. They stand midway between the Philosopher and the Historian. Mr. Symonds sums up the position assigned to poetry with his usual felicity when he says, " If philosophy is too much occupied with the universal, history is too much bound to the particular." We have here a concise summing up of this portion of Philip's argument.

Love has ever been the theme of poets, and it could not be ignored in this *Apologie*. Gosson's " poets, pipers, players, and their excusers " had no cause to regret their champion. Utterly scouting, with some heat and a real eloquence, the libellous attacks of the ignorant and impertinent, certainly Gosson's knowledge, if he had any, was not according to wisdom ; the advocate declares that even if "love of beauty is a beastly fault," it is because man's wit "abuseth poetry." His argument here is so clever that I shall quote it almost in full.

" Grant love of beauty to be a beastly fault (although it be very hard, sith onely man, and no beast, hath that gift to discern beauty). Grant that lovely name of Love, to deserve all hateful reproaches : . . . Grant I say, whatsoever they will have granted; that not onely love, but lust, but vanitie, but (if they list) scurrilitie, possesseth many leaves of the Poet's bookes : yet think I, when this is granted they will finde, theyr sentence may with good manners, put the last words foremost : and not say, that Poetrie abuseth man's wit but that, man's wit abuseth Poetrie. . . . Doe we not see the skill of Phisick, (the best rampire to out oft assaulted bodies) being abused teach poyson the most violent destroyer ? Dooth not knowledge of Law, whose end is, to even and right all things being abused, grow the crooked fosterer of horrible injuries? Doth not (to go to the highest) God's word abused, become blasphemie ? Truely a needle cannot do much hurt, and as truely, (with leave of Ladies be it spoken) it cannot do much good. With a sword, thou maist kill thy Father, and with a sword thou maist defend thy Prince and Country. So that, as in their calling Poets the Fathers of lyes, they say nothing : so in this their argument of abuse they proove the commendation." Here we are face to face with a brilliant argument, one not easy to rout. Philip shows, also, a sense of humour, as indeed he does throughout the essay, which his serious conduct and speech has not prepared us for. If the *Apologie* did nothing else, it proves that its author had a pungent sense of the ridiculous at times. And his argument in defence of poetry is an admirable one against all faddists who would condemn a thing or a custom because abuse and misuse leads to trouble. This idea animates him when he asks why England, " the mother of excellent minds, has grown so hard a stepmother to poets." His answer is ready, and cannot have given pleasure to a number of people. England, he asserts, does not dislike poets ; what she objects to, and with

reason, are bad ones.  In a very candid sentence he
declares : " I do not remember to have seen but few (to
speak boldly) printed, that have poetical sinews in them."
For Lyly and the Euphuists, though he does not mention
their leader by name, he has nothing but scorn.  These
elegant people were told frankly that he found far more
merit in the works of "divers small-learned courtiers."  It
is difficult at this day, when they are more than half-
forgotten, to understand how great was the influence of
Lyly and his school.  A great deal of courage was needed
to declare that language was given us to reveal and not to
conceal thought.  With a boldness almost unequalled he
reminds his reader that kings, captains, and senators were
not only the cause of poetry in others, but desired, and
tried, to be poets themselves.  The drama is not neglected.
He reviews it with some care.  Unfortunately in his day
the theatre was in its infancy.  Pleasant as it is to muse
over his admiration for Shakespeare, had he lived to see
"Hamlet" or "Romeo and Juliet," a day-dream is not
history.  Truth to tell, there was little in the drama of his
day that was worth consideration.  Philip saw what the
stage might become ; he was not spared to see what it
became.  But even his vision was limited, and in a longer
life he might, one thinks, have relinquished some of his
inordinate admiration of Seneca and Italian tragedies.

This " incke-wafting toy of mine " ends with a fervid
peroration.  Philip felt he had pleaded a good cause, so
he quits argument for declamation.  He bids men no more
scorn the mysteries of Poetry ; Aristotle had recognised
them as the ancient treasurers of Divinity.  Civility, he
reminds us, sprang from their efforts, and he agrees with
Scaliger that Virgil can make a man honest more easily
than the philosophers.  He finishes thus :—

" To believe with me that there are many mysteries
contained in Poetry, which of purpose were written darkly,
lest by profane wits it should be abused.  To believe with

368 SIR PHILIP SIDNEY

Landin that they are so beloved of the gods, that whatsoever they write proceeds of a divine fury. Lastly, to believe themselves when they tell you they will make you immortall, by their verses.

"Thus doing, your name shall flourish in the printer's shops; thus doing, you shall be of kinne to many a poetical Preface; thus doing you shall be most faire, most ritch, most wise, most all, you shall dwell upon superlatives. Thus doing, though you be *Libertino patre natus*, you shall suddenly grow *Hercules protes*—

'*Si quid mea carmina possunt.*'

Thus doing your soul shall be placed with Dante's Beatrix, or Virgil's Anchises. But if, (fie of such a but,) you be borne so neare the dull making Cataphract of Nilus, that you cannot hear the Plannet-like Musick of Poetrie, if you have so earth-creeping a mind, that it cannot lift its self up, to look to the sky of poetry; or rather, by a certaine rusticall disdaine will become such a Mome, as to be a Momas of Poetry: then, though I will not wish unto you, the Asses eares of Midas, nor to be driven by a Poet's verses, (as Bubonax was) to hange himselfe, nor to be rimed to death, as is sayd to be doone in Ireland; yet thus much curse I must send you, in the behalf of all Poets, that while you live, you live in love, and never get favour, for lacking skill of a sonnet: and that when you die, your memory die from the earth, for want of an Epitaph."

How far this whimsical and witty passage, with its exhortation and threat, influences the ordinary business man may not be known. That it created an impression among the authors' contemporaries we know on good authority. Philip, hard up often, was not at a loss to find the necessary moneys wherewith to pay his printer. Moreover, a great part of his writing was worth the expense. No

better defence of poetry, certainly no wiser one, has come
down to us.   A poet's just claim to be taken seriously has
had no cleverer advocate.   His determined rejection of
what was bad or indifferent went far to strengthen his plea
for what was good.   His own style, if we make allowance
for the curious punctuation, was of the finest order, some
sentences, as, "you shall be of kinne to many a Poetical
preface," may claim cousinship with the happiest phrases
of Stevenson.   To English ears, unless wilfully deaf,
poetry has been wittily, logically, and wisely defended.
Nay, more, it was Philip who first showed us how noble
poetry is, and how necessary if we would be brave and
prosperous and happy.

It is always with this truth uppermost in our minds that
we should think of Philip Sidney.   That is why I reiterate
it, now that he and his companions have, pageant-wise,
passed before us.   Not only was he a poet himself who in
his own verse reverenced truth and beauty, but his life was
a poem, and the begetter of poetry in others.   Poetry was
for him "the great C major of life"; and his so-called
defence is a pæan of homage and triumph.   There were,
he saw, many things a man could do with profit to himself
and his country, but the seemingly intangible claims of
poetry he feared were overlooked.   Yet a knowledge of it,
and a love of it, nay, even indifferent practise of it, were
an essential to all true success.   "If he doesn't like an old
ballad," said the late Professor York Powell, of an indifferent fellow, "kick him downstairs, and thank God you
have got rid of a knave."   Philip knew that it was idle to
ask men to fight life's battle worthily unless they could
rally to such a trumpet call.   Just as the singer David
drove away the madness of Saul, the King, by the music
of his harp, Philip believed all mad and base thoughts
could be vanquished.   A knowledge of the beautiful
thoughts proclaimed by the men whom God had directly
inspired was a sure shield.   The arrows of the wicked fell

harmless, as the hushed storm and the calmed waves of the Psalmist. So his defence of poetry was much more than the eulogy of an exquisite accomplishment; it was a proclamation to the busiest, the most heedless, the scoffer, and the ignorant. He might well have headed his treatise with the words, "Serve the Lord with gladness: come before His presence with singing," for assuredly he was one who joyfully obeyed both these commandments.

# INDEX

375

Sidney, Sir William, 8–9, 236
Sidney-Sussex College, Cambridge, foundation of, 15
Sidney, Thomas, 52, 236–237, 239, 245–246, 249
Simier, du, 146, 278–279
Southampton, Henry Wriothesley, Earl of, 268–269
*Spaccio de la Bastia Trionfante*, dedicated to Philip Sidney, 199
Spain and Catholicism, 30–31, 111–112, 153–154, 175–176, 187, 201–203, 214, 222, 259
Spenser, Edmund, and Ireland, 189, 192, 260, 267, 269–271; on Dyer, 251; friendship with Philip Sidney, 251–252, 260–261, 263–266; and the Areopagus, 253–254, 261–262; his poetry quoted, 260–262; and Elizabeth, 261; and Gabriel Harvey, 262–263, 266, 362; *The Shepherd's Calendar*, dedicated to Philip, 263; Philip's criticism, 266; in London, 263–264, 267, 270; *Colin Clout's come Home again*, dedicated to Raleigh, 264; and Essex, 264, 270; private secretary to Lord Gray of Wilton, 264; Clerk of Decrees and Recognisance in the Chancery Court of Ireland, 266; Clerk to the Council of Munster, 267; discontented, 267–270; and Lodovick Bryskett, 267; *The Faëry Queen*, 268–270; speedy recognition of, 269; "Heavenly Spenser," 269; Disraeli on, 269; marries Rosalind, 269; composes the *Epithalamium*, 269; meets Shakespeare, 270; offends James I., 270; Sheriff of Cork, 270; death in a tavern, 271;

tribute to Mary Sidney, 341; on the *Schoole of Abuse*, 359; otherwise mentioned, 190
Stage, the, and the Reformation, 29; condition of, before Shakespeare, 156–162; granting of first royal patent, 159
Stella, *see* Devereux, Lady Penelope.
Stow, John, quoted, on Philip Sidney, 231
Stuarts, the, 317–318
Sturm, Johann, 27
*Supposes, The*, Gascoigne, 161
Sussex, Earl of, on Leicester, 274; otherwise mentioned, 129
Sussex, Frances Sidney, Countess of, 15
Symonds, John Addington, on Sidney's portrait by Veronese, 80; on Philosophy and Poetry, 365

Tarleton, 160–161
Thornton, Dr., Epitaph of, 48
Toleration, lack of, 2, 25, 28, 31, 94, 187, 208, 288, 290, 298
*Trueness of the Christian Religion, A Work concerning the*, Du Mornay, translated by Philip Sidney, 134, 197, 200, 302–303

Veronese, Paolo, portrait of Philip Sidney, 6, 80, 301
*View of the Present State of Ireland, A*, Spenser, 260, 270

Walpole, Horace, on *Arcadia*, 76, 168–169; on Shakespeare, 169; character and opinions of, 345–346; Dr. Johnson on, 345; on Philip Sidney, 346–348